Wadda Life

D E R E K   M A S S E Y

First published in Great Britain in 2025 by
The Book Guild Ltd
Unit E2 Airfield Business Park,
Harrison Road, Market Harborough,
Leicestershire. LE16 7UL
Tel: 0116 2792299
www.bookguild.co.uk
Email: info@bookguild.co.uk
X: @bookguild

Copyright © 2025 Derek Massey

The right of Derek Massey to be identified as the author of this
work has been asserted by them in accordance with the
Copyright, Design and Patents Act 1988.

All rights reserved. No part of this publication may be
reproduced, transmitted, or stored in a retrieval system, in any form or by any means,
without permission in writing from the publisher, nor be otherwise circulated in
any form of binding or cover other than that in which it is published and without
a similar condition being imposed on the subsequent purchaser.

The manufacturer's authorised representative in the EU
for product safety is Authorised Rep Compliance Ltd,
71 Lower Baggot Street, Dublin D02 P593 Ireland
(www.arccompliance.com)

Typeset in 11pt Minion Pro

Printed and bound in in Great Britain by CMP UK

ISBN 978 1835741 917

British Library Cataloguing in Publication Data.
A catalogue record for this book is available from the British Library.

For Gabby, my wonderful wife. Not many women would have agreed to go on this crazy adventure of a life with me. For that, I am forever grateful. And my children: Dirk, Tamika, Kristina and Gavin, I couldn't have asked for a better family.

ONE

The Start

October 2, 1940, was not a particularly auspicious day, other than WWII going on, and the Blitz. However, my mother felt differently, as she was able to get me out of her innards. I am not sure I was able to breathe fresh air considering with what I was used to, so I probably got a smack on the bum by some nurse or other. Anyway, it happened and I have no regrets because I have had a great life.

I was number four of the batch, and with number five arriving eighteen months later, they decided that five male kids on a farm labourer's salary would not provide an exotic lifestyle. We moved house before I was five years old, which you might say was good training for my future lifestyle. So, with a favourable bank manager's agreement, in 1944 father was able to ask via a banker's prerogative to take on a farm rental. Soon after moving to the farm, numbers increased.

Mother's wish for a daughter was again ignored. After that, I think my parents decided that six made an adequate number for family labour and quit trying for more.

Prior to the move to the rental farm, I have only two memories from that abode, one when we arrived from a visit to Uttoxeter on the weekly 'Green' bus to find our vegetable garden seemingly full of rabbits.

Another was a WWII memory; a plane was seen to be having trouble and crashed into a field not far from our cottage. Dad, being in the Home Guard, grabbed his army-issue 0.303 calibre and his bike and then, putting me on the cycle rack of the bike, and accompanied by two other cyclists with guns, set off to see who had come down and what help could be required. It turned out that the pilot was English and, as he was not badly damaged, he sat on the back of one of the other cycles and we all went to the pub. I remember sitting on a log outside the Red Cow whilst the four adults poured beer down the pilot's neck as they awaited his rescue squad, a taxi. I sat outside for what seemed to be an age.

When we moved houses a couple of times and eventually to the farm, apparently somewhere along the line my favourite golliwog was lost and I am told I cried my eyes out. Does this have anything to do with my staying in Africa for so long, or is it just coincident? I guess I will never know.

The farm my parents rented had been misused during wartime to produce as much as possible whilst trying to forget about trivialities such as weeding, fertiliser, fencing or building care. In short, it was a wreck. The house itself was a three-storey mansion that had reached the end of its usefulness long before we moved in. It did not have electricity or indoor toilet or bath, and all water pipes were lead. Twenty-four rooms and five cellars – that sounds good, I guess, plus the excitement of a residential ghost. This ghost was there not just for us. The house was well known to be haunted. As people walked home from the pubs in the evenings, whilst passing our house on a close road their singing rose in volume, or they ran past our house to the stretch of road beyond, which was lit by one gas lamp. This ghost was interesting. Three of my brothers claim they saw it; it was a ghost who lost her fiancé and would sit on the front doorstep crying. One of the other occupants of part of the house was a policeman and he claimed that he often saw her there when returning late at night after a late shift.

There were also two unrelated families lodging in the right wing, and we had the run of the rest of the house. These lodgers either died off or were tired of our behaviour, or perhaps there were innocent reasons, but they all disappeared. I was too young to care and I scarcely remember them. The place was considered unsuitable for human habitation when we moved in, yet we lived in it for 25 years. So, you can maybe imagine what it looked like 25 years later. As kids, we adopted a hedgehog that we found on our farm in the autumn. We took it home and it did not hibernate at the end of that year. We fed it mainly on bread and milk and it hunted down all our cockroaches, which seemed to have a base at the back of the ash-hole under our coal-fired stove, which went around four feet – long enough for mice, cockroaches and even room for hedgehog.

The owner of the Old Hall soon realised that he should have sold it after the war for housing construction and consequently refused to spend any money on either the house or the farm buildings, hoping we would move on. It was so bad that if a window fell out, not just a pane of glass, but a whole window, we would just move into another room. The only heating was the coal fire in the 'living kitchen'. We had a billiard table in the main hall where we used the ceiling as billiard chalk, that is until the ceiling collapse, and the main hall was large enough to play a sort of soccer in when it was raining. In other words, we were ruffians.

Bathing was a flat-bottomed tin bath situated in front of the fire and partially filled with 'a bucket of warm' water from the fireside 'boiler'. I guess we shared the water when it was bath day. Later on, as we grew up, we took a trip to Newcastle-under-Lyme and bathed in one of their slipper baths. Not sure what the 'slipper' means, but it was enjoyable. Initially we had two workhorses for the heavy stuff, so we all knew how to enjoy having carthorses around and especially taking them to the blacksmith for a new set of shoes when needed.

After the birth of the sixth son, my parents seemed to give up trying for a girl and concentrated on ninety-six acres of mixed farming, and all of us six kids were expected to help from an early age. I think my oldest brother was not too happy about the labour input but then he was always an oddity. He claimed he was teased by pupils at school because he smelled of cows. Farm work was considered a mixed blessing among my brothers but tolerated by most. I liked and still do like the odour of cattle. As kids we had pigs, poultry and calves to feed before school and the same when we returned.

The farm was close to a built-up area and people would walk their dogs over our fields of grass. There was no damage in walking their dogs, but occasionally some idiot would let one run free and dogs like to chase cows, which is a no-no for a dairy farmer as it reduces milk production due to adrenalin rush, and cattle can get bitten or lose a calf by abortion or even get a twisted gut. When it got to the point that too many loose dogs were in the fields with the cattle, father would shoot one or two chasing the cows. I remember one dog owner getting very shirty with him and said he would call the police. Dad told him there was a sergeant living in police housing across from our drive into the farm. The man stormed off and returned with the sergeant, who listened to the tirade. When the complainant ran out of words, he was told that it was quite legal to shoot a dog worrying cattle. The man stalked off only to be called back and ordered to take the dog's carcase home.

At the border of one of our fields was a coal mine, Brymbo by name, at the foot of the 'dirt tip', where unwanted rock, shale and other underground rubbish mixed with coal was dumped. The tip was quite high, perhaps a hundred feet or more; it was a mini mountain to us kids. Among the shale, a certain amount of coal would come down from the top mixed with rock, dangerously fast on, usually taking an erratic course and sometimes hard to avoid. Just occasionally attempted avoidance was not sufficient, RIP. Coal picking was illegal and risky, but postwar such things were tolerated; however, deaths did occur. Boulders from the coal tip would finish up in our fields, and because of this we were allowed to collect coal. As our house was extremely 'well ventilated', free coal was an asset. The coal tip was also a place to hunt for fossils. Not knowing anything whatsoever about a fossil, it was just an interesting pastime for us kids and we found a lot.

As I got older, I moved my bed to an empty room on the north-east corner when I needed space doing my homework. In winter it regularly got iced up on the inside window pane. I slept with as many blankets as could be found and on occasion fully clothed or, in extremis, an army greatcoat. Sleeping fully clothed had the added benefit of not having to dress for school. In a word, I suppose you could call us ruffians.

As kids we spent a lot of summer time sitting in the top branches of mature beech trees growing on a mini cliff at the entrance to the farm and close to a road. Occasionally, we would put a long, thick rope on a particular branch that hung out towards the road below. It made a wonderful swing out over the road by about seventy or eighty feet above it. Father had numerous complaints from car owners and he suggested there was no chance of their running over us kids seventy feet up, so go away and not to worry. Or perhaps he moderated his 'chat' if he thought we kids could hear.

I enjoyed school, which was in the village, and I enjoyed fighting. I lost as often as I won and also fought my brothers, but usually lost to older kin. The younger ones were not really worth the effort. My hair was rather different in those days, in that it stood straight out from my head. It was cut short by Dad in a 'brush cut' and occasionally it was a remarked upon by a fellow pupil. They would call me 'bristle bonce', and I would fake umbrage and demand a fight. If accepted, it was an after-school event which many pupils and even teachers would come to watch. Fighting would end when one of the pair wanted to stop. I would get home with bruises and cuts; Mother would ask, "Fighting again. Did you win?" followed by, "Go and clean yourself up."

Being farm raised made healthy, strong and active children; this came in useful on entering secondary school. I am not sure how it happened but our junior village school usually sent five or six pupils to grammar school, but my year were a bit of a surprise and sent thirteen. I believe to this day that I was number thirteen; it became my lucky number. At junior school, I was often sent off in soccer for being too aggressive. At 'big school' I found that rugby was to my taste and the sports master labelled me as a number fifteen immediately, with the advice that I could tackle anyone having the ball. When playing rugby I was a wing forward. In life, when the partisans were numbered the other way round, the full back was numbered one and I would take the number thirteen shirt, as the other flank forwards seldom wanted thirteen. I was happy with the number thirteen shirt (nowadays a number seven), and he gave me permission to scrag anyone I could catch so long as he had the ball. Rugby became my game.

It was on the farm that I learned how to shoot, when to shoot and when not to shoot, gun care, and the responsibilities of owning a gun of any type. There was always a loaded shotgun hanging on slings above our kitchen door. This came in useful when occasionally a loaded gun was needed. Coming home late from a night out, we would go hunting rats. We knew where to find them and would often get three or four each evening. I was introduced to guns gently. I had a Diana air pistol but could hit nothing with it. I then graduated to a Webley air pistol, once again not able to hit anything. Then came a 0.177 calibre pellet rifle, and the next one 0.22 calibre Webley rifle to keep the starlings and sparrows in control, both considered to be pests. I later got a sixteen-bore shotgun and then the big one, a twelve-bore calibre. Throughout my youth I was lectured on what to shoot, when to shoot, and what I might hit if I missed my target. I was also taught the necessity of keeping the guns cleaned and oiled, lessons which stayed with me. And never to point a gun at anyone or anything even if you think it is not loaded. After a day of shooting, on getting home the dogs were the first to be attended to, then the gun and then myself. I later in life I used this mantra: never point a gun at anyone unless it is necessary. Incidentally, our entrance door, the back door, was never locked or bolted. The front door was never used; it was not needed.

Late one night, just before Christmas, I did take the gun out. I was sitting late in the house reading a newspaper when I saw headlights coming up the drive. We usually kept about thirty or so turkeys for sale at Christmas time and there had been a police warning that thieves were operating in our area, stealing close to Christmas. I quickly switched off the light, took down the gun and waited to see why the driver was coming to the house and for what at that time. No action, so I went out to take a look and walked to the van to see who was inside. A policeman rolled down the window and asked who I was. I told him that I lived in the house. He told me I was very lucky as he was about to let the dog out. I told him that either he or his dog were very lucky. He asked why that was, then I showed him the gun. He left.

At Christmas time I learned to kill poultry for sale and also how to dress a bird. Living on a farm did have a few downsides. We usually kept the biggest turkey for ourselves for our Christmas dinner. As this one particular year we were having guests for the new year, we kept the last one after the others were gone. A couple of days before new year, on a snowy night, I heard the gander making a lot of panicked noises. I hopped out of bed, stuck my feet into a pair of wellies, grabbed a coat and gun and ran to the turkey pen. In the moonlight I just saw a fox dragging the turkey across the field. I chased him for about half a mile before he left the dead bird, and I doubt if I would have fired a shotgun, as we did not appreciate lead pellets in turkey drumsticks. That turkey tasted good, as the fox had only damaged the bird's head.

Fog in the Potteries could be very bad, and with fog came pollution from the numerous factories, forming smog. During the winter the atmosphere got very nasty and very unhealthy. The smog regularly slowed traffic on the nearby A34 to walking pace. One particular day we left school and literally could not see our feet. We had to walk with one foot on the pavement and one on the road. It was rather difficult, because if you missed taking a corner you were lost, with roads joining the A34 and later through the village. A group of us went the way we needed together and we all got home successfully. We took the next day off school on the spurious grounds that it was still bad smog the next day at our village.

At school there was a cadet's group, and also a scout troop which I joined rather than the army cadets. I had a brother who made me believe the army was not my cup of tea. I joined and enjoyed the scouts, including, of course, the two weeks of camping during the Whitsuntide holidays. The time of year ensured that it was not necessarily nice weather and we were washed out a couple of times. I remember Galashiels in Scotland, the Llŷn Peninsula near Caernarvon. On one trip we also spent a night sleeping on Crewe railway station on our return from camping in Northern Ireland. It was a period when the IRA was active and I thank them for waiting until we left the campsite before the they blew up an electric substation, situated in the next field, the following day. The scouting also helped me a lot in my career, including the roughing it on Crewe station. I like to think a lot of now-elderly folk have spent a night on Crewe station. Palatial in 1954 it was not.

My father was basically tied to the farm and seldom left home for long; absent days were usually on Saturday when Stoke City played at home. Father had played for his village in his youth. One of the Stoke City team lived in our village and kept a few pigs on our farm to supplement his salary which was comparatively poor compared to later years. Frank (B) was marginally close to playing for England and did take part in a tour of Colombia (Bogotá) with England the A team.

The pigs were housed individually in a small enclosure with a brick floor, drainage and a boundary wall with a wooded door about four feet high. On the farm, we had our groceries delivered by the local grocer's shop. Len Taylor had a van for deliveries and we always knew when he was on his way long before he arrived. He fed the pigs with his unsold bread and the pigs could hear him coming from far, far away and would stand on their hind legs at the sty door squealing for bread. Then it was (in the vernacular), "Aye yup Len's cumin, put th' kettle on." How the pigs got to know the sound of Len's van on the A34 faraway among all the other traffic noise I have no idea.

At one stage we were improving the footing in the cow sheds on the farm. This involved a serious amount of concrete. One Saturday, when Stoke happened to be playing at home and father was away in Stoke, for some reason I was the sole person at the farm and out on the tractor haymaking. An unexpected full load of ready mixed concrete was dumped in the middle of the yard. A friend who regularly exercised his dogs on the farm found me down the fields on a tractor and told me about the concrete. I unhitched the turner and drove back to the farm at the top speed of eight miles per hour. True enough there was a full load of concrete which was seriously going hard. A hosepipe and tap were quickly set up, and with a shovel I set to work re-damping the load and turning it all over and over to delay hardening. Of course, there were no mobile phones in those days and our house phone came later. So, I was seriously knackered before anyone came to assist.

At secondary school I had a long-standing feud with the careers master who taught German. Nowadays he would be called a bully but it was tolerated by the regime in those years, and with my behaviour I would have been kicked out of school; therefore, it was not helpful to complain. My oldest brother had attended that school and was a good French-speaking student. Teacher Earnest (K) tried for two years to get me to enjoy learning German. After two years we were allowed to drop some subjects. I dropped German mainly because of (K). Most of the school, of around six hundred boys, knew about the friction between us. The German teacher was also the careers master and it was part of his job to offer advice as to what line the individual leavers should consider. Just before I left school as a senior, I decided I was not taking any career advice from him. As it happened, he stopped me in a corridor one day just before I left for home and said, "Massey, I expect you will want to come to see me about a career." A small crowd of my classmates were listening in as I told him, "Not so, and if you ever speak to me again, I will floor you." This enmity was known to most of the school to the extent that the usual end-of-year rugby match of staff versus students was cancelled, as many knew that I and the German master were not the best of friends. The school was afraid that I would break his leg(s). The physics master quietly agreed with me in this; he was a rugby fan and a good friend of mine.

PRACTICAL FARM WORK

After grammar school I enrolled at Harper Adams Agricultural College, which demanded that I did twelve months' practical work on a mixed farm before entry, regardless of the fact that I had been involved in farming all my life on a mixed farm with both crops and livestock. I tell myself that I did not learn much during that year on the farm where I was classed as a farm pupil; i.e., a low salary. The experience I needed most was farm accounting. I never got any and I still wonder if my employer was fiddling the books or just did not want this kid, daft enough to work for 'nothing', to know too much about his business.

I cycled six miles each way, six days a week, in rain, snow, fog, the lot. My parents did not have a car and turning up on a Fordson Major with a top gear of eight miles per hour was not on; besides, the home farm needed it. I had Saturdays off work, so I filled Saturday with rugby. The farm manager had just completed the course at Harper Adams so I did learn a lot from him. After I knew him, he tried to take on his own small farm, without much success, so he became a magician, entertaining children at parties and such. Odd.

I learned my biggest lesson one morning whilst fetching the cows in for milking. As I was rounding them up to drive them into the cowsheds, I saw that four or five cows were not getting off the floor, so I wandered over towards them to give them a nudge, and without getting too close I realised that they were dead. A clue was the fact there was the electric pylon in the middle of the corpses. I skirted the pole and realised that I was getting tremors in my legs, so I went and wasted no time in telling the farm manager, Roy (Watts). That was my introduction to the maxim, "When seeing something dead, try to find the reason it is dead before getting too close." This served me well in later life.

That later incident was useful when I was off-roading in Botswana, when I saw a dead wildebeest which looked to have died very recently. I got out of my truck and climbed through a fence. I walked just a short way and stopped, wary, then I spotted the lions watching me in the bushes, so I walked slowly backwards to the truck, wished them "Bon appétit," and scarpered.

I loved rugby and did my best to keep fit, running almost every evening on my regular three- or five-mile route. I was in the Harper second team for most of my first year, but filled in for absentee first team players. The first fifteen lost about half their games where we, the second fifteen, won nearly all of ours. Late on in the term the second fifteen challenged the first fifteen to a match but the firsts declined, which was almost the same thing as knowing that they would lose. The first fifteen was made up almost exclusively of second-year students. A match was arranged for a game of first year against second year. The first year beat the second year. I only remember one incident of that game and that was with my friend Stuart the other wing forward. He and I picked up the opposing scrum half and threw him at the ground. He was the college captain and went on to play for the Wasps and later England and the British Lions. He, Clive (A), later admitted that ours was the hardest tackle he ever received.

I loved college life. I was second youngest in our year and I soon had to lay down my marker not to be messed with. Early on I had a letter from a female cousin/friend and someone grabbed it and passed it around the class. No lecturer in sight, so when the biggest guy in class had my letter, Jack, I went for him and after that I had no problems. Had I not had that session with

Jack I was afraid I would have been teased. However, after that episode I believe he held a grudge. I was the second youngest of that year's intake but possibly the roughest.

The college frowned upon facial hair; no beards were allowed to be grown at college, so I grew one during the first Christmas holiday. Then I took it back with me to college, which was like a red rag to a bull. The only other no-no was long hair, which crowned the head of a guy in our year whose weekend fun was motor racing. John had a Frogeye Sprite which he used on the road to get to the races, but it had a high ratio gearbox and an engine which oiled up at less than 6,000 revs. It was quite noisy, so we knew when he was coming to college. The second year caught him one evening and cut his hair but they did not catch me; I suppose I was faster than John when he was not in his car. His hair was hung up as a totem. The second-year lot did not catch me though they tried regularly. College fun.

Exam time at the end of the first year was not a success. I was almost sent home for poor results in the first-year exams, but I managed to convince the principal at 'The Principal's Tea Party' that I would manage the coming year better. So, I stayed on and had fewer pub visits. At the end of my second year, I got a second-class result, but no one at Harper got a first in the national exam and I think there were only four firsts in the country that year, with none from Harper. However, sports were my priority, but I also enjoyed taking the piss out of old Etonians, though one, John (M), was a good friend. I irked one guy, a baronet D(N), so much that one day he came at me in my room with a set of brass knuckles, ready for action. Fortunately, I was in the process of slicing meat to make biltong. I picked up a meat hook, the S-shaped tool used to hang meat up in a butcher's shop. It had two sharp ends I used to hang strips of meat until dry – English biltong. Fortunately, he thought the better of his action and backed off and that was it, except that I lost my meat hook. It was confiscated, but I am not sure of what happened about the brass knuckles. However, as I had four more meat hooks in a drawer, I was not overly fussed.

One attempt to catch me for a shave which nearly succeeded was when the athletics team captain called me for a meeting to be held in his room in a separate building. It was a period when they were determined to trim my beard down to the skin, so I was hyper careful. I walked down the corridor, very quietly, and as I got close to the captain's room, I heard doors open behind me. On turning I saw two of the main people I recognised as wanting my 'facial fungus'. As I got to the captain's room I saw two doors, one on either side, opening with emerging people. I then started to run, a well-used rugby hand-off with each hand, and away I went, chased by a group. Down the stairs into the reading room, and luckily there was an open window. At a run I dived through the window onto the grass lawn, back onto my feet, and away down the road. The best runner of short distances on the athletics team chased me, but gave up before long. I got back to my room via the college farm fields and farm buildings. I think afterwards they just about stopped trying to kidnap me.

During my second year we had a very good rugby team; we had no stars but won almost all of the college long-term fixtures, mainly because we were a team and we lived almost like brothers, as there were only about 120 male students. I remember once we played against Tern Hill air force station; they had fourteen international players of varying ages. We lost, but not badly. I remember one incident of that game which still makes me chuckle. Some Harper player had booted a long ball down the pitch very close to the end of this tight match and close to the touch line. I chased the ball and so did a mountain of Irish muscle. We caught the ball up inches from the line together and my opponent stuck a boot into it, which sent it over the changing rooms. The ref admonished our Irish hero as to why he had kicked it so hard and wasted time so close to the end of the game. My Irish friend's excuse was, "I was kicking for touch, sir."

I graduated from college with a second diploma and after finding out that only one first scholarship was awarded that year from all agricultural colleges in England, I did not feel too bad that I came second!!!

So, what to do for a career? I wanted to remain connected to farming but was well aware that the nearest I could get in the UK would be as a farm manager and would never get a farm of my own and have a decent life. I considered the police and also the army, but neither could offer anything agricultural, and I also knew I could never accept the discipline of either. Looking back on my two years of college and chatting with other students, and in particular to the guys from various parts of Africa, a visit there seemed attractive. As I did not have the cash for a look-around visit, I decided to look into getting a job somewhere over there to 'test the water'.

The *Farmers Weekly* once more came in useful when the ladies' hockey team won a match when there were only about twenty female students. The ladies challenged the rugby team to a game of hockey. I was warned beforehand by friends who had participated in a female versus male hockey match as to what extra equipment was needed. Items such as a well-padded cricket box, shin pads and gum shield were essential. There was a new set of rules for this 'game': the rugby team could only pass backwards, could not hit the ball forwards, no bodily contact, etc. We were thrashed.

My parents always had a weekly delivery of the *Farmers Weekly* magazine, which had a section covering jobs available in England and occasionally abroad. Not more than a few weeks later, there was an advert from the Crown Agents saying they were recruiting for Tanganyika. I applied and was successful in getting a job with the Ministry of Agriculture. I do not remember being interviewed but I did enter their offices in London at some time or other. The post was for a hides and skins officer and, deciding that I had to start somewhere, I left for Africa a couple of weeks afterwards, on my twenty-second birthday. As I was broke, the payment of half my salary whilst afloat was a Godsend.

TWO

To Africa

Setting sail from London Docks on a Union-Castle cargo/passenger ship was the start of my African adventure. Accommodation was OK. I was sharing a cabin and the food was very good for a farm boy, but I desperately lacked exercise. The first stop was Gibraltar but by this time I was stir-crazy. Finding a likeminded body on board, we decided to run to the top of the rock, but found this less than satisfying. So, we ran down again and at the bottom we just looked at each other and did the return trip again. After that, I had no problems, so thank you, Gibraltar. Next stop was Naples, with which I was not enchanted, the adage 'See Naples and die' was true for me, except I would have died from boredom – my lack of culture perhaps.

Then through the Suez Canal. My only lasting memory from Egypt was having to put an Egyptian postage stamp on an aerogram as demanded, which made it heavier, so we had to put another on it too, and the miles of sand for a view. I think Egypt were unhappy about the recent war over the Suez Canal. I now realise that Egypt was short of cash and charging for a stamp was low as they could get.

By now the temperature was rising and the sea more tempting. We stopped off at Aden, where I took a taxi to Crater and bought duty free goods – namely a small radio and a camera. Our ship was anchored offshore, the Mediterranean was crystal clear, and we were in the small ferry taking us to our anchored ship. We watched as a recently purchased camera, far more expensive than mine, slowly sank to the bottom of the Med with a trail of bubbles. As expected, the owner was less than happy. We then trudged southwards to warmer seas and the ship's swimming pool now had water warm enough to enjoy.

The next stop was Mombasa, Kenya. It took three days to unload cargo, and many regular passengers took their mattresses or blankets from the cabin and slept on the beach. Next was onwards for a brief stop at Zanzibar, where I bought a pair of silver clove-shaped cufflinks which I have yet to wear. I was not on the island long enough to have a memory, good or bad. Then it was onwards, ever onwards, to our destination, Dar es Salaam.

THREE

Tanganyika (As Formerly Named)

After being ferried to the shore with my few belongings and met by government staff to handle my baggage, I climbed a flight of steps, sweating as I went. Customs was not a pleasant experience. My bag and trunk (an ex-army ammunition box) search was carried out by a Sikh who queried every item I had; e.g., "Why do you bring blankets? We sell blankets here? Why do you need kitchenware?" and so on. It was quite a while later that I realised he thought me to be rich or he wanted to impress port authorities in order to remain employed after independence, which was not far in the future, when Tanganyika would become Tanzania. At the time, I was quite a budding ornithologist and looked forward to seeing my first African bird. As I was going up the steps from the customs to the car, I saw a bird in a shrub. It turned out to be a budgerigar, obviously a tourist! I was taken to the best hotel in Dar es Salaam, the New Africa, luxury after life aboard. But when I watched the ship leave port, heading for Mozambique, I must admit I felt a bit like a castaway.

I spent a couple of weeks in Dar es Salaam being briefed and trained in hide valuation. As most disputes were between sellers and buyers of cattle, sheep and goat hides, my new job meant that I was supposed to adjudicate. I was also to ensure that storage sheds/huts were clean and tidy and nothing else was supposed to be in the sheds. I was eventually tired of imposing this and allowed for the necessity of safe storage of a bicycle. This was all new to me and I did enjoy the job, meeting people and discussing the villager problems. My area of operations was enormous, maybe 300 by 200 miles or more.

I was also to be present when crocodile skins were packed for export; the number and length of each was documented. Since leaving that duty I am led to understand that fifteen feet or so is classed as a BIG croc. I know that I watched numerous twenty-one-foot skins being packed when I was in the hides and skins department. I next bought a car in Dar using a government loan and set off for my duty station, Mbeya.

I was based in Mbeya, in the Southern Highlands, responsible for a massive amount of territory. I set out for my station, and was tootling along at around sixty miles per hour on the reasonably good tar road with almost no traffic. About sixty miles beyond Morogoro I saw a car coming towards me in the distance and as it got closer, I saw a rather good-looking lady driver. I was mentally admiring her as my car fell off the end of the tar road onto dirt. I thought I had lost at least two wheels! In fact, driving in Tanzania on dirt roads, bush tracks or no tracks at all made for easy driving, leaving behind all the problems of the UK. But it also had its own problems, such as livestock on the road. In the hotter season cattle and goats slept on the road, as it cooled faster than off-road. No roads were fenced off to keep animals away and cattle roamed freely in lion-free country. There were no catseyes set in the road, but cow's eyes and goat eyes in the road, shining in the headlights, did help. A major problem in the rainy season was of course mud, which was often impossible to get through without some bad language and sweat. Often there were empty roads, which were good unless you were having vehicle problems. There was no RAC or AA except in the cities. But other drivers could be very helpful.

One of the vets born in Tanganyika, Mike (H-W), took the trip from Mbeya to visit friends and relatives in Durban, which is near to the coast of South Africa. He and his wife set off in his Land Rover and were in the process of passing through Johannesburg city centre when he came to a major crossroads in the city centre and, in his own words, he just froze. Having no idea what to do, as he wondered what was legal, a member of the traffic police came up to him. "Move on." "I can't," he answered, "I don't know what to do. Look at my number plate, I am not used to all this traffic." The cop looked at the plate and said, "Where is that?" He answered, "Tanganyika," whereupon the cop opened the door and said, "Move over" in a rather threatening manner. He then got into the vehicle, drove it to the edge of the city, and got out after, saying to my friend, "This is the road to Durban. Now f*** off and don't come back."

I booked into a guesthouse run by a Scottish lady who knew everything and everybody, which was quite useful. As I was booking in there was an elderly guy ahead of me who was also checking in. He asked Nessie, the owner, if it was June or July and the reply was, "May." He asked seventh or fifteenth, and she answered, "No, it is the fourth." Then he wandered off to his room.

I later found out that he was a professional croc hunter who would take his old and battered Land Rover without doors into the seasonal dryish Ruaha swamp area, build a hut and park his Land Rover on a pile of timber. With the seasonal rains' arrival, the swamp filled with water and as the Ruaha River flooded, he had a boat and he stayed out there until the waters receded and then he returned to Mbeya to sell his crocodile skins. One year in the dry season he felt that a bit of company would help to while away the months on the swamp, so he went down to Jo'burg to find a wife. He returned with a woman who only had clothing suitable for the stage, as they had left in a hurry from the show. That is what she wore for quite a while, I believe. I have seen a book about this guy's exploits; he was quite a character.

He was a heavy drinker and after years so was she. The story goes that for a couple of years the pair had spent a lot of time at Mbeya Club and were completely sozzled when they set off to his camp at the edge of town. As I have said, his Land Rover had no doors, and when he swung around a roundabout at speed, she fell out, screaming, as she had broken her leg. He heard her screams and backed up, running over her other leg, breaking that one too. I feel that was enough of an excuse to say goodbye. So did she.

My operating area was from Songea to Sumbawanga – the whole of Southern Highlands Province, quite a chunk of territory. Another part of my job was to teach farmers not to brand livestock where the hot brand mark would damage the most valuable part of the hide, but to brand lower down the leg, which was of less use. The place to get the biggest audience for my advice on this was at the cattle markets. Before I could be of much use I needed to learn Kiswahili, which was spoken by almost everyone, but each tribe had its own tongue too. I was sent to enjoy a three-week course in the north, in Arusha. We got a basic grounding, to which we added vocabulary as we went along in the tour.

The course instructor enjoyed shooting and asked if I would like to come with him to get a few guinea fowl, which were plentiful out of town in the open range. The idea was to have me walking along the top of a valley with a .22 rifle and to drive the birds across the deep and steep valley. This, in the local lingo, is a *donga*. Not a bad plan, but after walking about four hundred yards through dry grass slightly above my knee height I got a surprise. A lioness walked out of the grass about six feet in front of me and just stood and looked at me. I stood as frozen for a different reason and just looked at her, me in terror and her as if pondering if I was fit to eat. She looked at me as if daring me to run, which I could not. After about what seemed an hour (one minute max) she just turned and walked back into the grass. There was a distant herd of cattle, which I believe she thought would be more fun, and she wandered back there. She perhaps unwittingly saved the lives of a few guinea fowl, as we immediately went back to town, not knowing how big the pride of lions was.

I had another entertaining experience the following weekend. Four of us students decided to climb an interesting hill which was capped by an immense egg-shaped rock. It was in a game park where no guns were allowed so we each took a panga, a two-foot-long bladed tool originally used by the Tanzanians for cutting sisal or sugar cane and enemies. It came in useful as the hill was covered in short scrub and we were all in shorts. On the way up we heard what we thought was a leopard but we didn't see one. We decided that climbing the rock was beyond us after a walk around it, and after a short rest, started down. Eventually it was my turn to go first and slash the thorny plants on our descent. Part way down I saw a small patch of dried grass, and just for the sake of avoiding a few scratches, I decided to walk across it. Halfway across I must have almost, or maybe I did, tread on a very large black mamba, which was sunbathing and was a trifle annoyed by my rude wake-up method. I did not blame it when I heard a rustling noise close behind me and, with the leopard on my mind, I jumped away, turned with raised panga, and saw that the snake had struck at my back, and its head had missed my chest by around six inches due to my twisting jump. It was a magnificent creature but I did not hang around to admire it; I was gone. The snake then chased my three companions up the hill. They told me it was travelling not on the ground but was on top of the scratchy shrubbery. I had antivenom in my truck but that was much too far away to be of any use. I later found out that the amount of antivenom I had was nowhere near what would have been needed if anyone had been bitten. On later reflection I decided that the snake's reaction was just a little over the top. I doubted that an apology would have sufficed. I later found out that haemotoxin was useless for mamba bites. Neuro antivenom was needed and lots of it, much more than I was carrying.

With the end of the course, I drove the six or seven hundred miles home to Mbeya. When I returned, I found that the regional veterinary officer, a Mr Silcock, was back; he had been on leave to the UK when I arrived and as I had not met him yet, I went to see him in his office. I later found him to be a rather stuffy individual but not without reason as, according to friends who saw me at our first meeting, I apparently put my feet on his desk as we chatted. I still cannot believe it but I am afraid I was that sort of person, so it could be true.

I had been allotted a house and found myself a 'houseboy' by the name of Asulwesie, who was a member of the Wanyakusa tribe from Tukuyu to the south of Mbeya. He was a great help getting me used to their customs and we became good friends, with occasional spats. One of the spats that I still laugh about was that one evening, when I had explicitly asked him to be on time to cook dinner as I was having a guest, the cook did not show up. I therefore had to prepare something myself, spaghetti and something, which turned out less than a success. As I was about to go to bed, Asulwesie arrived rather drunk and I gave him a real dressing down. He then went away, unhappily, to his quarters. The following morning he got his revenge as my breakfast consisted of cold spaghetti sandwiches.

On one occasion I was the only senior staff member in the office when a report of a rabid dog was brought in. I loaded up a couple of veterinary assistants and a couple of shotguns and went hunting a rabid dog. A local man led us from village to village that it had passed through and we eventually found two men sitting by a fire with the dog spitted and roasting. The conversation went something like this: "We want that dog." The reply: "You cannot have it; we saw it first." A couple of shotguns were sufficient to settle the argument and, after an explanation, the villagers thanked us for saving them. I guess the dog could have been edible if cooked well enough, but that is usually not the case in that society, nor was I about to try out the belief.

Mike H-W had hunted for quite a while and, being Tanzania born, the opportunities were plentiful. One of his yarns involved the Itigi thicket, which was just as named. It was not a favourite hunting ground but there were a few big elephants in the thickets. Getting to them meant crawling along water channels which were usually only just wide enough, shoulder width, to make any progress. Mike had heard elephants, decided to take a look, and set off crawling along a dry water bed with his gun, and as went he encountered a tree stump. He was about to crawl around it when he noticed it had toe nails. Crawling backwards is not well provided in our DNA but Mike reckoned he had the Tanzanian record.

A couple of interesting memories of Tukuyu come to mind. I was travelling there when there was thunder about and it started to rain – not just rain. It poured so hard that I could not see beyond my Land Rover, rain pouring down and then back up again. After a while I was able to see a few yards ahead, enough to keep me on the dirt road, and going down an escarpment. I could watch whole tea gardens of an acre or more sliding down into Lake Nyasa. It was said that day Tukuyu had twenty-four inches of rain in twenty-four hours. The lake level rose to the extent that people were scrambling onto the roofs of their thatched huts and the crocodiles were dragging them off. Then some brave soul found a motorised canoe and we went round the villages to take people to dry land.

Another time when I visited the area, I went to see a butcher who had a hide store. I checked it out and complimented him on its cleanliness. We chatted a while, sitting on a hide, and he invited me to take a cup of tea. He called to some woman to make tea for us and we sat and talked away. There was a large group of children of various sizes running around and I asked which of these kids were his kids. He took a look and said, "Most of them." In answer to my question as to how many children he had, he calmly replied, "Well, last year, when we last counted them, there were seventy-five." Me: "From how many wives?" The answer: "Ten."

There were three other Europeans in the office. Two were very helpful, but not the regional vet, and I suppose I can't blame him. The other two became lifelong friends and we hunted together numerous times along with a family of French/Germans born and bred in Tanzania on the Usangu Flats – the bottom of the Rift Valley – and our usual prey was birdlife, geese, duck and guinea fowl being our standard pot. Soon after leaving the road and out onto the flats we would collect a couple or so of guinea fowl and then swing north to Maji ya Moto (hot water), a hot spring. We would tie the guinea fowl legs to a long rope and fling them out into the place where the water was hottest, and then go looking for other stuff, returning to retrieve our cooked dinner. It was more like game watching than hunting, camping out using a camp bed and a mosquito net, with dogs to let us know if there was anything nasty in the area. In the part of the flats we frequented, there were no lions, but farther east there had been the hunting ground of a notorious pride of man-eaters around Igawa, Njombe district, during WWII. I believe there were about ten to twelve lions in this specific a pride in the area, and they hunted and killed many people before the game warden, George Rushby, managed to shoot the last one. He shot many of them but was unable concentrate on getting the lions, as he had other duties during the war going with Germany. It is reported that the lions killed 1,500 people before the pride were all shot out over a twelve-year period or so.

Apparently, lions are not overly fond of human meat and my personal close encounter did not turn the lioness I met at close quarters into a yummy-yummy hungry feline. Few lions are man-eaters. As with snakes, if they hunted humans there would be no more humans on the planet. The Njombe lions would break into houses, drag the screaming people outside, and eat them there and then whilst other villagers watched in terror. Alternately, they would drag the body away and picnic in peace. The norm would then be to find the nearest source of water and afterwards look for the place they intend to sleep the day in the shade.

As with many things in Africa, nothing is straightforward, and this Njombe problem was tangled up in local chieftainship and witchcraft. The colonial office had sacked a chief who was also a witch doctor. He claimed that he controlled the lions and that the killings would not stop until he was reinstated as chief. The game warden was overburdened and understaffed due to WWII, with troubles throughout the Southern Highlands, and could only deal with the Igawa lions when other duties allowed him to be away. The lions travelled over a wide area and he had to walk long distances to get to the latest killing(s) and then try to catch up with them. Meanwhile, the ex-chief/magician was telling tribesmen and women that the lions were magical and he would not stop them until he was chief again. Eventually the game warden was able to shoot the last lion – about two weeks after the chief had been reinstated. That is Africa. One reason for the long reign of terror was that the villagers were afraid to shoot them because of the believed connection with the magician's spells. They believed the witch doctor would kill them by some spell or other. Poisoning was the normal route the witch doctor took to get rid of the whoever had upset him or her.

In East Africa, there was a belief that witch doctors could turn themselves into lions and prey on people; alternately, they could control lions to attack people. Trackers would track the lion spoor after the killing of a person into the bush and then after a while the spoor footprint would become a human footprint. Then the tracker would stop and return afraid. As late as 1964 the lion-men were operating in eastern Tanzania and the government demanded it be stamped out. I was not involved, but heard later that troops tracked the 'lions' to their lair. They found a cave with youths in pens, the roof so low that they could not stand. When these people were sent out on a mission to kill, the youths had lion paws attached to hands and feet or knees. The 'lions' were heavily drugged on something or other and it is believed that the military shot them all, including the handlers. That seems to have been the end of 'lion-men' in that part of Tanzania.

There was also a similar belief of leopard-men in Congo, and that they could possibly still be operating in the rural areas. I have not heard anything lately of such activity there.

It was in Mbeya that I met my future wife, Francis, aka Gabby. I came off the golf course and she was shivering in a corner of the clubhouse, so I threw my sweater at her and went and joined the golfing group for a shandy. We did meet again after a few days, as she returned the sweater and I learned just why she was so cold. She was raised in southern California and was teaching in Mbeya. She returned home in the States after the end of her contract. We kept in touch until we found it sensible to get married. She still gets frozen, especially in our British winters. Poor soul. We did not marry for five years as she was in the American Peace Corps and had returned to her teaching.

I had never played golf in the UK, but in Africa it was something to do after work. We had a threesome; the other two were the veterinary office guys, but not the boss man. Between us we had four dogs which accompanied us, and we wondered why other golfers gave us a wide berth. As I played, I got into it and was not doing badly until I developed a 'banana' shot. This was so bad that when I played a shot it nearly hit me on the back of my neck. I tried everything to correct this but to no avail and eventually I was driven to quit. I walked into the clubhouse, threw my clubs into a corner, and informed all that I was quitting golfing for good. A coffee farmer, Gordon (E), asked if I really meant what I had said and could he buy my clubs, and I said, "No." Pause… "You can just take them home." (I have not touched a club for the last sixty-six years and do not intend to do so.) The result was that the next morning I found a hessian gunnysack of coffee beans at my door – it took forever to use them all. Thank you, Gordon.

I started work and, having camped in the scouts and done my share of hand milking and farm work on a less than highly mechanised farm, I was able to relate to the customs of the local people, and my language course helped tremendously. I then set off on my first 'safari', which means a period of work (in the bush) and not a holiday jaunt, as seems to have become the meaning of late. I was equipped with a tent, a rolled-up table, a folding chair and a camp bed. I obtained the necessary kitchen items and food plus the essential water container, but this proved far too small. I later graduated to a forty-four-gallon barrel and later in life to two such barrels. I was about fifty miles from Mbeya and thinking about what I needed, then suddenly remembered I would need to cook and had no matches. Being a nonsmoker, I just forgot. Rubbing two sticks or two boy scouts together was another option, but I decided to try matches first. I stopped at a *duka*, a small wayside mud-built shop. I walked into the shop and a woman appeared from the rear, a child on her back and naked from the waste up. Her breasts, which showed signs of wear, were tucked into the top of her *kanga*, which is basically just a piece of cloth around the waist of respectable length (a sort of wrap-around skirt). I requested matches, which she had in stock, and then her baby started to cry, so she pulled a breast from the top of her kanga and handed it to her child over her shoulder. It was all part of the learning curve! I then drove onto the Usangu Flats.

The story is, and it seems to be true, that during the time of Shaka Zulu of South Africa he sent an *impi* north raiding for cattle. They got as far north as the Usangu Flats and drove the Wasangu tribe westwards from their territory, rounding up as many cattle as they could find. In addition, they had noticed a small smoking hill of volcanic activity and decided to take it home as a gift for their chief. They dammed a small stream for a water supply and started digging. Eventually they gave up and returned home because of a series of deaths amongst them, due to a fouled water supply. The ditch they were digging could still be seen when I was shown the site by a local man.

After a few of my monthly trips to the cattle markets on the Usangu I got to know my way around this trackless expanse and to know the local people quite well. Cattle markets were held at different villages weekly, spread over the area, and were held every other day in a constant pattern. I therefore had a day of work and then a day left to myself. Every other day I would therefore drive to a new camping spot, sometimes near a village and other times completely in the bush. I had a favourite campsite, with a tree that had hanging branches which started twelve feet up the trunk and then drooped the twelve feet back to the ground, so that it left a lot of space for a campsite. I cleared all the thorns away and cut a gap to get my vehicle inside the foliage and I stayed there regularly. It was about fifteen yards from the Ruaha River, which provided food. Birds such as guinea fowl, partridges, ducks and the occasional goose were all on the menu. Occasionally I would fish for my breakfast, and one small fish I loved was a nine-or-ten-inch silver fish that tasted beautiful if eaten immediately, but if left for more than thirty minutes tasted and smelled like dog poo! How did I know? My dogs told me. There were larger fish in the river, mainly barbel. I would use bits of meat as bait and, being alone, I fished naked to keep cool. One day I was using a hook attached to a piece of steel trace attached to my line and I was above waist deep in the river when I cast to the opposite bank of the Ruaha River and I got a familiar tug on the line. Then the line went dead, so I reeled it in, only to find a clean-cut steel trace. It did not take me long to realise that my delicate bits were under water, and a rapid retreat was needed. To this day I do not know what could have cut that trace. I took up fishing in khaki shorts, standing yards from the river, from then on.

 I would wash in that river using my government issue bath. This I would sink into the river and sit in it to keep the sand and mud out of crevices. I occasionally saw small crocodiles watching me as I bathed, and now I realise how big a risk this was: baby crocs have mummy and daddy parents. I was told that the Ruaha croc only ate fish; I did not try to prove it either way. I also heard this about the Okavango swamp crocs before they were heavily hunted; croc shooting is now banned in the swamp. The Ruaha is, I believe, now a game reserve, so all hunting is banned.

 Diversion: I had recently received an email from Australia

about a youngish couple who were walking along the bank of the lake near Darwin, discussing their pending divorce, splitting the home effects and funds, etc., when a twelve-foot croc charged out of the lake and started to chase them. And crocs are unbelievably fast. The croc was gaining, then the wife remembered she had her 0.22 Ruger pistol in her handbag. She took it out and fired just once and that was enough, and she walked happily homewards. No man can run fast with a bullet in the knee… pertinent joke.

There was one local individual I knew well and we fished, swam and wrestled together during off days, but I could never get him to act 'sensibly' when I was on duty. I would be at an auction when suddenly I would hear a loud howl and he would come racing up and jump onto my back, or drag me to the ground wrestling, or just start punching me. He was obviously a local character and the crowd would laugh. I guess it helped me in my work, as they saw that I was not at all pompous, and when I was talking to them about the branding, they would take notice. I did do branding occasionally as a demonstration, which also helped. They understood that I knew my business and would then ask for help with other livestock topics. Being as young as I was, with little experience of Africa, with hindsight now I realise how tolerant the local farmers were towards me. In the office there was one elderly local with long experience of the duties required who could not accept me, a complete novice, as a boss. I now realise I must have upset him because I had usurped his job and he got himself transferred. So, Rajabu, I do apologise.

Usangu Flats were desperately hot for much of the year and, when it became too oppressive, I would go to the Chimala Escarpment and face the twenty-four hairpin bends to the top of the Elton Plateau, where it was cool, and could even have frost at night in the winter. The road was tortuous and used by traders bringing down the harvest of pyrethrum flowers using forward control Land Rovers. It necessitated that on almost every corner they would be forced to take two full lock attempts to navigate the bends. My Peugeot estate always needed to take a rest on the climb; I guess it was overheating due to the rarefied altitude and hard work. One of the advantages of going up there was the streams of clean water that had been stocked with rainbow trout during wartime, I was told. The few local people there thought they were snakes, so the trout were unsophisticated and readily took a carefully offered wet fly. After a couple of days, I would return to work at the bottom of that scary hill.

I was in Tanganyika when there was a diplomatic spat with Rhodesia. It turned out that fuel imports for Zambia had to be routed through Dar es Salaam and southern Tanganyika, soon to be renamed as named Tanzania, and southwards. Also soon to be renamed as Zambia was Northern Rhodesia. Unfortunately, Tanzania was having a particularly heavy rainy season and the road became a four-hundred-mile bog. Wheel tracks in the mud were very deep and only lorries and four-wheel-drive trucks could dare to try to get through; it became well known as the Hell Run. Trying to avoid the Hell Run led to other traffic problems. Traffic tried using the dry season swamp road and it would take three or four days to travel the two hundred plus miles to Iringa. Local transporters had a profitable year and many new transport 'companies' sprung up who had seriously aged trucks which 'caught fire' on the way. It is reputed that drivers sold off the drums of petrol on the way and then fired their vehicles and claimed a new lorry from the insurance.

Part of my work area was Sumbawanga District, which was actually a part of Western Province, but due to it being a difficult place to get to from Tabora it was handed over to me. I would travel southwest through the coffee farming area south of Mbeya and into Northern Rhodesia, as there was no direct road from western Tanzania to Sumbawanga. It was a matter of miles of dirt road, along the Northern Rhodesia border on their side to Abercorn, then back into Tanzania and from there north to Sumbawanga. No passport required. On one of my trips in a heavy rainstorm, wallowing through puddles on the dirt road, I almost ended my activities. It was dark and very wet but, in my headlights, I saw an unusual puddle. After taking a closer look, I got my fishing rod and found it was about four feet deep and flowing rather fast. So, I backed off and slept in my car and waited for morning, which obligingly provided a bulldozer to fill the 'puddle', as the flash flood had ended. I could then continue, pass through the border barrier, and on to my duties.

Sumbawanga was not far from the escarpment of the rift wall. It was a very friendly town with very little going for it. It was a colonial 'punishment' station due to its location. There was a cattle ranch nearby, which had been established by a German character sometime in the late nineteenth century. Eventually he got lonely, which didn't surprise me. In the early twentieth century, he walked the five or six hundred miles to the coast, travelled to Germany by ship, and found a wife. He arrived back in Sumbawanga with his new wife after walking the six hundred miles back again from Dar es Salaam. It was not long before she was less than impressed with the lifestyle and, preferring Germany, she set off on foot back to the coast. After a while hubby decided he had made a mistake in letting her go and set off after her, and got to Dar es Salaam before she caught a ship. How he managed to convince her to return to Sumbawanga is not known. They then walked the six hundred miles back to Sumbawanga and home.

It was rumoured that he was a less than pleasant man, and one story claims that he took a raft load of oranges to market across Lake Rukwa with two paddlers, which is quite large. Lake Rukwa is a shallow lake and subject to violent storms. It has no outlet but is fed mainly by the Momba River. After a sudden storm that wrecked his raft and lost almost all the oranges, his journey ended. Local anglers eventually found him in the reeds, after floating for almost a month on a waterlogged wreck of a raft, living on what few oranges were left on the raft and drinking lake water. The raft could only support half his weight and his legs had been heavily gnawed upon by barbel fish as they had been trailing in the water all the time. There was no sign of his paddlers. Rumour has it that when the lake dried up a few years later, as was not uncommon, as it depended on the climatic whims and the lake had no outlet, two skulls had been found with a bullet hole in the head of each.

He met his end quite a few years later so I heard, when he was in Northern Tanzania and got into an argument with the locals, who are a very proud tribe, and he succumbed to the sharp end of a Maasai spear. He was not the only European to suffer similarly. Some white guy working in the same general area had a shot a lion which had been giving villagers a really hard time, and in gratitude one of the villagers offered his wife for the night to him. He said, "No, thank you" at which the warrior got really angry and shouted, "What is wrong? Is my wife not good enough for you?" and speared him. I learned that if I was ever in that situation, which luckily never occurred, the answer could be, "I am sorry but my wife died two weeks ago," so, I am in mourning. If the Maasai lost a wife, it was no sex for six months.

I arrived in Sumbawanga not long after that. His wife was still around and their son ran the ranch. His ranching business was going well, and his mother usually sat outside where she overlooked most of the ranch with a pair of binoculars, spotting lions. If she saw one the info would be sent to the son by radio, so stock losses were low. They sold their beef to Abercorn, just over the border in what is now Zambia. The son usually carried a holstered handgun on market and travel days, as he often had to carry quite a large sum of money. He used the gun once when a cow went mad in the auction ring and he shot it with just the one bullet, which impressed the local people. A second incident occurred when he was driving down the road with local people on the back of his truck and he encountered a flock of guinea fowl crossing the road. He stopped, took one shot and blew the head off one of the birds. After that he was considered someone to be respected.

Sumbawanga had its own local character. It was a girl of around sixteen who walked about the town playing a tin whistle whilst stark naked. Her roots were not known but she was cared for by everyone and anyone. If she asked for food, she would get it. She was fully accepted and watched over by residents. The townsfolk would try to give her clothes, but she rejected them. One day some travelling male turned up and he raped her, which was not clever. The locals hung him.

When the sisal grower's union in Morogoro was giving the government problems, their union leader was rusticated to Sumbawanga and we shared the guesthouse. When I left, I offered to bring him anything he would like from Mbeya, and he replied that he would appreciate a pineapple, and was supplied some. He was later jailed and moved to the north and never seen again, as far as I am aware.

When I was in the area, initially I occasionally slept in the station wagon and once, on stopping on the edge of the rift wall, I was able to read a newspaper in the car due to the almost constant lightning flashes. On returning to base, I decided to exchange my Peugeot for something more robust, so I bought my first Land Rover series one, a pickup, which served me well despite its age.

There was a tourist hotel on the northern side of Lake Rukwa, called the Outspan, Afrikaans for a stopping place. The hotel had an immense rock wall behind it, the rift wall, and in front close by was the lake. Once when I visited, due to the heavy rains, the lake level was unusually high and had started washing away the foundations of the hotel. So much that we guests were sitting in the dining room with rod and line, fishing for breakfast. Before the flooding, there had been a swimming pool between the lake and the hotel, which was now filled with lake water. On starting the day one morning, I was told that there was a hippo in the hotel swimming pool that was unable to clamber out. It had probably been wandering along in the shallow lakeside in the night near the hotel and suddenly dropped about three feet or more. It was surprisingly amiable for possibly the most lethal animal in Africa. After breakfast we engaged all residents and many men from a nearby village to fill the shallow end with rocks from the cliffs. The hippo watched the activities nonchalantly and was still there in the evening, but had gone by the next morning without so much as a goodbye kiss.

I would occasionally visit Songea, a small town to the southeast of my working area on the Ruvuma River, between the Indian Ocean and Lake Malawi. I would take the road to Dar es Salaam and then turn off into Njombwe District to the south, onto a poor road. The main population were descendants, remnants, of an *impi* of Zulus who had no wish to return to South Africa. They reasoned that they had fought for the cattle, so why should they turn them over to Shaka? The Matabele of what became Zimbabwe are part of the same group who stayed behind, but at the time the Tanzanian group thought it too close to that headcase, Shaka, and continued northwards. By now the Tanzanian contingent decided that it was necessary to put more space between themselves and Shaka's warriors, where they would be safe. They eventually settled north of the Ruvuma River after politely 'asking' the people there to leave using their assegais.

The way to Songea is rough terrain, and it is rumoured that a group of four Chinese surveyors set off to explore a route for a railroad, and were completely got lost for six weeks before they gave up surveying and were eventually rescued by the locals. Not long afterwards, a road was built to Songea on a route surveyed by Rope Soled Jones, and a bus route established. The bus to Songea had three fare rates – first, second and third. People could sit where they wished and the seating was uniform throughout the bus. However, if the bus had a problem, got stuck in the mud or slipped off the road, etc., the third-class passengers had to get off and shove, the second class got off and walked, and first class could remain on the bus. During the dry season, obviously, most people bought third-class tickets.

On one of my trips, I came upon a Mercedes lorry blocking that road on the escarpment with a very deep gorge on the right and a mountain on the left. The lorry was on its side and fully blocking the road. It had suffered a broken half-shaft. Very soon a bus arrived behind me and there were cars coming from both directions, so a pow-wow was held. The driver, who was unhurt, had lost the forward control and rather cleverly reversed into the rock wall to the left to prevent him careering over the edge. It apparently had a broken a half-shaft. The decision was made to chuck the truck over the edge and into the abyss; this was accomplished after unloading it and then using numerous jacks and plenty of muscle. I later found out that the lorry belonged to some Christian mission, but just where I never found out.

On arrival in Songea I booked into the only hotel, but the owner said he could not supply a meal unless I gave him ten shillings to go shopping, as he had only that day been released from prison. We shared a decent meal.

I had been told of a fantastic waterfall about a two day's walk away so I set off to take a look at the weekend. On the way I saw someone on the path, it turned out to be a European. As he got closer, I recognised him: he had been at college with me. But instead of the banal greeting, "Dr Livingstone, I presume," we ignored each other. We then walked a bit, then turned around laughing.

Back in Mbeya we heard that a convoy of trucks was on the way from the north. It was shortly before Kenya achieved independence; the convoy was made up of mainly Boers and their families who were leaving, heading for Rhodesia and South Africa. It was a very long convoy which passed through Mbeya, every adult carrying a rifle, and nobody had asked, fifty miles south at the northern Tanzanian border, to see passports. Apparently, at the Zimbabwean border no one asked to see visas or passports for leaving Tanzania or for going south for entry either. Not a surprise, really.

At the border post there was a small but decent hotel used mainly by people not achieving the closing time of the border post. Needless to say, it was rather boring for the three youngish Rhodesian border staff. One night just after closing they heard someone knocking on the door. They ignored it for a while, but the knocking persisted and got louder, so one of the staff answered the door. He was faced by a rather beautiful young lady wanting to get to Kipiri Mposi. Asked why she was so desperate to get to Kipiri Mposi on the Copperbelt that night, as there was a rather comfortable hotel across the road, she said she had to be in the town for a show later that evening. On being asked which part she played in the show, she admitted to being a tassel dancer. The guy's eyes lit up and in no time appropriate music was found; the counter in the office was cleared and used as a stage, and the young lady was later on her way with border control's best wishes.

Mbeya, the regional capital of Southern Highlands, had a rather nice railway station with a decent platform – but no lines. The nearest line was four hundred miles away. It was decided that it would not be commercially viable carrying anything, after it was built. The line was eventually put in many years later, long after I had left, built by the Chinese. The roads in Mbeya were tarred but quickly became dirt roads once leaving the town, which quickly turned into a 'washboard' and were poorly maintained. To avoid this washboard effect, a driver could travel at over fifty to sixty miles per hour, which eased the punishment, as I believe only the top of the washboard rib was touched; it only skimmed the ridges. The government employed a man with a tractor who would try to keep the corrugations to a minimum: a bushy tree would be cut down and dragged behind a tractor. This method did work after fashion but it put up clouds of dust whilst the tractor was there and the thorns left behind were a hindrance, and punctures were plentiful.

Another village, called Kamsamba, close to Lake Rukwa, was a place I regularly visited and I occasionally stayed at the Catholic mission there. It was staffed with three Canadian missionaries who I got to know very well whilst working in the area. When checking the hide storage facilities, I was quite amused in that I could catch one or two and sometimes three traders with an utter mess in their stores. And then the drumming started, and within an hour every store would be completely acceptable. On hearing the drums I knew all stores were clean and it was pointless visiting any more villages. The talking drums were an efficient means of communication and spreading news, which I found out when a ten-year-old child had drowned in the river. His body was found and the talking drums gave a whole group of local villages the information that the funeral was on, and hundreds of people arrived the next day for the sad event, from an area that I had thought was thinly populated. The Father Superior was reputed to understand the drums.

I had been given an introduction to another Catholic mission. It was usually staffed by three French Canadian White Fathers.

The mission was located close to the Momba River which is the main source of water for Rukwa Lake. When I arrived, a lone missionary met me gladly. After a short chat he saw my guns in the truck and asked if I would like to shoot a few ducks along the river. I answered, "Gladly", so off we went. He told me that he was short of food there so we got a number of ducks. On our return to the mission, he offered accommodation, which I accepted happily, as it was getting dark. He set to on one of the ducks and, thinking he did not realise what day it was, I gently reminded him that it was Friday, which was a meat-free day for Catholics at that time. He agreed it was a no-meat day and, as ducks ate fish, they were therefore fish, so he was allowed to eat duck. It was a good dinner, as he was good cook and a decent shot, if not a good Catholic.

Father Poel was also a French Canadian missionary. He had escaped from the *Simba* (lions) guerrillas in the Congo where there was a full-blown attempt to kick out the government and was quite violent. I believe it was Mobuto who employed a mercenary usually referred to as Mad Mike Hoare. He and a few others like him helped to squash the attempt at takeover, but things did not improve by much. Father Poel had escaped by crossing Lake Tanzania in a dugout with two oarsmen and four nuns. All four nuns had died on the journey across the lake due to their treatment at the hands of the Simba rebels. He had been granted a year of rest from his work in Africa by the Church to get over the ordeal. He subsequently left the ministry and married in Canada.

On his death years later, by which time he had left the church, he had asked Father Phillipe of Kamsamba to care for his wife and, as Phillipe had also left the Church, he was able to take her under his wing.

The Father Superior, Phillipe, became a very good friend of mine, who never tried to convert me to Christianity and even less to Catholicism. Incidentally, I have no faith, which could have been an asset when working as no one was pressured. We fished and hunted together and even went fishing for trout on the Elton Plateau after visiting his boss, the bishop in Mbeya, and could get lost for a few days. On one fishing trip, accompanied by Father Martin Poel, we arrived on the Elton Plateau on Saturday evening and fished on Sunday morning. Fathers Poel and Phillipe tossed up as to who would say morning mass. Phillipe lost and Poel went fishing. Phillipe found a place where the stream bank had slid down to be almost at the water. He then stood on the slipped piece of land at his chest height and spread his altar cloth on the ground, which was at an adequate height to act as an altar. He was halfway through mass when Poel came back and stood swinging a string of good-sized trout in front of his face. Phillipe was going full stream in Latin when I distinctly heard him suggest to Poel to go away in anything but religious language.

Phillipe told me that during the previous week he had called into one of the villages as usual on his small motorcycle, to hold a service as was the norm, but the normal number of people who would come to greet him were just not there. He waited a while then went to the house of one of his congregation who he knew well, and knocked. No answer. So, he knocked a bit harder and eventually the door opened just a slit. Phillipe said, "Hello," and the woman whispered, "Is that you, Father?" "Yes, it is me." "Is it really you?" "Yes, it really is me. Why do you ask?" "Promise you are not a ghost." "I promise I am not a ghost." The door then opened a little wider and the rest of the family came out to join in the conversation. Apparently, the last time Phillipe had passed through the village, which had a very sandy path, a lion was chasing him. As he was battling with the sand, he was going slower than usual, and the villagers thought they would not see him alive again. Phillipe mentioned later that he had heard an odd noise behind him, but concentrating on the sand had prevented him from looking behind.

Phillipe also told me of an incident where he heard a shot when in the bush, then nothing, then another shot, and this went on for a little while. He decided to investigate, and saw that there was a hunter with an old muzzle-loading musket who was being chased around a biggish tree by a maddened buffalo. Once the man had got his gun loaded again, which is quite a feat when being chased around a tree, making sure you do not trip on an exposed root or such, he would get off another shot. Eventually Phillipe rode his motorbike close enough to get the buff to chase him instead of the hunter so the hunter could leg it away. A close encounter of the less than enjoyable kind.

Father Phillipe had a visit from an old school friend who wanted to go hunting and I was invited to go with them as a backup gun. No one should hunt elephant without a backup gun and I was the only fool around who had the capacity for that role. It was as hot as Hades and we took what we thought would be enough water, but it turned out to be insufficient. We ran out of water, even though it had rained a short while before and the water there was in such hollows as elephant footprints. Phillipe and I were happy drinking this water but his friend refused to touch it. After a while he got into trouble, and on the way back to the mission he had to be carried in a makeshift stretcher and 'hospitalised' at the mission for five days afterwards. My reasoning, which he had rejected, was that he could be treated for an upset stomach but not death. However, I had a priest with me if the worst happened.

On one of my visits, which usually ended up with a decent story, he told me of a rogue elephant which frequented the track from numerous villages over the Momba River. The animal had killed quite a number of churchgoers as they walked to and from church, and Phillipe asked if I would back him with my heavy rifle. I asked him if he had ever shot an elephant and he said had not. Neither had I, so I agreed. Mad? I asked how we should find this particular elephant; his reply was a bit worrying when he said, "Don't worry, he'll find us." Jumbo did not turn up for us on that day but was later shot by a game scout. It was a tuskless bull and the theory was that the tusks were in-growing, which put pressure on the brain, and they became mad.

On one trip in that area, I was travelling through the bush with no track to follow down close to the Momba River, and not far from the Zambian border, when I heard a very strange noise. I decided that it was not my truck and got out to find where the noise was coming from. It sounded like a concrete mixer. I thought I knew my area but when I came upon a hive of industry building a bridge across the Momba River, I was rather surprised. I was a member of the Southern Highland Development Committee but knew nothing about a rather large building site. On enquiring, I gathered that the intention was to build a bridge over the river at this particular spot because it was the best route to build a road to Sumbawanga and save having to go through Zambia. The chief engineer in Mbeya had asked me previously if I could recommend a route up the escarpment across the river. I had told him of an elephant track used by the jumbos when coming off the top of the escarpment down to the Rukwa plains. So, it was my fault, but as nobody told the elephants it was my suggestion, I was not harassed by them. No one else on the Southern Highland Development Committee left the office if it could be avoided, so there were no other suggestions. My cook told me often when I caught him washing my Land Rover that if I was seen in a dirty vehicle, I could not be important, as I had to go to the field and not sit in office every day. It did seem to be logical and very true.

At the time of independence for Tanganyika, people were

worried about what would happen and it seemed that Julius Nyerere was taking over from the Brits. The expats were not sure how the locals would behave during and after the event, so most of us took ourselves into the bush, taking food and drinks for a four-day party. About twenty-five of us with went to the Usangu Flats with enough beer and all the clobber for a fun camping trip. On the first day, a bunch of us had decided we would go and look for buffalo. Early the next morning some of us took a walk to where we thought we would find buffalo. I am sorry to admit I had consumed well over the recommended alcohol limit for a walk with the big gun. I felt dreadful, my guts were unhappy, my head hurt, I was bleary eyed and felt as weak as a kitten, i.e., not the best condition for taking on a buffalo or a jumbo (otherwise known as a tembo). I guess that, luckily, we did not find any. We stayed about four or five days before returning to the Mbeya, where all was good and safe as previously. We enjoyed our four-day barbeque, mainly duck and partridges or guinea fowl, and bathing in the river water and a few game-spotting drives. The only game of note was a cheetah ambling along at a stately thirty miles per hour, driven by the Mbeya magistrate, also an expat. We were rattling along trying to get closer to see just what speed he could get up to but gave up after he got up to forty miles per hour, as the truck sounded as though it was about to fall apart on this black cotton soil, and the animal carried on without a care.

The story is that just after the change in Tanganyika's government from colonial rule to independence, the first official visitor was the president of Egypt. He was met at the airport by Mwalimu (Teacher – the local name for Tanganyika's president) and they travelled together to the state house in Dar. On arrival there, the Egyptian, seeing the security fences and walls, commented, "I suppose all this will be taken down now." Ooops. It had only just been erected!

I was visiting the north of my area when, nearing Chunya, I saw an odd sight. There was an extremely large acreage, thousands of acres, of planted pine woodland, said to be the second largest area of planted forest in Africa. It was usually a rich green, but when I saw it, it was all brown. I was a little worried and when I got back to Mbeya, about four days later, I told the forestry officer, who got into a tizzy, and we went together to look at it. He almost had a fit – he just could not believe it. It turned out that it was some sort of viral attack. We turned around and went to Mbeya, him to the telephone and me to the club for my normal shandy.

On another trip, returning from the north, I was passing through Chunya, which pre-WWII was a prosperous gold mining area. The mines were a hangover from the time when Tanganyika was a German colony, but Chunya was now a ghost town. However, there was a pub with a beautiful bar of polished wood, curved and long. There was one woman in the bar, sitting on a stool, who turned out to be the barmaid. I asked about business and she replied that there was almost none, she had sold almost nothing, but had a lot of stock left over from wartime and when many of her patrons (Germans) were interned or the Brits and South Africans joined the allies. I asked the prices of the drinks and they were still pre-war prices, so I bought a case of gin and a case of whisky and returned to Mbeya. I casually remarked that there was cheap booze in Chunya, which is about forty or fifty miles up into the hills, and then watched as people slowly made their excuses for leaving the club early and went hell bent for Chunya. It took me many BBQs to dispose of all those spirits and I was only occasionally blamed for the headaches.

Mike H-W was driving through Chunya one day on duty and noticed a dog lying in the gutter, and for some reason which he could never explain, he stopped. The dog was at death's door and Mike asked who owned it. The locals said it was a *shenzi* (an unowned mutt). They said as nobody owned it, if he wanted an almost dead dog, he was welcome to it. The dog was virtually bald, puss oozing from its eyes, worms, and could hardly stand, never mind walk. So, Mike turned around and went back home where he could attend to it. He nursed it back to full health and it turned out to be an extremely good pointer. He would fetch anything shot down except ducks. Why? No idea, but a few guesses.

At the end of my two-year tour, I felt that I was now able to take care of myself, and when asked if I would like to return after taking leave, I had no hesitation but to agree, with the proviso that I would in future deal with livestock, not with hides. This was agreed and I would be transferred to Central Region. Whilst on leave I spent a couple of weeks attending a course for Land Rover maintenance, which I found useful. On the course I met a couple of university students with their fiancées who were intending to travel from England by road to see as much of southern Africa as they could, so I told them to look me up. Once I understood their route, I suggested they would find me if they asked the first European they met on entering Tanzania; they were sceptical. As it happened, the first guy they met was the owner of the garage where I had bought my Land Rover. Robbie Rosevelt was a very good friend who was able to tell them I was in Dodoma and just where.

It was a saying that after your first tour you would be able to settle back in England, as little would have changed: the pub would still have your favourite stool and you friends would mainly still be single. However, it went on that if you took a second tour, that would be it, you would not be able to settle back in Blighty, everything would have changed and you would go back to Africa. I went back to the lure of Africa and South Asia for fifty years.

CENTRAL REGION

I was transferred to Central Region and based at a veterinary research station in Mpwapwa, where they were studying cattle and goats, plus grasses, as Central Region was relatively dry compared to the Southern Highlands. I settled in and shared a house with an American Peace Corps guy of about my age. We got on well. Joe and I played pool on the club billiard table regularly. The table had belonged to another club about sixty miles away at a ranch called Kongwa. It had previously been the site of a large programme run by the Brits to grow groundnuts, also known as peanuts. It was intending to provide the UK with margarine after WWII. The attempt was a disaster. The project was abandoned. All it managed was to kill around five thousand rhinos, so it is said, and to clear a lot of bush, which by the time I got there was good cattle range. There were rumours that the failure was due to lack of expertise and that could well be true, as many farmers are growing groundnuts even to this day in the same soil. Stories of cement being used as fertiliser and not one agriculturist among the complete military staff were very possibly true.

Kongwa ranch was the first to use artificial insemination in cattle in southern Tanzania. They ordered one thousand straws, and one of the European staff carried out the inseminations. The local staff of the ranch were very undecided about the inseminator. They were unsure if he was successful or not as a bull; he had inseminated a thousand head but he had only five hundred calves for his efforts.

There were only two members left in the Kongwa club clientele, which had a European population of two and no other snooker table with a British table within a radius of fifty miles. They were due to leave at the end of their contract apparently, and the Mpwapwa club agreed to buy the snooker table for the grand total sum of 10/- (50p), but it was buyer collect. The roof was taken off the club, and a large crane lifted the table out of the club and put it on a Bedford truck and took it fifty miles to Mpwapwa. My story on this topic ends here because I never did get to hear how they got it off the truck, nor how it got into the club without having to take down a wall. The effort succeeded, however, and the table was a lovely one to play on, with a slate base and wonderful cushes – 'cushions'. Obviously the military looking after bored squaddies.

I only shared accommodation with Joe for a short while, as he was due to leave just after I arrived. There was one memorable incident worth relating. It was a normal evening at the club where a number of South Asians were playing snooker and watching. Joe and I were watching too. There was a radio on in perhaps Urdu or Hindi but not at all any use to Joe and me. Suddenly the game stopped. Some of the people went to one side of the room, others went to the other side. They picked up cues and billiard balls and the room was quiet. Apparently, India and Pakistan were at war. Joe and I slid under the table to an ominous silence. One Indian started talking, saying that they as a group of Asians had lived as friends for many years and what was happening 'back home' should not create mayhem in Mpwapwa, and other such good sense. Eventually they left the club in their respective groups, minutes apart, and Joe and I played snooker.

My duties were not on the research station but about thirty miles away on two ex-European farms, which I was to turn into a fattening ranch for cattle. The two previous owners were cousins and had reputedly left for a holiday in South Africa and had sent a postcard back to the Tanzanian government saying, "Merry Christmas" and that they would not be returning. The government took over the farms and loaned the land to the Central Region Co-operative Society for use for fattening cattle.

One lucky thing was that the farms were close to a railway so that animals could be railed to the abattoir in Dar.

Initially I would go to the ranch daily as I got things organised. There was no fencing, but boundaries were traditionally well established and the labour force of previous years was re-employed. Cattle corrals were constructed and the cattle dips were cleaned out. Meanwhile, cattle buyers were getting ready to sell animals to the Co-op and we were getting ready to receive them in the corral/*kraal* (the word used over much of Africa), which is made of timbers from trees that quickly regenerated once stuck in the ground. Before long we were faced with six hundred cattle to be fattened and destined for slaughter.

These cattle were from local farmers and had never been through a cattle dip. They were not immune to East Coast fever (ECF) and so to keep losses down we had to dip them regularly to prevent a build-up of the level of tick infection which carry the disease. This entailed driving the cattle through a 'race' and at the end the only way was to go was forwards into the water, which contained the pesticide Gamatox acaricide. This was filthy from the mud and doubtless some manure from the feet and hides of the livestock. Almost all animals will take to water with their head held high, but not all. Many refused to jump until pushed in, which was usually enough to get them to go. One cow went in with head down and came up to the surface of the water upside down. I jumped into the race to try to get her back to upright, hooves down. I grabbed her by the nose and tried to turn her over. She shook her head to such an extent that I landed on top of her and down we went. I stayed on the bottom, as I suspected flaying hooves might be just above my head. I swam slowly along the bottom and, arriving at the stepped ramp for the cattle to get out of the dip, I put my arm above my head but felt no feet and so carefully climbed the steps. The staff were searching for me at the entry end, and as none of them were swimmers they probably thought I could not either. I saw a row of very worried faces likely wondering how to explain this to the government. There was a swamp not far away where the water was obtained for the dip and I went and splashed in the muddy water to get rid some of the Gamatox. Then I went back to the house and got my cook to pour water over naked me to get rid of the rest of it. After that we tried to work out how to restore an upside-down cow in a dip, and we searched the livestock manuals available without success. We never had a repeat of that episode and I never caught ECF!

There were two houses on the ranch, around four or five miles apart. One was spacious and made of timber with a sheeted roof. But I chose the other one, which was stone built with a thatched roof and a little smaller. The view from the house showed me much of the ranch. Access was just off the dirt track and it had a water supply. There was a stream some hundred yards from the house and the water was pumped by a ram pump, which does not need an electric motor, or to be driven by petrol or gasoline. The water was pumped by stream water pressure and as long as you could hear the thump-thump you knew you had water at the tank up at the house. If not, I had to get the spanners out and keep at it until it worked again. It needed a new leather washer or two on the ram reasonably regularly. Where does one commence finding leather washers in central Tanzania? The answer is, my boots.

The house was very comfortable, mainly clear of mosquitoes and dangerously poisonous snakes. Euphorbia trees, which for some reason unbeknown to others lined the lane leading to the house from the dirt track, often had boomslang snakes in their branches. I asked the locals if they understood why these trees were the preferred perch in the daytime for the boomslang, and it was thought that due to the trees' open branches birds often came there in the daytime. This snake is green and poisonous but it is a back-fanged snake and for many years was not known to be venomous. I guess nobody allowed the snake long enough to chew its way over a hand until it got its fangs in touch with flesh. Even then, it was not normally deadly.

Rabies was a problem in much of Tanzania, and we had one episode whilst I was there at the ranch. I was at the house when I heard the howling of a dog. My dogs raced for the house and hid under the bed. I closed the house door and I jumped into my Land Rover as the howling dog came running down the lane. I drove up the lane and it attacked my front wheel. End of anecdote.

Later in my work in Africa I was invited back to Tanzania to manage a rabies eradication vaccination programme. All was ready: contracts signed and local teams appointed and ready to go. I was packing my goods and chattels when I got a phone call telling me that it was all cancelled. Why? It seems that the airport staff were not told that the vaccine must be refrigerated all the time, and the vaccine had been sitting on the tarmac of Dar es Salaam airport for two weeks. Dar es Salaam is a very warm all the year round.

At this time, I had bought a large old kerosene/paraffin fridge. It worked fine until it was left unused for a while. This meant that after I had been away for over a week or so it had to be taken for a ride on relatively rough terrain. I would put it in the back of my Land Rover and take it on a drive around the ranch. It entertained the staff and then when back at the house it would be working well.

I had one unhappy episode whilst running this ranch. I was getting too many dead animals, cows and bullocks – just an odd one weekly, and it seemed to me to be very odd. East Coast fever caused the deaths; I could not understand how ECF was rife when we had regular dipping programme. After I got the tests back and they confirmed it was ECF I thought I ought to investigate the dipping regime. I took a walk to the ranch dip rather than driving and, before I got to the dip, I found half a dozen animals grazing among the trees quite happily, instead of going through the dip. The staff were intentionally leaving a few animals undipped to ensure that they died from ECF and then the village would not be short of meat for a while, as the carcases were given to the staff. I gave them a very strong lecture and told them that anymore of that they would all be sacked, and I would bring a bunch of Maasai to come to work on the ranch. These men were said to be handsome in the eyes of the local females and fearsome in the eyes of the males. Dead animals were buried thereafter. It worked a treat as I think they did not want it known that it was their fault that a dozen or so Maasai warriors were living in their village area.

One day I saw a single Maasai warrior walking along just outside Mbeya. There were about four local men armed with spears following at about a hundred yards behind him. This guy was just taking a look around before returning to Maasailand. I doubt if anyone queried his intentions but he was followed everywhere; he walked for at least a thousand miles.

Once when I returned to the ranch after a longer than usual time away, I walked into the house and could not focus on the floor. It seemed to be hidden in a mist. The dogs would not come in and I eventually realised that I had a problem with fleas, which were jumping in glee in anticipation of a decent meal. I had Gamatox 'bombs' in a cupboard. I grabbed them and matches, as the bombs needed to be burning to give off the smoke. I used about five bombs throughout the house. I then went to find a guinea fowl for dinner, by which time all the fleas were dead and it was safe to come home. I also sprinkled Gamatox powder onto my bedding when staying in local hotels; otherwise I got carried away by bed bugs. Unpleasant creatures. It has since been found that Gamatox is a rather nasty chemical, which I believe has now been banned for years. I also wondered if bed bugs, etc., that suck our blood could be considered to be at the top of the food chain. Sucking my blood indeed!

Apart from the predatory hyena there were a number of leopards in the locality that would occasionally take goats in the night. The research station had a pack of ridgeback dogs with a handler who would track the leopards the morning after a killing; they had middling results, but it seemed to scare the leopard from the area. The dogs would tree the leopard and the handler would shoot it. The pack of about thirty was a rough bunch of animals and interbred ridgeback. Someone had a bright idea of getting some bigger males for breeding and ensure bigger progeny in the future. The old males were taken out of the pack and the six new males introduced one evening. Next morning there was no sign of the new males and it turned out that the pack had eaten them. They were an evil bunch and nobody other than the one 'master of hounds' dared to go into their pen.

The main contact I had within the Central Region Co-operative, which owned the ranch, was with a Nigerian accountant. One day he met me with a big smile saying that he had managed to procure some metal sheets to roof the ranch house. He just did not understand why I said I would leave if the thatch was taken off. Just after I left Mpwapwa, they found a rather large discrepancy in the ranch accounts and asked the accountant if he could explain it. His reply was that he was a chartered secretary and not a chartered accountant. So, no action was taken. However, he left the posting for elsewhere.

I was asked by the Ministry of Agriculture to go to the west of Dodoma and find a sparsely populated area where a million-acre ranch could be located for fattening animals. I found what I considered to be a starting place and camped close to a small village. My cook disappeared to the village as I went to bed. In the night, I felt quite ill, and on exploring my body I realised I was suffering from appendicitis. I could not locate my cook, who had gone to the village for what was his business, so I loaded up and drove quite a number of off-road miles to the main road. I got more and more ill as I drove and arrived at the hospital in a pretty poor state and sat on the step of the clinic. After around forty-five minutes the doctor arrived and asked what I was doing sitting on his office step. I asked if he had many patients for surgery in the day and he asked, "Why?" I told him I feared I had an appendix problem, and I was immediately admitted. Apparently, the doctor, John (B), having just finished his training, had never taken out an appendix. He requested the doctor from a nearby mission hospital, who had never done one either. I learned later that one had held the book whilst the other carried out the cutting job. He had to admit that it was not a keyhole job but it had not burst, and I still have a delightful scar to prove it all. I was dismayed that he had forgotten my tumultuous predicament when he visited me here in England recently.

I was hospitalised for a few days before I was allowed home, but was permitted to attend a 'do' at the club so long as I was back in bed by 10 p.m. I thought I was pretty hard, but a lady of about my own age, of statuesque physique and blonde, who was working at the mission hospital as the theatre nurse, also went down with appendicitis a day or so after me. She was the only nurse with surgery experience, so a curtain was draped across her chest and the equipment trolley alongside. She then handed whatever instrument the doctor required. Tough? She was up and about, even driving a tractor on her father's farm whilst I was still in hospital.

Mufindi is a small town, which exists mainly because there is/was a company producing tannin for treating hide to make leather from the bark of mimosa trees. The trees are grown to the appropriate size, then cut down, leaving all the branches on the ground. After being stripped of the bark, the wood is then burned. I understand that the seeds of the mimosa tree need to go through a fire before they will germinate. The bark is cut from the wood and boiled, using the branches for fuel. The end product is tannin with a rather nasty smell, definitely a nasty smell.

One man I enjoyed when playing rugby against in Mufindi was a South African with very limited education who was in charge of the cooking of the bark. He was a rough guy. I was told he would curse and swear at the labourers who loved him. I never did understand why he was so popular until it was explained to me that he was, on that day, unable to play rugby. Apparently, he could not play because the wife of one of his labour gangs was at the hospital in labour and my friend was doing the shift for the father, thus ensuring that the father-to-be could be at the bedside and not lose any wages. He put in a shift of throwing logs into a furnace to keep the vats boiling. Maybe his bark was worse than his bite.

Most of the senior staff was from South Africa and there was a senior school for local children. During the early days of the American Peace Corps, two male teachers were based there, along with a Brit male. One of the Americans (MR) had played American football and the Brit had played rugby, so they taught the larger and older children to play rugby and a match was organised against Mufindi factory staff. The Mufindi whites must have outweighed the schoolchildren at least twice or even three times and were proud of their rugby, and it was assumed that the factory team would win. They didn't. They were able to carry the game so long as they had the ball, but once the schoolboys got the ball they were away, faster, fitter and unafraid. I still have a mental picture of this very large South African chasing a sprig of a child down the wing, cursing and threatening a nasty death: "When I ******* catch you."

The American Peace Corps rugby trainer was ex-marine corps and an American footballer in the US. One day whilst out hunting with a group of Peace Corps friends, they spotted a kudu entering some thorny bushes and he jumped off to stalk it. He was never seen again. Intense searches of the area were carried out and local people questioned but no information was forthcoming, despite large sums of cash offered for information, and also large numbers of cattle. He was never found, and it was supposed he had fallen into a game trap with sharpened wooden posts in the bottom and he had lost the grip of his rifle, with which he could have sounded the alarm. The owner of the trap would have found him the next day and filled the hole in. A nasty way to go. Another possibility was that a lion had taken him by surprise and he was unable to use his gun for either the lion or as a signal of distress. Any local would have taken his gun away as a 'souvenir'. I think the first guess would be the correct one.

It was whilst I worked at the ranch that I was permitted to attend the Nairobi Agricultural Show. I drove to Nairobi, no passports needed, and camped in my little pup tent on the show ground with my Land Rover parked there too. I took my guns with me and left them in the truck. Over my three days at the show, nothing was taken from the tent or truck and I did learn quite a lot about livestock husbandry in the tropics. I found that, with better management, crossbred exotic cattle would survive and prosper. I was learning as I taught farmers about cattle management; they knew their environment much better than I did.

I decided that much of the information I gave to farmers was not only from my agricultural background but also from what I learned from the various Tanzanian farmers in discussions. I was learning as I went along; in fact I was learning all through my working life, because I was continually meeting up with new situations.

After around a year later I was transferred to the regional office of Central Province as the regional agricultural officer, with duties both in agriculture and with livestock.

SNAKES

There was a saltpan south of Mbeya, not too far from the Mbosi coffee growing area, and I met the owner one day at a cattle market. We got chatting and before we parted, he told me he would like me to drop in for an overnight stay for a longer chat than we had had. Six weeks or so after our meet, I dropped in on him close to dark. We spent a few hours chatting, partly about how he had diverted a small saline stream into a shallow pool and the sun evaporated the water. Simple. He then saw me to the guest room. It was nothing palatial – a comfortable enough bed but little else other than a very large wooden chest. During the night, I heard a noise similar to someone exhaling, and over breakfast I asked what it was. He laughed and apologised for forgetting to tell me the previous night. He lifted the lid of the bedroom chest and I saw a heaving mass of snakes. It was mainly puff adders, which I had heard puffing, but the mass included other species. He then explained that he caught snakes and when he had accumulated a large enough number, he would send them to Johannesburg where the snakes would be 'milked' for the venom, which somehow or other was used in the production of antivenom. I forgot to ask how he fed them, if at all.

My experiences with snakes have not always been bad. I was sitting on a riverside bank just upriver from Maun with picnickers. There were perhaps twenty of us when a spitting cobra came through the well-spaced grouping. The snake was very nervous but slid between picnicking people until it got to its hole and then down it went. At the same spot on another occasion, at Tlapaneng Bridge, I saw something I could not identify close to the water, so I prodded it with my fishing rod. It turned out to be a sleeping python, which uncurled at a fantastic speed and disappeared into the river.

Swaziland is/was the place for snakes, said to have the most *nyoka* per acre as anywhere in the world. I met up with a few. When on horseback you could see them moving away from the hoof beats. Thirty-nine thousand acres gave snakes a lot of room.

One day in Swaziland/Eswatini I found that a spitting cobra had climbed up my rear door and was trying to get though the gap on the hinged side of the door. It was already about fifteen inches through the gap when I saw it. I closed the door to trap it and then thought I would club it with a stick. NO CHANCE. I tried to whack it on the head but it evaded every attempt when I tried an up-down stroke. But it was slow on the left-to-right swing. It did not spray me with the 'spitting' half of its name, so I would suggest they have to be coiled to do so. I was lucky, I guess.

Mike H-W, a work mate of mine, was in the bush, before I knew him, with his wife and children having a weekend break. The parents were establishing a camp by the river and the kids were playing nearby when the little boy came to show his parents a 'worm' he had caught. It was actually a baby spitting cobra. The parents quickly checked the toddler for puncture wounds and, finding none, allowed it to leave camp.

I woke one night at the ranch and went to the toilet stark naked, as was my wont for bed attire in the heat, and as I walked past the kitchen doorway, I heard an odd scraping noise. On checking by turning on our feeble lighting system, I saw it was a snake crossing a thin piece of wood – the side of an orange box. I found a sweeping brush to use as a weapon and in the dim light I tentatively identified it as a brown house snake, which is not venomous. However, having decided that

I did not want the snake around inside or outside the house with us, because we had three quite young children who were not able to identify one snake from another, and who had been told to avoid snakes, rapidly and completely, I decided to end its days. I called my wife, asked her to bring a torch, and then whacked it with the brush, which upset it! So, I retreated to the top of the kitchen table and whacked it again and again, eventually killing it. I picked it up in a dustpan and dropped it in an outside bin. End of snake and end of story, except a neighbouring farmer (nine miles away across the mountains, thirty-two miles by road) passed by and identified it as a spitting cobra. So much for my snake identification skill. My excuse? It was only a feeble light.

I love rugby and played whenever there was a game on. One was arranged between Mbeya and Mufindi on one weekend. When we arrived, the pitch was not quite ready and a local man was driving a tractor to mow the grass. We all stood around chatting when the driver jumped off his tractor and ran over to us, saying there was a big snake in the last small unmown patch of grass. A group of us ambled over and found it to be a rather large python. On deciding that it was not the best place for a spectator, the ref said, "Send it off." A few tracksuits were collected and ten or so of us walked over to the patch of grass. The snake did not seem to be at all aggressive, and when a bundle of tracksuits was flung over its head, followed by the rest of us throwing ourselves on it, it did object a little. Once its head was secured, we picked the snake up like a length of hosepipe, deposited it in the bush surrounding the field, and then got on with the game. We lost.

I did not kill snakes except in self-defence or for the safety of my family.

Just after I left Tanzania, there was an outbreak of what was said to be bubonic plague. The place was overrun with rodents, as the locals had killed off most of the predators: snakes and jackals, which lived off the flea-carrying rats and mice. The snakes were killed because the locals were afraid of them and afraid for their families. (Since then, it has been thought to not be carried by rodents and their fleas.) Many of the local people were not able to distinguish between poisonous and non-poisonous snakes. The jackals were killed off in the area, as in winter the fox-like animal had a dense, warm coat, which also made an excellent, warm *kaross* – a very soft, snuggly, warm and hairy blanket. Many local people died from the 'Black Death' before it was diagnosed and dealt with. So, I respect snakes and they seldom attack unprovoked; if they did hunt humans as we hunt them, we would be extinct by now. I am not sure that bubonic is carried by rats, but it seems this was the latest thought on the matter. The carrier of the disease would not be rats, as the rats do not travel at anything like the speed of the spread of this disease. It is now thought to have been perhaps anthrax, not bubonic.

One of my favourite stories was when a local mixed-race Tanganyikan fishing friend of mine was travelling to Dodoma from Dar. He saw a dik-dik, a very small antelope, in fact the smallest in Africa, at the side of the road and shot at it with a .22 rifle. It ran off the road and died under a large tree. When George saw it fall, he went over to pick it up when something smashed him across his back and sent him sprawling. It was a big python hanging from the tree. George left the scene immediately.

There is a tale which I cannot guarantee as true but is highly plausible. A driver coming into Dodoma town ran over a snake on the road but could not see it in his rear-view mirror. He had hit a rock in the road during the trip and afterwards he heard a clanging noise. The car was overheating when he arrived in Dodoma, so he went straight to a garage he used regularly and asked them to check it out. He put it over the inspection pit and the garage owner told a mechanic to take a look. He was hit by a mamba and died; they could not get to the hospital in time.

I visited Mombasa with my family, and the hotel we were staying at had put on a little show about the different snakes in Kenya. It was a pleasant little show and the children enjoyed it. One snake on view was a python, about five or six feet long, which the children were encouraged to stroke. After playing its part, the snake was left in the middle of the circle of seated people and it kept trying to leave. It would be dragged back into the middle of the stage. It came towards me after a while, so I went to the snake and picked it up and sat down with it on my knees. It coiled itself comfortably, and tucked his head under my arm, and slept until the end of the show.

DODOMA

Dodoma, now the capital of Tanzania Central Region, was a much drier area than the Mbeya region, with varying lengths of rain-free periods each year. I soaked up the local history and got to know the locals, who had a very different culture from the Southern Highlands. One tribe, the Gogo, copied the lifestyle followed the Maasai, even though they were of Bantu stock. There were also different tribes similar to Southern Highland tribes, so there was no real problem adjusting. Dodoma had more Europeans than I was used to, and numerous Americans.

The American Peace Corps personnel were engaged mainly in education. The lucky ones were posted to towns and the less lucky to villages, which made a harder life for the volunteers. In my travels I met up with many of them and one female I knew slightly was in a very distant bush village. She rescued a puppy one day which village children were stoning and took it home. The puppy later died and so did the volunteer – from rabies.

My office was in the fort built by the Germans many years

before. It was a pleasant place, as it had battlements to walk when trying to solve a problem and was high enough to catch the breeze if a breeze was wanted. It also had a well in the centre of the compound, which presumably was used for water supply by the previous occupants, but the only thing it was used for when I was living there was to throw old files in, which for some unknown reason I had to witness.

On a quiet weekend I took a few days off and went with one of my colleagues to take a look at the Ngorongoro crater in Lake Manyara National Park. That night at the hotel there were few visitors, but all night long the hotel cat was making a dreadful noise. She was on heat and was desperate for a male to visit, but apparently the nearest male was about twenty miles away. The crater next day was all I imagined and more so. It was wondrous on its own, but with all the game ambling about to entertain, it is something that cannot be forgotten. But I did feel sorry for the cat.

One of the game scouts told us about the local elephants roaming around out of the crater, which was all national park. Nearby there was a village called Manyara, which the elephants considered to be their banana shop and would too regularly go into the *shambas* (local farms) and feed on the fruits. The locals complained to the game department and wanted protection. The game department fenced the elephants away from the villages; however, the animals were not impressed. The fence consisted of forty-four-gallon drums filled with concrete and sunk in the ground with a telegraph pole set into the concrete. The jumbos walked up to it and just threw it away, according to a watching game scout. Then someone had a bright idea! An electric fence. After a while, one was erected between the game park and the village. Later, the elephants turned up for their banana treat and one heard the clicking of the fence. It grasped the wire in his trunk and did it have a shock?! The watching game scout swore the elephant jumped into the air (elephants are the only animal on the planet that cannot jump), swung around in the air and was galloping before it hit the ground. I do not believe it, but it makes a good story.

The elephants left the scene but returned about a week later, and when they reached the fence two or three cows started pawing the ground, raising dust and trumpeting. A young bull came in with the bravado of youth to see what the problem was and pushed between two cows, intending to take over and show them what to do. As he passed between the cows, two of them joined trunks behind him and flung the bull, yelling, through the fence, and the rest ambled through to yet another banana feast.

In East Africa the 'bride price' varied between tribes, town, country, and the economics of the people involved, and was usually paid in cash, except in rural areas where the payment was usually in cattle. The husband-to-be, or often his father, would pay the father of the bride, and usually the transaction was amicable. Some of the weddings were major social events. However, one of the tribes close to Lake Tanganyika had developed a different system. The ladies were considered to be extremely good-looking and they paid a 'husband price' for their men. The wife-to-be would be earning good money by 'working' in Dar es Salaam for a couple of years and then return home to find a husband. This accomplished, they settled as any man and wife. It could be true. I never met any problem in the arrangement in the short time I spent in that area.

Dodoma had quite a sizeable expat population, many of whom were working for the government and many were volunteers, which made quite a change. It had a very active club, golf, numerous shops, tennis and rugby. It was whilst I was in Dodoma that I was selected to play for the Scorpions, the East African 'Barbarians'. We lost against Blackheath on the way to South Africa to get mauled.

I worked all over the Central Region for months and things were looking to be improving on the livestock side. I was visiting Singida district when we got a message that the president would be visiting to look at projects in the province. Big panic ensued, as senior staff left district HQ infrequently and were not known well. The people in the villages were all jazzed up to greet the president, but the staff from HQ had little idea of what could be laid on for Mwalimu.

I had been visiting many projects in Singida district and spent time in training field staff, talking to local farmers and being shown around their individual area of operations. Their training was not overly good because the trainers were not well trained either. When visiting one village, which had a new 'livestock assistant' based there and had fenced in a rock outcrop, I asked the purpose of it. He told me it was to demonstrate rocks being weathered down to form soil.

I had promised to be a stand-in for the father of the bride to give away a European woman in marriage in Dodoma that coming weekend. That was the reason that the SH(one)T hit the fan. I had been travelling around Singida district for a couple of weeks or so and decided to get back to Dodoma to prepare for this wedding. The evening I was due to leave, the district officer told me that the president would be coming to visit Singida in a few days' time and I must stay in Singida to help with the preparations. I agreed. Next day I learned that the minister of agriculture would be arriving the day before the president and he would like me to show him around in case his boss, the president, asked him any questions. Next, it was the head of agriculture in Singida and then the regional commissioner. Lastly, the man who ought to be the one showing visitors around, the district agriculture officer. He asked if I could show *him* around! He had been in Dodoma for a number of years, was loathe to leave the office, and obviously knew sweet f.a. as to just what was happening in Singida district. There was no way I could do all this tour guide job and get to Dodoma for the wedding.

That was when I lost my rag and told the district commissioner (DC) that I was being asked to tour with him, then the regional commissioner, then the head of agriculture, and then the minister of agriculture, and then district agriculture officer, and then the bloody president! And that was it. I could have put the 'bloody' anywhere in that sentence as it was only used it for emphasis – but I was told not to leave town. Some clerk had reported me and it became quite an issue. Actually, the clerk was not thanked for reporting me. Firstly, the regional commissioner said he could not attend, then the minister of agriculture said he would not attend, followed by the president, and the clerk was rusticated to the worst posting (punishment post) in the country, Sumbawanga.

Two days later we found ourselves in Morogoro outside a café at breakfast time. All the passengers and I got off the bus and went in to eat. I do not know what I ate but I did get a decent cup of coffee, and then I left the café but I could not find my escort to tell him that I was going for a pee. I then found him sitting on the kerb and when I asked if he had eaten, he said he had not. I asked why not. He told me that they would not let him into the café with his gun. I offered to hold the AK forty-seven for him whilst he ate, so there I was, sitting on a kerb in Morogoro at the crack of dawn nursing a rather lethal loaded assault rifle.

Eventually we arrived in Dar es Salaam and we were dropped off at the cop shop, the Central Police Station. I was shown to my 'quarters': a place of four spacious cells each side of a central passage, with one tap and a urinal, and the gate at the end of the central passage – with the only lock to be seen. I had about thirty cellmates, mainly sailors around my age, who had gotten drunk and their boat had left without them. There were also a few people who claimed to have lost or had their passport stolen, but nothing in the way of high crime except for one who was being held for murder and had managed to secrete his knife in a hole in the ceiling by a light fitting. He was said to have achieved that on a tower of cellmates. It was quite spacious, no overloading. It was not a jail, just the police holding pen.

As evening approached, a policeman came in and asked what I would like for dinner. Now that was a new one on me, as I was fed rice in Singida, so I asked what was available, whereupon he pulled the menu from the best hotel in Dar from his pocket. I looked at it and gave him an order of top-line fodder, starting with lobster and on from there. When I had finished ordering food I asked if I could get a crate of Coke. "Yes, sir" was the answer. I cannot stand the stuff but my new mates loved it. It was the best meal I had in Tanzania, and all I had was a spoon to eat it with.

I spent a full day in the cells and I suspect it was being debated as to what to do with me. The next day I was told that I would be going to see the secretary of agriculture on the following day, so I asked for my shaving kit and was looking halfway decent for my meeting. We started speaking in Kiswahili, but when I understood the severity of the issue, I asked him to speak English, in which he turned out to be perfect. The upshot was that I was told I was to leave Tanzania. I asked how soon must I leave and he surprised me with, "How long do you want?" I asked for a week and it was granted. It was a pleasant way to be deported. He said that someone would see that I was on the plane.

Back to Dodoma to pack up, find homes for my dogs, get rid of my Land Rover and a VW Beetle. The VW had been bought for my girlfriend, now my wife, but she had left before this fuss. I also had a Citroen Light 15 given to me by an old timer. It had only driven twelve thousand miles and not moved since his wife died twelve years ago. I had managed to get it running and was quite proud of it. He gave it to me as a non-runner. I checked it over and found a bent pushrod. I hammered this straight and it was running perfectly after that. I asked the Welsh guy, who I considered a friend and who bought the VW, to send the Citroen to me by sea and I would repay him for the expenses, and I let him have the VW quite cheaply. I used to call him Huge Moans. He told me by phone when I was in the UK that he was not sending the Citroen to me because I had not told him that the VW had suffered an accident. It was second hand when I had only bought it recently, and it had not seen a garage whilst I'd had it, and I was not aware that it had suffered an accident. I still believe that the VW had no trouble. It was a reliable runner and Huge Moans did not disagree with that. I do not know what to call his bit of skulduggery but I would like to meet him today. If anyone knows where I could find Huge Moans (or something sounding like that), I would appreciate it. I now use many different names for him, *mavi* (Kiswahili for manure) being my favourite, and I would appreciate it. He will be perhaps seventy years old or more, as a starter in the hunt.

I disposed of my unwanted stuff, giving much of it to locals, and hopped onto the plane as expected along with my valued items. On arriving at Heathrow, I was met by a phalanx of reporters who rapidly peeled off when I told them I had not been abused but, on the contrary, I had been well treated. The only problem I had was getting my bank account sent from Tanzania to my UK account. I eventually called my MP, Mr Steven Swingler, and my cash arrived within days. I called him to thank him and I asked how he had done it so quickly. He told me that it went quite high in government, and Tanzania was informed that if the cash was not transferred, the amount would be deducted from the next grant payment.

FOUR

Twixt Contracts

When not employed overseas I have carried out numerous temporary jobs. Nothing brain stretching, you can be assured.

After Tanzania I worked on the family farm for a while, undertaking whatever father wished. However, along came an outbreak of foot and mouth disease (FMD) and I felt that I could help. I called the Ministry of Agriculture and offered my services. They asked if I had any experience with FMD. When I told them that I had seen FMD on the ranches I had been running, I was gladly welcomed. "You start tomorrow!" I was told to report to an ex-water affair building taken over for the duration and was advised that there could be a berth in Congleton, Cheshire, which I decided would be fine. My berth was distant from my home near the Potteries, but I could not go home to the farm due to the big risk of spreading FMD.

The job itself was simple enough; initially I was to teach contracted drivers how to read a map and how to decipher map readings. I then got a gang of people recruited with Land Rover–fitted crop-spraying apparatus and taught them the same task.

The method employed to control the disease was that once a farmer suspected FMD, a vet would visit the farm, and if it was a positive diagnosis, a police officer would be sent to prevent anyone unauthorised from entering the farm. In places where burying cows might pollute the ground waters used by the Water Board for domestic use, carcases were burned. Burial was only used to get rid of dead animals where it was considered no threat to drinking water.

Once a farm was confirmed as infected, a slaughter team was sent in and all cloven-hoofed animals were shot using humane killers. I knew of one incident where a vet shot all the cattle, and then shot the dog which had rounded the cattle up. I felt he should get educated; dogs are not cloven hoofed, which should be knowledge to all but the odd (very odd) VET. The carcases were then dragged or carried out to the fields to be buried or burned. This needed heavy plant, diggers and 'drots', perhaps a local name for a tracked machine with a large scoop/bucket in front, which could carry up to four dead animals at a time, hired for the duration. Once all the animals were out of the farm buildings, the heavy plant would dig a hole, the carcases were dropped in it, and then the ground would be levelled. Where burning was to take place, the dead stock would be put into heaps and accelerants were used with straw bales to set it all alight.

The heavy plant would then need to be washed off so as not to carry the infection elsewhere, a job for the fire brigade with their high-power hoses. Once clean, the Land Rovers would arrive to disinfect the plant by spraying disinfectant, and then the heavy plant would be loaded by their drivers onto low loaders as soon as one was available. The machines were returned to a pool where the heavy plant was held. The drivers were collected by taxi and dropped off at their lodgings. The police officer was also returned to duties. On the farm, the next activity was a team of usually men who would disinfect the premises, and then the farm would not be able to bring in fresh animals until the area was considered to be free of FMD.

This system worked rather well, but there was one incident, which exposed a weakness. The drivers had come from all over England and maybe Wales too and were strangers to each other. One farm was finished with and the heavy plant digger driver was waiting for a low loader to collect his machine. The driver put it onto the low loader and that was the last we saw of it; the low loader was not one working on the eradication team. So far as I know, the machine was never found.

The pressure was on to find enough people to take on the task of scrubbing up the farm buildings to get rid of the virus. The Labour Exchange could not find any more labourers, so the military were asked to help. The North Stafford's were to be taken out of Yemen, Aden, and promised they would be home for Christmas. On arrival in the UK, they were immediately sent to Cheshire to scrub up cowsheds, which was not a pleasant Christmas surprise. I visited many farms checking on progress and ensuring that the 'scrubbers' had all they needed. One farm I visited where the army were working and met first with the farmer to hear how he was coping. He took me to the building where the army were working only to hear the refrain 'Old McDonald Had a Farm'. He said when he first heard them, he wanted to cry, but decided that having come through months of hell in Yemen and thinking they would be home for Christmas they were entitled to unwind.

It was quite hectic at times, and the easiest way to handle farm visits to supply lighter, urgently needed equipment was by helicopter, which was on standby in the car park.

I was in a team of three working very long hours at the peak of the infections, so much that we were knackered, so tired that the police would not allow us to drive home in the evening. We would be dropped off at our digs by police cars and picked up next morning. It happened quite often, drop off and pick up next morning, or sometimes later in the night. My landlady told me that the neighbours were getting rather nervous about my frequent involvement with the police and she was getting a bad name in the area for putting me up. I promised I would calm the critics down and turned up back at my lodgings that day by helicopter, dropped off in the field just behind her house – that and being collected next morning by helicopter. After a few times, transporting me to my digs in this way seemed to appease the locals.

The FMD outbreak lasted over Christmas and, as I visited all farms early on to assess what equipment was required to handle each particular case, I met many distressed farmers. On duty on Christmas Day, I was invited to join them for Christmas dinner, as they had invited guests, but non-infected farmers thought it better not to attend the offer. As a result, the farmers had an abundance of spare 'dinner' (it would be called lunch down south). I was invited to share and, being infected, this happened three times! Which meant I was not worried about not being at home. There were a few entertaining happenings during the three months in which I was involved.

Labourers were often seen to be munching on chunks of meat taken from the fires; pork seemed to be the preferred meat. FMD is not transmitted to humans and there has only been one human, so far that I am aware of, who ever tested positive for FMD. I think it was in 1952. So, they were probably safe whilst chewing a leg of pork, each.

There were a couple of Irish heavy plant operators who refused to go to a farm without his mate. One drove a drot, a bulldozer type with a wide-bladed shovel, the other a digger. One Sunday when it was quiet, I saw them in a field fooling around. They drove straight at each other; the drot was trying to lift the digger by getting his bucket under the tracks of the digger. The digger then swung his hydraulic arm over the cab of the drot and tapped his digging bucket on the roof of the drot. The drot put him down. I checked the roof later and found no dent at all and only a very small scratch mark.

I was leaning on a roadside village name one day, I am not sure why, when a truck working on the FMD eradication effort stopped to ask the way, showing me a note with *CHUMMLY* written on it. "Can you tell me the way to Chummly?" I told him he had found it. He replied, pointing to the sign, "No, that says CHOLMONDELEY." I said that is because they can't spell in this area.

At one farm I was sent to, I arrived just after the vet, who I found sitting on a straw bale. The cattle shed was on fire and the cattle were tied up facing the hay storage, with nothing but a walkway between them. I asked if all the stock were dead. He said no. I asked what he had been using and he pointed to a handgun by his side. It was loaded, so I grabbed it and a handful of bullets and ran down the gap between burning hay, shooting cattle as I went. Running out of bullets, I left the shed in a bit of a hurry. I did not go back in and then the fire engine arrived. I left the farm shortly afterwards, radioed in, and stopped at the gate to talk to the police officer who had also just arrived. I asked if he was OK and he said he was and then said, "I heard they were burning cattle but I didn't know they burned the farm as well."

I was carrying drag chains urgently needed at a farm quite a distance by car (the helicopter was busy), on a route taking in Sandbach on market day. The centre was jammed with traffic and I was in the middle of it, close to a phone box. (Yes, they did work in those days.) I called 999 and told the person handling emergency calls that I needed a police car/guide to get me through Sandbach, but she said she could not pass the message on, as it was only for emergencies. I told her that I was involved with the FMD outbreak which was classed as an emergency and I was in a hurry. She accepted this explanation. A police motorcycle arrived soonest and he asked where I was going. Then started the drive of my life, wrong side of the road, along pavements – we hit nobody, I think – wrong way on one-way streets, the wrong way around roundabouts, overtaking on the inside, etc. Once clear of traffic he just wheeled away with a wave and was gone, leaving me sweating and wondering how many laws we had broken.

At the end of the FMD disaster I disinfected my car with some concoction brewed up by the veterinarians. I did it on my last day and slept at my digs that night. Next a.m. I headed for Scotland for a few days so that I would not be taking the virus home. I did keep away from cloven-hoofed animals in Scotland, as I had no interest in being blamed for starting another outbreak. It was a very cold day and I had to drive with my windows open – the gas left inside the car from the disinfection was nasty. Nottalottafun!

One incident which may amuse you happened when we moved farms from the Potteries to a place not far from Blackpool. We had a sow which was due to farrow (produce piglets) and decided that it would be better to move her with piglets inside rather than outside her, so she was the first of the livestock to be transferred. I had a Morris van and we put her in the back with a sack of feed and a door between her and the feed. Halfway up the M6, late at night, I ran out of petrol. Idiot. I called the AA for rescue help and asked them to hurry as the sow was getting unhappy and trying to eat her way into the cab. The AA man arrived and whilst I was pouring fuel into my tank, the AA man opened the door to take a look. "You said you have a pig in here." The sow immediately backed out and onto the motorway. Chaos! He got onto his radio and had the motorway closed. Two or three police cars arrived and a couple of truck drivers joined in the fun. That sow was determined to get some exercise. The anatomy of a pig is such that it does not provide many handholds, and she was very determined not to be manhandled. After half an hour she decided that running around dodging various people she did not know and who used abusive language towards a pregnant lady was not much fun anymore, so she walked up to my van, walked up the door I had placed there as a ramp, and lay down. Job done. The crowd dispersed amid laughter and I drove on. Shortly after this episode I went to—

FIVE

Botswana

I arrived in Gaborone knowing little about the place except they had a desert and more livestock than people – approximately 600,000 people to six million head of livestock, and meat provided ninety-five percent of the national earnings. The best cuts of meat went to Europe, next best went to South Africa, and the less attractive cuts went to the goldmine labour. The first and newly installed president, His Excellency Sir Seretse Khama, had been exiled to the UK for a number of years and was married to an English lady. I also found that there were only three government officers in the livestock department, and I was the third.

I was posted to Mahalapye, which was about 130 miles from the capital and 150 miles from the second largest town. One advantage to living in Mahalapye was that it had a railway line entering from Rhodesia and then exiting to South Africa. A few miles from the border into South Africa is Mafeking, which was the place to shop. I would send a shopping list down the line in the care of the train guard, who handed it to a 'super' market, which I never did see. Back came a box or two of supplies two days later. Almost home delivery similar to Waitrose, only by train.

Mahalapye was a coaling station for the steam engines plying the route. The trains always carried as much as they could, a little extra of which fell off the tender and dropped on the line as soon as they left Mahalapye station. A short walk through the bush gave access to the rail line, and in the cold winter months I reverted to my old task of 'coal picking', but without the experience of getting clouted on the back of my head by a boulder.

My position was in the veterinary department and initially I was consigned to training and equipping mobile units of trained staff to go out into the desert to educate farmers and their labourers. Now is the time to let you know that the desert was not really a desert. In the wet season, the last three months of the year, there was a fantastic growth of nutritious grass, followed by nine months of dry. The end of the rainy season was a rapid cut-off of rain and the grasses dried up quickly to become standing hay, which was quite nutritious.

Also, during the period when it rains, the water fills up dry 'pans' to allow some odd little fish to 'hibernate' in the soil at the bottom of the water later on when it dries up, waiting for the next wet season. If there are no rains they stay underground until it does rain. The bigger fish, such as barbel (this freshwater fish has four thin projecting organs that protrude from the upper lip), can also go through a dry season in this manner. I never did eat this one, as they tend to have parasitic worms which are rather off-putting when cooking, rather like strands of spaghetti.

There is a village where there is a small lake, a pan which normally never dries. The lake belongs to the village chief, who allows the villagers to catch fish one day every three or four years. It is not a deep 'lake' and the villagers have developed a way of fishing. They split a piece of cane about two feet long (sixty centimetres) and put a twine down the middle tied to a sizeable hook. The twine has a metre or so which is tied to the wrist of the fisherman. They then wade through the waters, swishing the cane backwards and forwards until they hit a fish. The fish is then unhooked and thrown to the wife on the shore. The normal weight of a barbel is around four or six pounds, but there is occasionally a giant barbel, which can get up to around sixty pounds. In that case, the fish tows the fisherman through the water. He yells and the hunt is on. Everyone runs to the side of the lake and collects a spear of some other weapon and chases the fish until it is killed. Then it is party time. The barbel is said to travel between sources of water using a snakelike movement, but is seldom seen in transit. I have never encountered one.

I soon settled in and into the new culture. The office was about a hundred yards from my house, and as I walked to the office one day, I found a chameleon and picked it up. I walked into the general office and said, "Look what I have found." As soon as my staff saw it, one sidled out of the office and another, Shoka (Axe), went through the luckily open window. He did not return for a week. I found that most of the locals were afraid of chameleons; I think it was the eye movements, and they were sure that they are poisonous. I had a very well-educated friend with two MSc degrees from the UK who admitted that he did not fear the chameleon, but he did not like them.

Before Botswana got independence, it was controlled by the Brits. It was never a colony, but it was a protectorate, and was administered from a small enclave that was British, in Mafeking, in South Africa. Before my time there, Botswana eventually got its independence, but not without a struggle. King Seretse Khama eventually took over as president. His predecessors had been kings of the Bamangwato for years, the most powerful tribe in the country. He had been rusticated to the UK for years and his people wanted his return, which was a problem for years. After a lot of agitation, in a protest demonstration one or two Motswana policeman were killed 'accidentally' – I never did find out what that word meant in this instance.

This was not the first time in which the Brits got upset with Bechuanaland, as it used to be called. One upset was caused by a couple of British traders who would not keep away from the king's wives. They were called before the king, who told them to leave his wives alone. But this was not enough, and the men continued 'pestering' the ladies. The king then had the white men flogged, resulting in the two miscreants complaining to the British government. The Brits decided that Bechuanaland should be punished for treating Europeans like that. The British navy had a couple of cruisers sitting in a South African port and the navy were ordered to take one of the big guns to Serowe and shell the village. The guns were put on the train and sent to Palapye and offloaded. It was the rainy season and the thirty miles of road to Serowe was deep mud. The navy and guards of the punishment team were unable to manhandle the heavy weapons, which were stuck in the mud. They tried to hire bullocks to haul it along but, not surprisingly, none were available. By this time the naval officer in charge heard the true reason for the flogging and sympathised with the king. He got his wish to hire bullocks from the king and after a lot of effort arrived at Serowe. He loaded up his gun and fired off most of the ammunition they had brought, but it was pointing in the wrong direction and moved a few rocks around on the hillside. Mission accomplished, they went back to their ship.

The Brits arrested eight men thought to be the ringleaders of the protest for his return and imprisoned them. To show that the trial would be free and fair, a judge was sent out from the UK. The trial was held in Serowe and as the judge, who had never been to Africa, could not identify the eight individuals, during the trials they were each given a number, one to eight. Every morning before going to court they swapped their numbers, which confused matters and amused the locals no end. As the trial seemed to be getting nowhere and the matter seemed to settle down, the Brits agreed to allow Seretse back, but if there was any more trouble they were told that they would never see him again. There was a bit of in-country haggling because he had married a white woman but she soon won the hearts of the people. "And they all lived happily ever after." (Well, almost).

I decided to take a trip to introduce myself to the veterinary field staff in the districts. It went well until I went to Serowe. Trying to explain to the district veterinary officer in Serowe why I was sending teams out into the bush to help livestock owners and their staff was difficult. And as he was in station, what could I do to improve matters? I must have sounded like a greenhorn as I toured his district and asked so many people what their biggest problems were. The district officer though it was unnecessary, as he was in the village in his office. I was welcomed everywhere except at the district office, based in the largest village in the world. (Please do not ask who measured and how, but that was what was understood.) The agriculture officer there, Bosile (T), was rather unpleasant and less than helpful, but as we were operating in his district he had to be informed. He told me I should not go into the desert, as Europeans did not know how to drive in such conditions, and sleeping out I would be lion bait, etc. One day I got so mad at him I punched his metal filing cabinet as I walked out of his office and after that he could not open the dented drawer. He was very soon 'retired'.

My fiancée (Francis) joined me and we married in Maun. I thought a marriage in Maun would be something different and the banns were posted. Two weeks later we were married by the European district commissioner. The licence cost 10/- (aka 50p). That was the best thing I ever managed. We stayed at a crocodile safari camp where I was known, just up the river from Maun, and as it was very hot, too hot to drive, the hotel offered us the use of their boat, which we gratefully accepted. There being no landing stage, we got to the office of the district commissioner in Maun, and I carried Gabby from the boat to dryish land. We then climbed the riverbank. Note, no steps, and I walked proudly, very soggily shod. The district agriculture officer (thank you, Richard) and his wife had agreed to be witnesses. As they lived next door to the office, they did not have to walk very far. After the ceremony we found the DC had brought a bottle of champagne, which we all glugged, and then we travelled back to the safari camp by boat.

Unbeknown to me, the safari camp had put on a wedding feast for everyone staying there at no cost to us. Everything was perfect except for the metal-framed beds, which made a screeching noise on the concrete floor with every move, so the mattresses soon went to the floor. The marriage has survived 50-plus years, which means it has cost less than 1p per year, and the best bargain I have ever made.

I did not take leave, so we carried on working around the swamp. I loved the area but my wife was not so enthralled. According to my wife, who does not like Maun or the swamp, she reckons the marriage as a calamity. I do acknowledge that my wife's experiences there were not overly enjoyable. Just two days after our wedding she came down with a bad case of diarrhoea and we were camping in the area of the Herero people, a people who dressed like Victorians. We were out in the open, no bushes to hide in or behind. She said it was just diarrhoea – in local parlance, 'dire rear'. I told her I reckoned it was amoebic dysentery but she denied it. I bet her a bottle of whisky and she lost. She got tired of pooping in full view of a crowd of sympathetic locals, so a visit to Maun hospital was needed.

Six months later, in Maun, she had another rather unpleasant incident when she apparently had a bout with a spitting cobra and lost. I was fishing just outside Maun on a bridge over the Matloutsi River and she yelled for me to come to her quickly. She told me what had happened. Having not seen any snake I decided it must have been a cobra and rinsed her eyes with diluted antivenom, but she remained in great pain. It did not seem to do any good so I threw all the camping gear into the Land Rover and took her into town. She was treated at the hospital there and a shot of morphine made it much better, plus antivenom eye washes.

The Herero were a large tribe based in West Africa (Namibia), which became part of the German colonies of Africa. Many of the tribe plus San Bushmen and Namaqua were killed in the takeover and the majority of the survivors – men, women and children – were driven into the Kalahari to die. Many of their descendants have returned to Namibia but some remain in Botswana. That German operation has now been accepted as genocide by Germany and reparation is currently being discussed.

The system of cattle management in the Kalahari is called a cattle post system. I was blessed with an American cattleman as the livestock part of a USAID program and I was to show him the ropes. He was an ex-cowboy with a degree and previously worked on King Ranch in Texas, which I believe used to be the biggest ranch in the world. After a couple of days, Jim had settled in and asked to see a 'cattle post' so we set off for the desert just a few miles out of town to visit a herdsman I knew. We arrived at the place and Jim asked where it was, little realising that a windmill, a water tank and a mud hut made up the title of 'cattle post'. It was obviously less than he was expecting. Jim had told me about round-ups in Texas and dragging cows out of the thorn bush using 'leopard dogs', which grabbed a cow by the nose and hauled it out into the open. Cattle recognised a man on a horse as OK but a man on foot could face serious problems. Jim told me a story of a calf branding job when the calf, feeling pain, yelled for Mother. Jim left the calf for the corral fence and jumped over it only to find a rattlesnake waiting for him, so he jumped back onto the corral top-bar and wobbled until it was safe to get back to terra firma.

He expected to see a corral, a holding yard, a cattle crush and all the trimmings as seen on TV and films in cattle country in the USA. The cattle were standing around and looking at us. Jim asked the herdsman how he could vaccinate cattle or treat them without a crush. I got the look from the herdsman as if asking, "Where did you find this man?" Jim walked well behind me until we stood a few yards from the cattle, who were being entertained by us strangers. Our friend called out a name and his favourite bull came out of the herd and stood quietly by him. He lifted a fold of skin on the bull's neck and went through the motions of sticking a needle into the fold of skin and depressing the plunger. The bull got a bit of petting and then was told to go back to the cows. Jim just stood there flabbergasted and said, "I might as well go home; we can't teach these guys anything about cattle management." And I think he was right. Wherever he went to next, I never heard of him again.

Normally late September or early October was the start of the annual rains. On one year the rains did not come, they were late and the drought was harming the few agricultural crops. The people would go to the church to pray for rain but none arrived. People got desperate and asked the president to go to church and pray for rain. He refused. A little later they strongly begged him to go to pray for rain. Eventually, he 'reluctantly' agreed and went to church. A few days later it rained and the rainy season was started. I met up with the president whilst discussing livestock a few days later and asked how he did it. "Do not tell, but I just call the meteorological department in

Jo'burg and they tell me when we will have rain." I was driving a government five-ton truck from Maun to Francistown one evening on the way home when the truck started playing up. I was about 130 miles from anywhere except a police post, so I pulled in and explained my situation. Camping was out, as it was lion country, and I wanted to send a message for a mechanic. The police were most helpful. They radioed in my predicament and a mechanic was promised for next morning. I was fed, we chatted, and I asked if they could provide a bed. They said all they had were cells and I gratefully accepted. I was shown to a much cleaner cell than I expected. The police officer carried my few overnight requirements and then left, LOCKING the cell door behind him. I thought, *Oh sod, what have I let myself in for*, when he turned around and handed me the key between the bars, with a "That is the regulation" and wished me a "goodnight." Next morning, I used the mechanic's vehicle to return to Maun, leaving him working on the truck.

A couple of years later I was lost in thick bush, looking for a dam to see what the water situation was; it was dry. I then decided that driving north for twenty or thirty miles, rather than eastwards, would put me on a road to Francistown. So, I started bush-bashing; it was completely devoid of any sign of a track, even a game track, and eventually I found a ridge of soil about five feet high. My Land Cruiser climbed over it and I found a beautiful gravel road in excellent condition running east to west. I stopped in the middle of the road and climbed out, trying to make sense of it all. There were no wheel tracks or any sign of usage. Nothing. So, I turned right, westwards, and after about forty miles or so the road stopped. In front was nothing but a mound of soil and bush. I then turned north again and after about five miles of bush-bashing, I found the main Francistown road. Next day I asked at our office in Francistown what the hell it was all about and I was told it is a secret road to the diamond mine at Orapa, and I was to say nothing, as the find of diamonds was not yet public knowledge.

I had a map of Botswana in my head and used the sun to navigate. Whenever I was 'lost' I would check the sun and my watch and I was off again.

It had long been known that there were diamonds in the sand of the Macloutsi River, but the 'mother lode' had never been found. Not sure where some interested person (I am not sure who) studied the map of Botswana and concluded that the Macloutsi River was too wide for its small catchment area; it must have been bigger in the past. He then tracked the river upstream and came to a fold in the ground which had diverted the river. Now the story gets a wee bit corny. He found some children playing with stones (marbles?) and at a newly dug well, he checked the dug-out soil and found diamonds. I am not sure the kids in Botswana ever did play shotties, or stonts, as I knew the game as a kid.

The story is that the first manager of the mines wanted a gravel path off the road to his house, and a loader and tipping truck were duly sent to where there was a heap of gravel left by the road builders. As he walked down his new gravel drive, he picked up five gemstones. Orapa become quite a place and obviously downgraded beef from its ninety-five percent of GDP.

There being little chance of keeping cash safely in the villages, and as the number of cattle owned was a status symbol from centuries back, cattle were treasured. There was a geneticist John (T) working on upgrading animals and as mostly cattle/oxen were used as draught animals, they soon turned to quality meat animals when an abattoir was opened in Lobatse. The conditions in the Kalahari were too harsh for exotic breeds. The project was exploring which breeds were most suited to use in cross-breeding for quality meat production. The head of the program, John, was a friend of mine, but we often fell out, as I had to try to get local cattle owners to accept his findings and to get cattle owners use them instead of the traditional manner. I had to translate his scientific findings into a language understood and accepted by local farmers with very limited education. I was able to manage a good argument for most people but I failed in convincing the top politician (the president) that a bull up for sale was a good one to buy. The bull had 136% (?) better growth rate than the average; it was an animal worth buying. His reason was that it did not look particularly male, to which I agreed, so much so that it looked to be too feminine and people would laugh at him, so one of his people benefitted rather than himself.

The Okavango swamp was a wonderful place, water game, fish, clean drinking water – just dip a mug over the side of the canoe and drink. BUT tsetse flies aplenty frequented the whole of the swamp. Tsetse fly could give humans sleeping sickness – it was rare, as few infected people went into the area when suffering from sleeping sickness to infect the tsetse fly, and few people spent a lot of time in the area generally. I did meet one guy with sleeping sickness. He worked for the government maintaining roads in the swamp. He knew he had sleeping sickness but refused to leave his job, as he loved being in the swamp, and said he would remain until God signed him off. Cattle were not allowed to enter the swamp area until efforts were successfully made to eradicate the tsetse fly, and eventually cattle were permitted in the swamp. A vast number of wild animals would spend their dry seasons in the swamp and with the annual rains would return to grazing in the desert.

I employed a guide who used to work for the last professional croc hunter, when it was legal. They hunted at night and from his description quite a hairy job. The best way to shoot a croc is a brain shot close to the eyes. As the eyes light up in a torch light, it was the best route to go. Once one was hit, the gunman or one other would dive overboard, hoping the croc was dead, and rope the sinking croc to be taken to land for skinning. He claimed that the biggest croc they got was twenty-six feet six inches. Nowadays sixteen feet is thought to be the biggest. I was in the game warden's office one morning and a young guy came in to report that he had had to shoot a croc, as it attacked his canoe. The game warden told him to bring the skin into his office. Whilst he was going out to get the skin from his truck, the warden told me that the young guy was the son of the last professional croc hunter. The warden had no doubt about the truth of this story but could not explain how so many crocs could recognise him.

Fishing in the swamp was quite productive, the most sporting being the tiger fish, bony and a predator with efficient teeth, which were situated on the lips (as I saw it) and would take a lure. Some of them would tail walk to shake the lure off, and if they walked for me, they went back into the water with a thank you. The fish for eating was the tilapia, a beautiful fish to eat, and they would take a fly and are said to be among the best in the world. I once fished off Tlapaneng Bridge not far from Maun. There was a continuous sight of fish jumping and finding something in the way of plentiful food, but they were not taking the lures which a number of European fishermen were using. I took a climb down to water level and realised what the fish were taking were small one-centimetre fries/tiddlers. I found a few guinea fowl feathers and made a few lures which were taken very quickly. I had plenty of fish for us. I sent baskets full to the Riley's Hotel in Maun and then started selling to pedestrians. I engaged a child to take them off the hook, as I was tired of the job, and he got every sixth fish. Another great place to find big tilapia was where the river entered Makgadikgadi Pan, where the water passed through a turbine and contained chewed up fish, so a bit of fish bait dropped into the outflow and it was teeming with fish which readily took a tilapia hook.

There is a river which feeds the main flow from the swamp to the pan when it is high water. When the swamp flood is dying down the water flows the other way. The river, however, has virtually no altitude benefit, so water is pushed both ways depending where the high water is, in the swamp or in the river. Needless to say, that is not a river for white water sports.

Makgadikgadi Pan used to receive all the water from the Okavango swamp but today little of the water gets that far. The pan is a large dry lakebed. I have yet to measure it but it is around a hundred miles north to south, two hundred miles east to west. It is flat and easy to drive on. At one time I did consider driving the north to south trip across the Makgadikgadi Pan. South of the pan was a village called Rakops.

There is a story which is likely to be true that the surface of the dam is only a crust. When the Francistown to Maun road was being built, they left a digger on the pan one night and next morning it was gone. Not stolen, just a funny muddy like surface to the patch of the floor, with a digger missing.

I often visited but I did not do the trip across the pan because if there was a truck problem it would be a long walk for help. I did do a short test run onto the pan; I drove about three miles or so out on the lakebed, then stopped. I stood on the roof of my truck and I had the strangest feeling in my gut. I could see nothing. No sign of life. No other wheel tracks, no game tracks, no grass, no clouds, no trees, no hillocks, no companions, no noise NOTHING except my wheel tracks. I have been to many odd places but that one is special, leaving me with a rather unexplainable gut feeling. I have never been to such a place before or since that experience. I have roamed a few deserts and the Himalayas but not got a gut feeling anything like it.

On another trip from Maun to Rakops I drove alongside the pan and parked up on a game track, got my bed organised and was sitting eating my 'dinner' when I heard a strange noise, crunch, crunch. It slowly came closer and closer until it bumped into my bed. It was a large tortoise. It had its head out, so I scratched the top of his/her head, which it obviously enjoyed as it quickly poked its head out again for more scratching. A little later on, after more petting, the tortoise backed into a clump of vegetation alongside my bed and settled down for the night. He/she broke camp as dawn broke and off he crunched. I too left, going south, and my friend went north.

I was asked by government to assist an American rancher from Kellyville, Oklahoma, who had an idea to ranch one million acres of northern Botswana for twenty years and then hand back the area to government. I was advised of the area and places he wished to visit and arranged to have ground transport when our plane landed. All went well. The pilot was supplied by the American Embassy; we landed where we could. The rancher had studied the area and its disadvantages concerning livestock in the north before he arrived. On the second night out, we were to literally drop in and stay at a road construction camp, when I mentioned that no one could just 'drop in' for a night's accommodation. He said, "Oh, we will be alright. I own the company." The food there was some of the best I have ever tasted; perhaps it was the locality. Breakfast was another steak.

One lesson he taught me, he always called me sir. I asked him why he did so. He explained that he always called everyone sir, so it meant nothing to him no matter how disgusting the man spoken to. He even called his gardener in the States sir. I took up the salutation and it helped many times in my career when addressing some pretty awful individuals.

Another day, when we were driving along a desert track about six inches deep in the sand, we saw a tortoise toddling along but obviously unable to climb out of the rut. We stopped and I saw that it was a soft-shelled tortoise. None of us had ever seen one before and out of interest we took him for a flight in the guest's boot. That night we were booked in at a safari camp in the Okavango and, being late, we had to climb to quite a height until we spotted the camp, and a rapid descent brought us to the airstrip. The safari camp had a very long communal dining table. We put the tortoise on the long table and she/he ran rapidly a number of times the full length of the table, then stopped and went to sleep. I heard later from the camp that it slept for four days. The rancher did not go through with his proposal.

There is a rather sad ending to this tale. The pilot finished his time in Botswana and went back to the States. After a few months we heard that he had killed his wife, mother-in-law and two children with an axe, and the last sighting of him was entering the Yellowstone National Park. The family were told that it is a common thing when people get to the point of no return. A tragedy, as he was knowingly devoted to his family and had a good career mapped out, and was also an interesting man to spend time with.

Another time when I was bush-bashing to find a dam built long ago, I was asked to see if there was water in it. My driver and I went through thick bush to look for it, as my driver knew of a place close to it. We stopped nearby and went on foot to find it. It was much further than expected but eventually we came upon it almost by accident. It was empty except for a troop of about thirty baboons or so sitting on the dam wall. I asked the driver which way to the Land Rover and he pointed across the dam, so that is the way we went. Halfway across another troop of a similar size appeared on the opposite side of the dam wall. Sixty baboons were more than I could manage, even if I had brought a machine gun, which I hadn't; it was one of the 'heart in the mouth' or 'squeaky bum' type of situations. We had to trudge a long way before we found our entry track off the road and followed our wheel tracks back to our abandoned transport.

A couple of fellow European employees were travelling from

Ghanzi to Lobatse. A north to south trip through desert sand with sunken wheel tracks used as a road, which were generally hard to get out of unless you found a hard patch of earth. The early Land Rovers had an accelerator lever by the steering wheel similar to a farm tractor and could be 'set'. One of them was driving. The passenger, Nick, went to sleep with the usual driving speed of about thirty-five miles per hour. After a while Nick, the sleepy one, heard his mate say, "Do you fancy a beer"? A sleepy "yes" changed to "WTF" when he opened his eyes and realised that the truck was driverless, as his mate was grappling with cans of beer in the back. Daft?

On the same route of around three hundred miles plus, heading out of Ghanzi on the road to Windhoek, I had been delivering building materials for a school for Bushmen children seventy miles or so west of Ghanzi, driving a 4x4 Bedford five-tonner truck. It was a horrible machine, as the transfer gear box had a tendency to come loose. I was returning home, driving through the night, and it was pouring with rain – it does so irregularly and it usually manages be there when I am – when I saw a small figure waving me down, and as you never drive on in the desert when someone is in trouble, I stopped. I stopped, opened a window, and he asked me where I was going; I then stated that he should tell me where he was heading. He wanted to go to Lobatse so I said, "Climb in," which he did and took his soggy coat off. I asked why he was out in this weather and this time of night when he would be lucky to see any vehicles at all before morning. As he was answering, I interrupted him and said, "Do I know you?" He then said, "You might do." I said, "OK, so who are you?" He turned out to be the vice president, Quett Masire. He was carrying a load of cattle down to Lobatse and was having trouble with his truck and needed a mechanic. At that time no one but the president was permitted to have use of government transport for personal convenience. Not even

Quett Masire. I dropped him off in Lobatse and went the last fifty miles to Gaborone and home.

Head of the department of animal production (KB) asked me if I knew anything about camels, and if so, he had a small job for me. I admitted that when I was about six my mother had taken me to a zoo so I knew that they had four legs, which was considered to be sufficient knowledge to allot me to the task as yet unspecified. The police had requested for someone from the livestock department to go and check out the camels at their Tsabong station and make a report as to improving matters, as their staff in the field were complaining that the camels were not up to the job of patrolling the desert as required. It was back to the desert again. Norman, a friend in the agriculture department, had a father visiting who said he would like to visit to the desert. I saw the old man as he arrived by air being helped down the steps from the plane and then using two sticks to walk; I was not overly enthusiastic as to his vulnerability, as it would be a tough trip.

Norman talked me into it and after loading his dad I set off back to the southern desert and the camel camp. Luckily the camels were not out on patrol, as these were weeks in duration. And even more luckily there was a guy there who had looked after camels all his adult life and knew exactly what was wrong. He taught me a lot and told me of their problems, just as a father would do when taking his child to see the doctor. Basically, they lacked vigour, their diet was not too good, not adequate, and the major problem was that there had been no new blood in the herd since the First World War. This trip made me the camel expert in the department. I rewarded my helper with a few cans of beer.

My report said more food, mineral supplementation, longer rest periods between patrols, addition to the browsing area used by the animals, and periodic visits by the veterinarians from head office. I stressed the lack of new blood, i.e., breeding males. I then went back to HQ hurried on by a couple of hornets who objected to my visit to the see the camels. Hornets hurt!

Back in Gabs, as it is/was called, I dropped Norman's father off, who had suffered not at all, and about a month later the old man went home with his two sticks tied to his suitcase and up the steps of the plane like a teenager. I believe it was arthritis or such and the dry air had worked wonders.

I handed my camel report in and heard nothing for a few months, then came a question from the police as to where could we get new camels. Being the camel 'expert', I pondered: Australia, North Africa, Saudi, Egypt, etc. It was going to be expensive and import restrictions in Southern Africa could be a problem, as they would need to be brought to Halifax in Namibia, then trucked five to six hundred miles to Tsabong in Botswana. I was chatting to an elderly Boer one day who was suffering from some untreatable wasting disease and he offered the information that camels used to be used by the South African police for patrolling until a while back, when they converted to Land Rovers. The camels were given out to any farmers who would accept them and it seemed that someone with some history told us that there were camels in the Gemsbok wildlife reserve which borders Botswana in the far south-west. The South Africa Game Department had offered, after a request from Botswana police, one male camel from the reserve.

So, with no discussion a decision was made. I got the 4x4 Bedford kitted out with high steel framework and attention to the transfer gear box, two drums of water, two drums of diesel and a pile of foam mattresses, plus a bundle of cash. I also took my rugby kit, as I was hoping to get to Mafeking in about ten days' time, where Gaborone was to play their team. At Gemsbok game reserve I arrived and surprisingly was expected, and there were a few male camels brought in for me to take my pick. I had been told that white ones tended to be easier to train and calmer. So, sensibly, I asked for the whitest one, which was duly rounded up and loaded in no time. I called him George and I had been advised by the game department that they could travel standing, which made life easier. The park people guided us to certain famers known to have camels, which was a big help. One problem on this trip was linguistic. Namibian farmers spoke Afrikaans or German. I was pitiful in Afrikaans and did have a few memories of German from school days. The little Tswana I had picked up was of zero use.

I had collected a couple more camels when it was suggested the next farmer up the road, about twenty-five miles away, said he had some. So onwards and found the house and farm as told. I managed in whatever language could be understood, mainly consisting of sign language, that I wanted to buy camels and he agreed that he had some but was puzzled as to why I wanted them. He was happy to show us the camels and I could select which I wanted. We saw quite a bit of game on the ranch/farm and we stopped and the farmer pointed out the camels. I just could not see any and told him so. He got a bit agitated and forcefully got me to look harder through binoculars. Still no camels, and eventually I got him to understand that what I was seeing were giraffe. In Afrikaans a giraffe is a *cameeldorp*, shortened usually to *cameel*. After a fair amount of laughter, he told me where I could find real camels. Onwards, ever onwards, I collected another couple, which gave me five, and I had a chance of getting to Mafeking in time for kick off.

Turning south, I hit a decent road but a comparative unending stream of trucks, tractors, lorries, cars, *bakkis* (pickups), even buses, etc. It got dark and it was not very warm, and in my headlights, after the traffic eased somewhat, I was not driving fast and I saw a very well-dressed police officer, obviously of high rank, waving me to stop. I had not long ago returned from a holiday in Brazil and had a smattering of Portuguese, and the police man told me in Portuguese, "Your people are staying down there," pointing to a turn to the right. I asked who he thought to be my people. He then questioned who I was and where from, so I suggested he took a look at the registration plate and he said to me, "Where that." At this juncture my Portuguese had slipped and next came Afrikaans. I owned up to being a Brit. He wanted to know why I had answered in Portuguese and I asked why he had spoken to me in that language, "Because you had started it." It turned out that I was in the panicked convoy flight of Portuguese from Angola, just after Angolan independence. Many Portuguese tried to use the coastal route but the sand and lack of drinking water sadly cost quite a number of lives. We had a laugh and a chat, then I moved on. He was a very pleasant policeman, obviously from HQ, probably out in the bush because of his linguistic skills and I suspect it had been a while since being on directing traffic duties.

I overnighted somewhere or other in an hotel and set off next a.m. for Mafeking, arriving just in time for kick off. By kick off my truck had disappeared under a hoard of children. I remember it as a good game and I left immediately for the camel camp, passing through a farm gate on a little-used road to Tsabong, Botswana. The camels were unloaded and into a kraal. Next morning, I called to George and he ambled over for his morning nose scratch. He had been running wild a few days ago and I had subjected him to all sorts of terrors and the abuse of being in the back of a truck for days. They had been fed hay and water but in a completely alien environment. I also doubt whether they enjoyed the rugby. We won.

On one of my trips to Momella game park (Tanzania), I was sitting on a bit of a hill overlooking a pool. Thick vegetation around the pool and after a while of looking at mainly birds, a sizeable antelope walked out of the bush and looked around then he was followed by a smaller (female?) second one. I had no clue just what they were but on getting back to a game book I realised I had seen a bongo, which is reclusive. Even then I was not aware how lucky I was, because I had never heard of them. Nor have I seen another.

My other encounter with lion was later in Botswana, when I was mates with Sekgoma Khama, the president's cousin. 'Sekki' was chief of the Bamangwato at the time and he was running thirty thousand head of his family's cattle out in the desert. He was having lion problems. "I don't mind them taking a few, but when they get too greedy, they have to be persuaded to go elsewhere." The only way to get them to leave is to shoot a female. I was driving one of the first Land Cruisers in Botswana and Sekki asked me if I would drive for him and three of his staff. I gave Sekki my 0.375 Magnum and left me with his 0.243 (considered a pop-gun) in the cab. With a bushman tracker we found them quite soon and I was asked to stop. Lots of bangs off the four guys in the back of the pickup, but I could see nothing. Then, looking out of my passenger-side window, I saw a lion trotting straight at us. So, I rapidly decided to see what the 0.243 would do to her. Just as she was hitting charging speed to go for the people on the back of my truck, I decided that no one would be trying to get into the cab on that same side as the lioness. I aimed for the neck/throat, but being so close the bullet went high and entered her mouth, chipped a tooth and into the brain, down she went, a particularly lucky shot, especially for the guys on the back. The lion had been hit by one of the men on the back of the truck, which set her on the track for revenge. I asked them why they had not fired anymore and was told they all had empty guns. I hate to think how I'd have explained to the president had my shot not stopped that lion. I am not proud to have shot a lion, but I think I did the right thing at the time.

I was a 'hero'. I was made to eat a part of its heart and then

I would have the courage of a lion. I was told to take the skin, which I could not refuse. Not that it was notable, and I never have felt happy about the event. I have just unpacked my tea chest of skins, 30-plus years later, and it is in perfect condition. I had bad dreams about that one for months.

I was getting to the end of my contract in Botswana and decided to go back to the UK for further education, having been denied a salary rise. University term starting dates in the UK were not what I wanted, so I asked if I could end my contract early without any penalty. My request was refused by some thick-headed Brit who was concerned with staffing. I got annoyed, as I had worked in the country for five years, nearing six, and thought I deserved a bit of lenience, but not so by my hero. I then told him that there was a project coming up for the next five-year development plan, and I was the obvious person to produce a plan and then he would be asking me to do the job. I told him that I could make a complete mess of the livestock program if he did not allow me to leave in time for uni. If given the promise of an early departure date without penalty, they would get a good program, as good as I could make it, and me leaving for the MSc university course in Reading.

I was way out in the bush with Sekgoma, chief of the Bamangwato tribe, and some of his employees, shooting wildebeest to feed the poor in Serowe over winter. The meat would be turned into biltong. It was a hard day and very hot, so in the evening, just when I had eaten and was settling down in the dark, my friend came to me and said, "Do you want to go to a party?" My response was, "Who, why, where, at this time?" I agreed. Could I refuse? We left camp still in a mess, clothing-wise, as I had been cutting up animals and had been walking/running for hours and all I wanted was bed.

We set off just the two of us, heading westwards, but by then it was too dark to see much until a soldier stepped out of the bush onto the track with a rifle, pointed at us. Sensibly, I stopped. A few words from my friend and we carried on. A mile or so later two soldiers stepped out, one from each side, and the same thing, allowing us to pass. Until at last we came to a clearing with a large bonfire. Sekgoma and I walked to the circle of people sitting around the fire. He said he would sit on a nearby seat. I was directed to my seat across the circle, where I greeted my neighbours, "Dumela-rra," on my left, and to the right, "Dumel—Good evening, sir." Gobsmacked at meeting the president out there. I sat next to him, with me not understanding a word of what was going on. After a while the group started to laugh and a few people kept pointing at me. I asked my neighbour what was going on. He said he would tell me later. He did tell me at the end of the meeting. What had been discussed, among other topics, was that in 1947 a South African bomber had come down near this village containing a crew of five, but the crash site could not be found by the South Africans after looking all over the area, until another plane spotted the crash site. An overland expedition turned up at the village and asked where the crew were. It goes like this, according to the story.

The questioning of the Batswana from Rakops by the South African air force:

Where are the crew?
What's a crew?
The people who were in that aeroplane?
What is an aeroplane?
That big metal plane that came down close by a while ago?
Oh, you mean that big metal bird?
Yes, that is it. Where are people that were in it?
Oh, there were no people in it.
Well, what was in it?
Just some white chicks who crawled out.

Where are they now?
We hit them on the head and ate them.

The reason the men were laughing was not at me, but they were teasing one guy who had taken part in eating of the flight crew members, and were asking what was the best part of me to eat, in his opinion. The left leg. That is what I heard on the evening, and my left leg was visible, as I was in shorts, so I patted it to stop it being embarrassed, which brought more laughter.

A little while afterwards all the villagers went back to their village, Rakops, leaving me and my neighbour alone to discuss livestock for about one and a half hours or more, considering the state of the pastures of the Kalahari and what needed to be done to preserve the livestock industry. My neighbour was the president; I was a UK farmer's son. We talked and he kept asking my opinion about land ownership in a fenced area, water availability, would they own the land allocated or pay rent to the tribe who were the 'owners', etc. I said that any fencing off would need to remain the property of the tribe and the individual cattle owner would pay a rent. I emphasized that the tribal elders would have to take responsibilities. We covered an awful lot of ground and it was getting late and I was no doubt very tired. I was getting annoyed with all his questions, so eventually, in exasperation, I said, "But sir, it's the only way!" He went quiet for a minute, or one and a half. I was wondering if I was going to be hung for ill manners but then he replied, "Yes, I agree with you completely, but if you ever tell anyone I will have you shot."

A short while later I was asked, as expected, to write up the livestock section of the next five-year development plan. I reminded the toad in the staffing section in Gabs that I would do it if I was able to shorten my contract without penalty. This was agreed, reluctantly. I gave him one of my 'F you' smiles and never met him again.

The government recruited an agricultural economist to help and this was agreed to. So, Ralph (V-K) arrived from Kenya and we set to. We made a good team; I knew Botswana pretty well after meeting many people, and got to know the potential and limitations of the range (desert). Ralph knew how to write it up so that it would attract a donor. The plan included a training school at Ramatlabama initially, for training in livestock management and grazing management and all the requirements for the Batswana herdsmen to change from running cattle on open range to ranch/cattle management. The proposal was accepted, but I was away very soon afterwards and did not feature in the implementation. One thing I found was my feeling of the best vehicle for the area, missing out wading, was the Chevy 125.

I then left Botswana with regret and went to—

SIX
University Of Reading

My wife and I bought our first house in the salubrious part of Reading known as Cemetery Junction. As usual, I found something to do to help put a crust on the table for the two girls. I became a pot walloper for a while at a nightclub and also worked for the GPO, and at Christmas time after the university course I worked for both. I had one entertaining spat. I had parked my Land Rover in the club carpark earlier and as the car park slowly filled, I got blocked in. Later in the evening as the entertainment was going on and I wanted to leave the club, I was unable to do so. I called three times on the deejay's foghorn, asking the owner to move his car, but no one showed up. I called one last time to the owner and gave them five minutes to move the car, as my Land Rover was going to leave on the dot of five minutes. So, I left on the dot, but as I left the carpark, I did see a man chasing and shaking his fist at me in my rear-view mirror.

Between Gabby and me we produced a little boy in Reading. Gavin is now six feet four inches tall, married, and has a Turkish wife and a daughter.

The MSc course in tropical livestock production was one of the last such courses in the UK, due to lack of interest; I was lucky to be admitted. There were three of us and we were the last course at that university. I was asked why I was taking this course and I said I wanted the piece of paper; I was told that they were sorry but they could not do that. Having spent ten years or so in the tropics, I was not stressed, and my dissertation was accepted. I find it hard to understand after so many years, but I did get 'my piece of paper'. I was looking forward to receiving information on genetics, with lectures by one of the top geneticists in Britain. I never saw him, and he died playing squash just after our graduation. I did not attend the graduation ceremony. I was busy haymaking for a local farmer.

After uni I worked on a farm near Reading for a while, until the British Ministry of Agriculture tried to find me a job. This was in my agreement when I applied for a grant for the MSc course. Their search came up with nothing, so I was released from the obligation.

SEVEN

Afghanistan, First Visit

I then found a job in Afghanistan. I knew little of the company hiring me or of Afghanistan. I even spelled 'Afghanistan' wrongly on my request for a visa at the Embassy of Afghanistan in London – not a good start, but the staff were kind.

The job was for a company in Bath who also really had little comprehension of Afghanistan. The post was advertised in the good old *Farmers Weekly* as working with sheep, but it turned out that the main part of the project was the construction of an abattoir. It was the only part in which my employer was interested. My posting was an add-on when some Afghan government official asked what the abattoir was for. So, my post was tacked on to keep the project acceptable to the donors, who also had little idea of what the abattoir would achieve. The idea was good but impracticable when any success would depend on the nomads as customers. Nomads were at the top level of the agricultural ladder. When a farmer had sufficient sheep to sustain a nomadic existence, he became a nomad, with due respect from farmers. So, trying to get him to return to being a farmer would be a big backwards step.

As late in the year as it was when we were to travel, we realised we would be there for Christmas, and among our luggage we packed a Christmas cake liberally soaked in brandy. Our luggage was being sent by sea, but was held up on the Afghan/Uzbekistan border and took about fifteen months getting through. Our luggage eventually caught up with us only a few months before we left. As they say, 'better late than never' and the cake was scrumptious.

My wife managed to get to Afghanistan via Afghan Air, which was seldom a fun trip, worn out with looking after a six-month-old boy and two girls. As she came off the plane, my office help went straight to the plane as people alighted and asked if there was anything he could do for her. He was immediately handed a child.

At that time, the 'golden' years, Herat and most of the country was happy. Women were being educated; dress was up to the individual, including whether to cover the hair or not. The female gender had freedom similar to the European lifestyle. We had local people inviting us in for tea; university students came to entertain our children. We had a house help, Gulam, who was far from handsome, as he was a usual case of a bad attack of smallpox. There was the occasional highway robbery, usually of bus passengers, but little violence.

The project was aimed at getting Afghan *kuchies* (nomads) to have their sheep and goats sold in Afghanistan instead of taking them across the western border to Iran and selling them in Tabas, as was the norm. There was to be an abattoir constructed in Herat using World Bank funds. The team numbered six but I was the only one to get out of Herat and off-road. My specific task was to encourage the sale of livestock through Herat, but no one had any idea how it should be done. The nomads were very nomadic; they would only spend two days in one place because after that the grazing would be finished. If someone in the group was too sick to ride a camel, they would wait another day, perhaps one more if high ranking, and if still too ill, he or she would be left to die alone.

Then, a couple of years down the road, the Russian invasion scuppered the whole idea. The nomads, kuchies, were almost wiped out by the Russian invasion, as the Russians were unable to control nomadic people who were not unused to guerrilla warfare. The Russians killed many animals by bombing, which ensured the kuchies' lifestyle was no longer feasible.

Herat was mainly Shia Muslim, which was at that time in Afghanistan perhaps less rigid than the Sunni branch. The Hari Rod River ran just across from the town and there often was a group of kaffirs/gypsies living in black tents; this was the Afghan version of Piccadilly Circus of old. There were buses in the town centre on a Friday which quickly filled up with 'gentlemen' who jumped up the steps to get on and were quickly taken across the river, where they rapidly disappeared among the tents. Not long afterwards, these same 'gentlemen' were seen to slowly walk, almost totter, back to the bus and were brought back to town. I doubt the wives dared to complain.

The king had his own rail line from his house in Kabul to his office, and an old very old steam train to carry him the few hundred yards to his office daily. But kings can do that.

Herat had at that time a very interesting mud fort of many years ago that was being renovated by a guy employed by the UN heritage branch. It was open to visitors and a number of tourists dropped in to look it over before travelling on to India. I do wonder if the guy who was repairing the fort would like to see it now. There were mainly two types of tourists, one of which was labelled as twinset and pearls, and the other lot labelled as pot heads. There was a swimming pool for residents and visitors and frequented by all, male, female, local or expats. A good mixing of the population, not to be seen for many, many years to come. If ever?

My job was to try to stop this over-the-border trade of sheep and goats. So how to stop this? As I have said, a farmer wants to be a nomad and no longer to be a farmer. Nomadism at that time was a farmer who got rich enough to have sufficient animals. The best I could hope for would be that the nomads would like to have a fodder store available for winter. I expected that a few farmers would leave one of two members of the family overseeing fodder production.

I compromised by obtaining a lot of acres of desert near to Farah, south of Herat, which had water not too far below ground for irrigation. I quickly realised that this project was to build an abattoir and not to worry about why. I knew the kuchies would not settle to farming.

Herat did at that time have the privilege of being one of the most conquered cities in the world, or so it was said. Armies going raiding north and others raiding south trampled on Herat. The locals talked about Alexander as though it was just yesterday. Herat was an ancient city which had suffered for centuries as the gateway to or from Afghanistan. Army after army marched over the city both ways. Most of the population of Herat were Shia Muslims and most Afghans were/are Sunni. These two have never been happy neighbours. The country was at peace in what is known as the Golden Years, peace and law abiding, which made it the gateway for tourists from Europe and hippies from wherever heading for India as the promised land for drugs of all sorts. There were numbers of 'twinset and pearls' tourists, too.

In my first year there I was met with my second coup in a country. All the action was in the east; we were not troubled by it. The king was usurped by his cousin and little damage was done. Herat had a fly-past of fighters to remind the town to be good and that was it.

We shared Herat with a number of less-than-friendly Russians who were said to be looking for oil in the north. I never heard of any success and in retrospect the explanation that they were oil prospecting was just camouflage. They had their own little Russian quarter. When the balloon went up and the Russians invaded, I am told that the Afghans threw hand grenades through all the windows of the Russian-occupied houses, but would not enter the houses afterwards in case they saw any women without clothing.

In an effort to understand the marketing system in country and more about the migratory restrictions, which were of long standing, I decided to visit the annual sheep sales. This took place in July; the nomads grazed their sheep into the higher central regions, slowly, to allow the new grass to grow before they arrived, finishing at a very small village called Chaghcharan, way up in the rolling hills. There was no accommodating hotel, as the only visitors were kuchies who brought their own houses with them. Having been told this, I took a one-man tent with me. I was given an armed guard each night I stayed there. I never sensed any animosity all the time I was there; all were friendly. I am unable to estimate how many sheep were there and how many were sold, but it would be in thousands or even millions. I am sure I only saw a fraction of them due to the rolling landscape.

The method of trading was not by auctioneering as understood in most of the rest of the world, but between individuals, and not verbal. The buyers and sellers would sit opposite each other on the ground and share a cloth hiding their hand from view. Presumably the price was decided by finger contact, etc., and the contract was not open to anyone but the two. It was a sort of blind auction.

I thought it would be educational to take another route home to Herat. On the map was a track though the mountains heading north which met the Hari Rod River, which later flowed close to Herat. The driver was happy to try it, and then we learned that the track had not been used for two years. But after discussion we decided to try it. It was a bit hairy, as much of the road was a track bulldozed through the side of mountains with a drop off of hundreds of feet down to a river. Occasionally we had to do a bit of road repair, and when both of us were satisfied with our efforts the driver and I took it in turns to drive over the dicey bit whilst the other walked, so one of us would survive to tell the tale.

After heaven knows how many miles, we dropped down into the valley with the river. I had heard of a minaret which was unknown to most of the world until a pilot got lost and followed the river to get his bearings. Over drinks he asked the name of the minaret up in the mountains. Apparently, it was named Minar-e-Jam and was said to have been built by a robber baron to thank God for helping in the destruction of his competition in the business of robbing on the Silk Road. Latterly it has been found to have been built close to a lost city on the hill overlooking the Minar, which has only recently been found since I left Afghanistan. In the absence of any controls in that area of Afghanistan, it is feared that many artifacts have been found and sold on the black market and lost to Afghanistan. The minaret was unusual in that it had two staircases, one for up and the other for down. It also had a very noticeable lean out over the river, so much so that I was a wee bit worried about climbing up the ancient steps to the top, but I did.

Leaving the minaret, we followed the river until we came upon a village across the river and decided to try to cross there. I took a long stick to use as a depth gauge and started to cross. Halfway across I suddenly thought of crocodiles, but I reasoned that I had not heard of crocs in Afghanistan, so carried on to the other side. We then took the fan belt off the Autodacia, as the fan blades would snap when wading through deep water, as had happened with other of the project vehicles. We crossed and wandered down the river for X miles and came upon a village which thrived on the takings of warm water from a volcanic spring and offered bathing facilities to passers-by. I then took a bath to arrive clean and volcanic smelly for when I got home.

The project accountant had brought a pair of pedigree Afghan hounds with him from England, and when it became known to the public the king decreed that they should not be taken out of the country. When our accountant left, he hired a plane to take him and his dogs to Pakistan. In Afghanistan there were in reality only two types of dogs – both were 'working' animals. There was the big fighting-type mastiff, which usually had severed ears. These were kept for fighting wolves when the wolves were hungry over winter and attacking the sheep and goats. The severed ear removed any bits of dog the wolves could grab in a fight. The second type was called a tarsier and were hunting dogs that had the appearance of a slightly heavier-built greyhound and a thicker coat. It was rumoured (which I still find hard to believe) to cost £1,000. Hunting what? I was told that there was a desert antelope somewhere in the deserts. I never saw any hint of a game animal, or birds for that matter.

In Afghanistan kite flying is a sport, not for kids but adults, who attempt to cut the 'strings' of other kites. The strings are fishing line, I believe, which is coated with glue and powdered (?) glass so when two kite strings rub up against another, one of them will be cut. The problem is that, when one string is cut, it drops to earth for a long way and can cross a road and stay off the floor when held up by roadside objects or bushes, and can and does cut the throat of motorcyclists. Some entrepreneur made a living manufacturing a frame to fit on motorcycles in front of and slightly higher than the rider, which would lift the fishing line over the head of the rider. Another Afghan sport is trying to entice pigeons to your 'tower'. Pigeon manure is a highly prized manure, so the more birds you have, the more fertiliser you will have.

The abattoir construction and fitting out was eventually sufficiently advanced that the employees were able to get lamb for Friday lunch, but the uptake of farming for fodder was going slowly. The kuchies showed little interest in going back to farming even if they could keep returning to their grass farm. In all it was a badly conceived project with inadequate pre-project analysis. The kuchies could not understand why they should be prevented from marketing animals in the old method they had used for many years, just for the sake of a government that had never done anything for them. They hated the return of becoming a farmer again, and when I suggested leaving one of their family to remain at the 'farm', this was rejected too. I had found a large shed full of road-making implements that would enable the opening up of large tracts of ground for farming once land and water was found. Another matter would be would the local owners of the chosen land allowing it to be farmed, which I found hard to believe. When I pushed the issue of using this machinery, I came upon a problem perhaps solo to Afghanistan. The door to the storage facility would be locked and had a paper across the gap between two large doors with a list of names. According to local rules, the doors would not be opened unless all the named people were present. The problem? Some of them were dead. My questions about getting round this were met with multiple shrugs of the shoulders, even of the highly ranked in government.

I have always said that the whiz kids who come up with such projects ought to be forced to ensure they are sound or even to spend time on implementation. Many project writers were not field experienced, and the people trying to get their daft ideas to function should be allowed a large amount of freedom in the development of the project. This project was a nonstarter from the beginning, in my opinion, and they were rescued by the invasion by Russia.

The company employing me were not interested in my tale of woe. The abattoir was almost finished and actually was able to slaughter a sheep or two for Friday lunch, but they stockpiled the carcase remains in the giant freezer. I was getting frustrated by the lack of interest, and the unlikeliness that the scheme was at all viable, when my counterpart advised me to go home. The political situation with Russia and Afghanistan was heating up and I was advised by my Abdul to get my family out of Afghanistan, "because we will have to take them on before too long." Wife and myself thought it would be fun to drive home instead of flying. I received cash instead of air tickets, packed up and said "Goodbye" to all.

I had purchased a Land Rover from the UN which was in better condition than it looked. The UN had held a sale of 'no longer needed' vehicles and got zero bids. In Afghanistan at that time if a vehicle was brought in duty free and sold in country, the buyer would have to pay the hundred percent duty, unless the buyer had duty-free privileges. Such as me. I asked the workmen and mechanics which was the best of the vehicles on sale. The actual price was a laugh. The UN staff guy in charge of making the sale asked me what price I was offering, and I said more than the offers you got at the auction. He smiled and said, "I was rather afraid of that." I offered £5 per wheel; he said that is £25. I refused, as one tyre was bald, so he gave me a new one. Then we counted doors and other bits and pieces, such as a steering wheel and floor pedals, wing mirrors, and eventually arrived at £97.

I had it checked over by the Land Rover workshop in Kabul

with no charge, as they were quitting due to the oncoming war. I loaded up and left. On my last drive from Kabul to Herat, I was driving at night and I saw some vehicle standing with headlights on high beam. Thinking of ambushes, I did not stop, but as I passed the vehicle, I saw a policeman and anchored up before they started shooting. I was able to explain in Dari that I was blinded by the headlights of the parked truck and walked him back up the road to prove it. The only light they had was a paraffin/kerosine lamp of about three candle power, if that, for informing oncoming vehicles.

EIGHT

The Trip Back To The UK

After adding a roof rack and a load of kit and fodder for five of us, we departed as far as the nearby border with Iran, only to have to stop for a VERY thorough search for drugs – and the searcher knew his job. At last, we were able to motor to the Caspian Sea, entertaining the children with playing around on the rear seat and listening to 'Puff, the Magic Dragon'. In Iran and a beautifully clean sea we got chatting with a local couple, who asked where we were heading for. We said Tehran and they said they had family there and we must stay the night with them and gave us an introduction note. We somehow easily found the head of PWD, a public works department again. A beautiful house, Persian carpet covering the floor of the guest room, and as we started to get dinner three ladies walked in carrying delicious food for ten. I still have a very high opinion of the Iranians. I have only met one other in my wanderings.

The roof rack was a bit of not the best Afghan workmanship. Almost every time we stopped overnight, we had to have the roof rack re-welded until we hit the tarred roads. We would motor into each town where we intended to stay the night looking for the flash of a welder's torch. When I mention Afghan workmanship, I really do a disservice – they were wonderful and full of initiative, but sometimes the initiative available fails. One incident was memorable, when we had a 4x4 Autodacia with problems that could not be fixed in Herat, so it was sent to Kabul on a lorry. I wandered over to the truck before it left and found that the roping of the 4x4 was less than I expected. They had passed a rope under the lorry, with the rope passing through both the cab windows. They had not even thought to put the brake on or leave it in gear.

We carried on with little mishap, getting insurance in each country we went through. We went until we hit the first country who could not decipher the Afghan number plate, so we drove to the UK with the supposed number plate painted in white on the front mudguard; somehow it was accepted all along the way. I therefore drove back to and got insurance as I went from country to country without a genuine registration number, including in the UK.

We carried on, loving the trip, until we got lost and found ourselves on a nice, flat, wide-open road, which turned out to be an airfield, and numerous 'dead' tanks dotted about until we got to Turkey. Then, driving south, heading for the Mediterranean, we arrived at a mind-blowing scene of Cappadocia. We spent a couple of days exploring underground cities, etc., and then went south to the Med, dawdling along the coast and turning north for the bridge over the Bosphorus and into Bulgaria.

I wanted to get through Bulgaria in one day, but somehow we got off the roads, with road signs we could not read, not in Cyrillic spelling. Lost in Sofia around midnight, I drove down a hill to a roundabout that had five roads going in, but nothing allowing me to move off the roundabout. Every exit had NO

ENTRY signs and no others, so I used the least trafficked one. I later came upon a young couple off the road a few yards away. I walked to them and asked if they spoke English. Yes, and they showed me the road. I know nobody who speaks Bulgarian and then we were lost again. I found a taxi and asked him to guide me to the border. A bit fast but no problem, and a five-dollar note disappeared, as did the taxi. Perhaps I paid him too much. Next morning through the gate and into Yugoslavia. No problem, very nice people, even the police. We got to the border and entry to Italy with no problem. We marvelled at the driving conditions on the Autostrada. We went looking for somewhere to lay down our sleepy heads when I met my only driving near accident. Just before we arrived at the campsite, I found myself driving on the wrong side of the road after going through a crossroad. Thankfully, we stopped, and so did a car coming towards us on his correct side.

We found a campsite that was closed for the winter but were allowed to camp for the night. It was cold, very cold – the only warm one among us was our last born, who had his nice collapsible, cosy, cot. Next morning we decided to leave early, though my fingers did not work well with ropes. Loading was achieved only just to secure our load on the roof rack, with a lot of hands in warm pockets, plus swearing.

Under the Alps and to Dunkirk with a night in a small hotel with a very kind owner. Next morning we had to hurry to make it to our booked ferry, and then just as we were at the loading ramp of the ferry the gearstick came off. I held it in place whilst driving onto the ship and fixed it as we crossed the channel and to Blighty. Nothing too serious, just a pin had fallen out of a ball joint at the bottom of the gearstick. The old Land Rovers were and still are treasured due to the simplicity of fixing the simpler problems.

When I sold my Land Rover in the UK later I found out that

one of the window panes was ordinary household glass. I and family had driven through Iran with the goat herding children who threw a rock at you if you did not chuck a cigarette to them. Luckily, I had been warned of this pastime of the herders. We managed to get through without a rock being thrown at us. I had bought cigarettes, as I had been told by travellers coming the other way to get ciggies. I eventually ran out of ciggies and had to pretend to throw a cigarette and fortunately we could get well past the rock. I went through London with the 'Afghan' Land Rover and got lost. I found I was going the wrong way, so I did a U-turn in Piccadilly, knowing that if any copper saw me, they would not be able to read the number plate, and if they could read Arabic script, they would not report it. My next assignment was Swaziland after a couple of months' leave.

NINE

Eswatini AKA Swaziland

My stint in Swaziland, which has since been renamed by the king as above, was almost a holiday. I consider it as playing cowboys. I was employed by the British government to rehabilitate a farm/ranch previously owned by a South African who unfortunately died with his wife in an air accident. He had flown to the Eastern Province of South Africa in his private plane to purchase things for the ranch and supplies for the home. One item he purchased was a 44-gallon drum of molasses for the cattle, which unfortunately was not completely secured. I was told that as he took off the drum of molasses rolled to the back of the plane, which caused it to crash tail first; both were killed.

Officially, I fell under the head veterinarian in the capital Mbabane. I think he was my best 'boss' of all that I'd met up to then. Usually there is a bit or a lot of friction between livestock production staff and the vets. The vets consider the livestock officers inferior because they do not, in their opinion, have an equal qualification. All vets are not equal, and many unnecessary livestock deaths occur due to badly trained vets. See my diatribe in the Pakistani chapter. I asked how often I would see him out at the ranch. His reply was, "Only if there is trouble."

I liked this vet on my first meeting. I did see him, but only once at the ranch, when his 'trouble' was he wanted some banana plants. He told me at my first meeting that they had a nice house in Mbabane for me. I explained to him that you cannot look after a cattle ranch if you live thirty-five miles away, that it is a twenty-four-hour duty. He agreed to have the ranch house cleaned up, which was one of the two houses on the ranch, and I had a very interesting two years there. My wife and three sprogs joined me and it was a very comfortable time. There were no lions in Swaziland except in the zoo, which took a load off my mind. The biggest threat to our children would be the snakes, of which there were too many.

The son of the previous owner, who had a farm next to Nyonyani Ranch, did not wish to take it over, and the UK government purchased it for the benefit of smaller Swazi cattle owners. The ranch/farm was 39,000 acres, i.e., an eight-mile square, sixty-four square miles fenced into sixty-four paddocks – where it was possible to fence, but not on some places as rock slides and cliffs. The road to town was dirt but not too bad. The road on the ranch was less well tended and was just a large circle. The nearest school was in Mbabane about thirty-five miles away, which in the dry season was not too bad but, in the rains, it became a bit problematic.

The ranch had both high veldt (pasture land) and low veldt, with an escarpment between the two ecosystems and a nasty drive, especially on the downward trip. Keeping away from the left edge, with eyes on the road watching for holes and avoiding loose rocks, was absolutely necessary. Driving my Land Rover down as usual, I saw a small greenish-yellow snake come out of the left-side heater vent, go across the dashboard and down into the right-side vent. Heart in mouth stuff. For three or four days I left the doors open and the bonnet up so it could escape this crazy refuge it had found.

A friend of mine who was working in Mbabane was arrested for growing marijuana in his garden. He had his court case about three weeks after arrest and was granted bail. At the court case, the charges were read out. He pleaded not guilty, stating that it was not his 'weed' that he had no idea there was weed there and it must belong to his gardener. He also stated that if he was guilty, so should the judge be. This statement was questioned by the judge and my friend said that he had seen weed growing it the judge's garden when he passed the house of His Honour that morning. The court was adjourned whilst they went to see the garden and sure enough there was weed growing there. Case dismissed. He told me later that he had planted it just two weeks previous to his court case.

It was not all fun on the ranch. We had two tractors and one had a problem – it was missing a mudguard. We needed poles to build a cattle crush at the dip. I talked the forestry department into letting me cut poles from the government forest. When we were cutting poles for the construction of the kraal (an open pen for cattle), we had been using rather old chainsaws that used petrol for fuel. The vibration was awful; my number two and I were unable to use our hands for much of the next day. I dispatched a tractor and labourers next morning to collect the poles from the forest. I specifically told the driver not to take the tractor which was under repairs with a rear wheel, so it was without the mudguard. Unfortunately, he did not carry out my order, because he thought it was the faster of the two. It was a cold morning and after they left the farm the driver told one of the labourers to drive whilst he stood on the hitch mechanism at the rear, putting his overalls on for warmth. He accomplished that and was then returning to the driver's seat without stopping the tractor. As he slid past the seat whilst the farm hand was vacating it on the other side, the tractor wheel dropped into a shallow gully made by rain, and this unbalanced the original driver. He sat down onto the rear tyre, which flung him ahead of the tractor onto the road between the front wheels in a sitting position. The tractor then hit him on the back of the head, slamming him forwards and breaking his neck. I was fishing in a pool on the ranch which I had stocked with trout when I first moved to the ranch. I was due to leave not far in the future and told the 'foremen' that I would leave them for the day to see if they could manage without me. I was called. I checked the man and agreed that he was dead and then sent his body to hospital for a post-mortem. The staff initially told the police that he had fallen from the tractor and was run over by tractor wheel. The post-mortem showed no bones broken except the neck, after which we got the original version above.

I was doubly horrified about this case because two weeks previously I had put him on a month's notice due to dangerous driving down the steep road. I had walked behind him after an earlier storm, which showed his tyre marks quite clearly, and I was angry about how close he got to the edge of the road a number of times, risking the lives of staff on the trailer. I was so distressed that I had put him under a dismissal notice; this meant he was no longer entitled to compensation for his family after his death. The ranch held a whip round and she got a gift from us, but not enough to last for long. His wife returned to her family.

The ranch was such that it had two ecosystems, the high veldt and the low veldt, and it was quite apparent; even over a short distance and height the difference in vegetation was noticeable. For example, frost occurred on the higher section but never on the low part. There was some open grazing land on the high veldt and bush, thick at times, lower down. These, added to the mix of mountainous parts, made management less than easy. I was in a new environment and it took some time getting settled in. The ranch had a drive-through road – one side was high and the other at river level. I used the high exit, as it went to the capital and from the house is an escarpment.

A month or so later I managed to get a government grader to tidy up that road. It was never accomplished, as very soon after the grader started work, the grader driver took a right turn where the road was straight and the grader fell off. It stopped about three hundred feet down and in a stream. The driver had abandoned the grader early, unhurt. The government had to bulldoze a track up the streambed for a couple of miles to rescue the machine, which actually suffered little damage. They did not offer to complete the road job and we had to carry on using the rather dilapidated hill road regardless. I was terrified that there would be a meet with one vehicle going up and the other one down. HELP!

The water for the garden and house came from a small stream that started high on the ranch, and I decided it would be clean; indeed, it was as good water as any available. It came by a pipe across some grazing land and then down to the level of the house. It was all installed by the previous owner. There was a small hump as it crossed the field, which would suffer occasionally, having air in the pipe. There was an upward-pointing release valve, why vertical I never found out. However, it was useful during the hot weather to allow the staff to cool off; they were usually stark naked when they were dancing in the 'shower'.

Once I decided to go and have a look at the stream at its source and climbed up the hill beside the pipe; I cleared a few filters, leaves and such, and carried on. I came upon a dead cow in the stream at a point where it was very deep and very narrow. The cow had obviously walked along the stream bed, which was narrower and deeper, until it was unable to clamber out and drowned. I decided to clear out the body. It was a tractor and staff enterprise now, and when we had everything ready to extract the animal, we found that the cow was rotten and was lifted out in pieces, quite an unpleasant task, until I thought of the house water supply with bits of rotten cow getting into the system. I borrowed a horse and galloped across the field along the stream path and then left the horse, slid down the hill alongside the pipe on my rear end, ran across the field to the house, and turned the pipe away which filled the storage tank. We therefore missed the stew coming out of the 'fresh' water tap indoors. I was surprised that no one was ill from the cow-flavoured water. I let it run for days into the garden before turning the inlet pipe back into the house reservoir. YUK!

One morning I went to the higher ground with the fencing gang and saw that there were lots of small white circular fungi in the grass. I wondered as to why we were blessed with such a toadstool crop. After helping with the fencing, I decided to take a look at the toadstools, as I had not noticed anything the previous years, never mind so many. I picked a few up and studied them, consistency and smell, and thought they may be a type of mushroom. All my staff assured me that they were poisonous. At the end of the day, I took a few to test them and I cooked them up and mixed them in the dog food for their supper. They ate them happy enough and were fine next morning. So that day I picked a hat full of them and told the staff I would eat them for the next day's breakfast.

It was a good breakfast and I convinced the staff that I had eaten them all. During the day I noticed that they were keeping an eye on me, expecting me to drop dead at any time. I was sorry to disillusion them and I never found out if any of them have tried to eat them.

On the road out of Mbabane there is a very large boulder

said to be the second largest rock in the world, following Ayers Rock in Australia. It has a name, which I have forgotten, but it is named after the man who fell off it. He was a local who, when talking to a South African, had said he could climb it if he could get a long enough rope. The South African and the local made a bet between themselves for a considerable amount of cash. A rope was found and tied at the top and dangled down to level ground. The local man was nearing the top and the white man was starting to get worried about the bet, so he cut the rope and the local died. The rock was named after him. Cannot verify the truth of this but it is what I was told by a local.

I was needing feed troughs to put bonemeal and salt in for 'licks', as the vegetation was lacking calcium and the cows like salt but not too much of that. For the cattle it was like a natural salt lick. I went around places where I might find empty forty-four-gallon drums and collected ten or so. I had heard some nasty stories about cutting these drums, dependant on what they had been used for beforehand. I took them to the public works department to have the drums cut in two. Head of PWD told me to contact their welder, and he was happy to do the job. I warned him to be careful, as I knew not what they had been used for previously. I then left PWD, saying I would be back to collect them in a few days.

Next day I went to PWD after hearing there had been an explosion there, and sure enough it was a drum blowing up. The welder was in hospital and, fearing the worst, I went to see him. He was surprisingly pleased to see me. He said he was comfortable and being well looked after. I asked what he wanted. He asked for some fruit and magazines to read, which I duly procured and dropped them off. From then onward, every time I was in town, I would take him fruit and magazines and whatever he had asked for. He told me he had been sitting astride the barrel when it went BANG, which made my eyes water.

One of the local politicians for some reason blamed it on me, claiming I was having drums cut not for the government ranch but for Europeans wanting barbeque stoves. He also said I never visited the man whilst he was in hospital to see how he was. The minister of agriculture checked on all this and told the politician to make sure he knew what actually happened after he visited the welder in hospital. It was the drums that verified the cuttings were being made across the drum, not along the height. The welder verified that I had warned him and that as a professional welder he should have known better, and it was his own fault. The minister also asked the politician how often he had visited the welder and the answer was, "None." Case closed. But I never heard whether the welder had fathered any children after the explosion. I never met the minister to thank him, but I would have liked to have done so. Politicians were not to my flavour but occasionally I met a decent one.

Swaziland (Eswatini) is reckoned by some to have the highest number of snakes per acre in the world. I must admit that so far as we could judge we lost no cattle to snakebite, or personnel. During our stay we saw enough snakes, thank you. We had a puff adder which lay along the house door, and as we had an outside loo, it was quite a pantomime. I reckoned that he wanted the warmth from under the door. Eventually we learned that if we thumped on the floor loud enough, he would go away and then return when the person venturing to the loo was back in the house. After the water in the stream feeding the orchard/garden was finished watering it was turned back into the stream, which had a resident python. We actually had two spitting cobras in the house but not residential. Having three small children, I was careful not to allow snakes too much free range around the house.

The ranch had about a hundred horses or so running loose on the high veldt. A few were trained for riding and had been used in the past by the herders, and I had my own mount. We seldom saw the herd and they caused no problems. One of the trained horses did not like going downhill. I made the mistake one day of taking him up the entrance road, which was no problem, but coming back was no fun. He refused to go downhill! After a while I gave up, took off all his gear, slapped him on the arse, and away he went. I have a feeling that his usual rider went and returned it to the trained herd. There was a beautiful stallion running with the herd. I saw him sometimes in the distance but only once close up. I was in my Land Rover and he was in a corral at a water trough. I drove up and blocked the exit. I looked at him for a minute or so he looked at me. He then backed away until his rump was touching the corral timbers. With little run up, he flew over the poles, which were around five feet high, and away he went, probably proud of himself. A beautiful beast.

Late one evening I heard a car go along the ranch road and was about five miles into the ranch. They did not come up our drive, so I thought they may be taking a shortcut through the ranch to Manzini, but from where to where I could not guess. A few minutes later I heard the car again, followed closely by another, then there were a few more vehicles all roaring along our ranch road. It seemed that drivers were continually driving the circuit and fast; I just hoped that the cattle would not want to watch the race. Eventually it all went quiet and next morning I got an explanation – and it was a story. I missed the racing cars. So, I never did see them. Perhaps I could have talked them into lending me a Mercedes for work on the ranch.

Apparently, the drug lords of Johannesburg (Tsotsi) had come to buy the harvest of the small plots of marijuana grown in the bush on the ranch. I knew where a lot of them were, as I found them as I walked the bush. Some were very small plots and one or two were relatively large. The car race was the police chasing the drug buyers, Tsotsis from Johannesburg, spivs and drug dealers. I believe they drove onto the ranch but could not find any exits, as they were driving too fast and had the cops on their tail. I believe it was two or three cars which were eventually abandoned and the 'baddies' took to their feet. The police took the cars away next day and for a week there were young men very snappily dressed roaming the area asking the way to Jo'burg, and never got a correct answer. It is now a local legend.

The staff of the ranch had a village of their own on the ranch, which was on the banks of the river the Black Mboluze, where they got their water and bathed. It was dangerous in that there were crocodiles in the river that were known to have taken women collecting water or doing their laundry. The water was very clean, being straight out of the mountains to the north. I was told that in the past a woman had been taken by a croc. And they told me that one woman had seen a large croc at the riverside. At my request, a game warden arrived to sort it out, but to no avail. I came to think that the croc had better eyesight than the warden. I thought I could stalk game but I had never tried croc. I would use my binoculars to check if the big guy was on his preferred sandbank. If so, I could get closer with stealth, but just moving a blade of grass would send him to the water. The game scouts gave up too, and so far as I know he is still around there in the Black Mboluze.

The staff at the village usually did a lot of drinking after payday; some drank far too much. Late at night one of the staff came to my house and asked to be taken into Mbabane when I went in the next morning, as he had a broken arm and the bone was sticking out. I offered to take him to the hospital right away but he said no. I gave him some painkillers and off he went and returned next morning. He asked to be taken to the village, as his brother-in-law also needed to go. We went to the village and the brother-in-law was on a mattress outside his house with an axe sticking in his head. We loaded him up and I made a careful trip to town and to the hospital, where the nurses took care of him still with the axe in his head. Apparently, they were both very drunk and got into an argument that one was not treating his sister nicely, and they got into a fight. Anyway, the man survived and was released from hospital after three weeks or so. He seemed OK but the staff said he became a little irrational at times. He continued in the ranch employment but I warned them that their drinking so much was a bad idea and with any more situations like that they would be dismissed alongside the axe.

Local farmers were allowed five cows per person, to get fat or stay to produce calves on the ranch; by now I had around a thousand head on the ranch but virtually all were cows and come breeding time I was getting worried about how to find even one, fifty being the required number for a thousand cows. Before breeding season there was a mini drought. The government ranches were running out of grazing land, and veterinary department were worried. I generously suggested I could take fifty bulls for a while. I had heard that the government stud ranch was very short of grass, and duly fifty Brahman bulls turned up at the ranch, which we gracefully accepted and turned loose among our cows.

After the bulls had been on Nyonyani for a short while, one of the herdsmen was worried that the bulls were not 'doing their duty'. He reported that the bulls would meet together all day, ignoring all the cows, even those on heat. I said I would see about it, as I had heard that Brahmans were 'shy' breeders. So the next late evening I took a horse. I usually took a horse at night, as they make more noise and ground vibrations compared to myself walking, so I was less liable to get bitten, as the snakes move away. In daytime you can see snakes moving out of your way at a walk. When I got to the grazing herd, the bulls were performing strenuously and sure enough the bulls were doing 'what they orter'. I had heard that the Brahman breed is a 'shy breeder' but did not expect that level of shyness.

Later on from the bulls episode I called (radioed) a veterinary friend I knew from a few years back – yes, I know I said I was not over fond of vets, but I do know a few who are reasonable – and asked if he would like to spend a weekend at the ranch, as I had a little job for him. He was enthusiastic and asked what he was to do. I told him he would PD (pregnancy diagnosis) a few cows. How many? "About a thousand." So, they never did get PD'ed. I complained that I did know how to do it, I had done a few, but like the vet I "became too busy." We had a satisfactory number of calves in due course, regardless.

Quite late one night, one of the staff arrived at my house saying there was a fire on one of the more mountainous hills. I had backpacks with sprayers ready filled with water for just such an emergency. I threw a few clothes on, hooked up the tractor with sprayers and went to the fire via the staff village, where I loaded about eight of the guys. We went as close to the fire as possible and loaded all the staff with the water sprayers and off they went, climbing up the mini mountain. I decided to join them as there were a couple of spare cans, so I slung one onto my back and up the hill I clambered. The climb was not too bad, as we could see by the light of the fire, and we managed to put it out without a lot of trouble. But the downhill part was not so easy, as there was no light except moonlight. I was stepping from rock to rock and progressing well when I thought to be stepping onto a rounded boulder. In the moonlight it looked like a boulder, but was in fact curled over leaves of a fern. I fell and landed on my rear end and it hurt. My back hurt. I finished the downhill bit on my rear end. It hurt. No kidding, it HURT. I could not walk and with help from the lads I got onto the tractor seat and took everyone home. I staggered into the house and crawled into bed. Painkillers helped, but by morning I could not get out of bed. With the aid of Sontu, my maid, I got through the day, but on the next day I had to see the medic. Thirty-five miles of rough road were enough to assure myself that my back hurt. He diagnosed a broken spinous process after an X-ray and, never having heard of such a thing, I agreed. The doctor said there was nothing he could do and suggested I should go home and go to bed. I decided I may as well see to a few business matters whilst I was in town. One of the main things was to go to PWD, where I needed to see the chief guy, a Yorkshire man, Paul, captain of our rugby team. I claim to be from Lancashire. (I did live there for six weeks perhaps, and I enjoyed insulting his county and people in it.) As I sidled into his office, he asked, "Why are you walking so funny?" I told him I had broken my back. "Then why are you not flat on your back or in hospital?" My reply, "Because I don't come from bloody Yorkshire, do I?" I had told him I was a Lancastrian; well, I was for a month or so. He never did forgive me for that one.

Quite often I went to town in the early morning and caught up with many school boys, but never girls, and I do not know why only boys went to school. I would allow these pupils to sit in the back of my pickup and I'd drop them at school. If they were coming out of school, I gave them a lift to their homes. They would tap on the roof when they wanted a stop. I would drive on until I heard a tap on the roof. That worked well until one child did not know about the tapping noise and tried shouting to stop me. On one day he was the last passenger but when I got back to the ranch he was not on board. I collected my number two and we returned along the road, asking people if they had seen a boy in the back of my truck. Eventually we came upon someone who had seen him, so we slowly drove back, looking carefully to see if he was lying hurt anywhere and asking people if they could name the lad. We eventually found someone who knew his name and where he lived and we went to the house. We met his mother and told her what had happened and she called her son, who arrived looking rather worse for wear but not seriously injured. Mother asked him why he had not been honest when he got home. He had told her that he had been in a fight at school. Some school!

There is/was an agricultural training centre in Manzini (the second largest town or even the largest, but not the capital) which has pupils from all over Southern Africa. I was asked to take a look at the place and make any suggestions to provide better courses. There was a course going on when I visited with male students from Namibia, and after half an hour or so there was a tremendous thunder storm, lightning and heavy rain for twenty minutes. As soon as it started all the students dashed out of lectures and, stark naked, jumped up and down, yelling and singing until the rain stopped, then went into the centre to find their clothes. They told me that they had not seen rain for four years; they came from Namibia. I did not join them.

Some 'holy man' with his own church and preaching his own form of worship visited the ranch weekly on Sunday. My housemaid occasionally told me what was going on after attending 'church'. On a normal Sunday morning she told me she had been to church and gave me the local gossip. But this time she had bad news for me; she claimed that God had told the preacher that someone (me) in my house was going to die. I had had enough of that type of religion in all the African countries I had worked in, and I knew the reality and power of witch doctors and their poisons. Unless I took action, there would be a death in my house; poisons are usually used. I had my family of wife and three children, plus Sontu, and if I let matters carry on without doing anything one of us would get trouble. I decided to hit the nail on the head immediately. I grabbed my twelve bore and half a dozen cartridges and went to visit the bastard. He was sitting at his table in his office and I walked straight in and let him see me put two cartridges in the gun. He got to be rather pale around his mouth and cheeks. I stuffed the gun into his face and tried to put it in his teeth, which were chattering by now. I did not manage that, but I let him know that if anyone died in my house from any cause, even a dog, I would come down to his 'office' and pull the trigger. At his next service he told his congregation that he had been told by his God that no one would die. End of story. Not nice, but very necessary.

Annually, the king of Swaziland holds a ceremony on his birthday, a reed dance, at which he chooses a new wife. Any young ladies who wished to take part would take a few reeds to the royal compound and the reed dance commenced. The girl/women numbered in the hundreds. Men were not allowed, perhaps still aren't, anywhere near the king's compound during the procedures and the dancing, in which I believe (Sontu told me) the women were naked. Well, I did not have to look for a new maid. The previous king had sixty wives, as he had been in power for sixty years. He was in some ways quite a character. When he was having meetings with people who thought they were important, he had a way of letting them know that he was boss in Swaziland. His official meeting hall being an imposing tribal hut, the entrance was set at a height that ensured the visitor had the crawl on hands and knees to get in.

The entrance to the fort of Zimbabwe, after which the country was named, had a similar entrance to the stone-built fort. It was designed so someone with a war axe would have the first meeting with the entrant. "Friend or foe???" When I visited the stone-built fort, I was intrigued to find that the four-sided fort was built with four walls which had no connections at the corners, just four high walls built individually and standing up, forming a square. Against the weaponry of the age, I assume that it would have been more than adequate.

The school run to town was getting to be a bit much for

my wife, as it was around thirty-five miles to the school, so we rented a house in town for them and I stayed at the ranch. The road to town meant driving through the hills and crossing the Mboluze River and one very steep hill of clay that turned to greasy mud in the rains. When it rained in the wet season the river became dangerous, fast and deep. There was no bridge, so it was your choice – turn around or risk it. On bad days a couple of the labourers would carry the children across on their shoulders. The kids loved it, but it was scary for me to watch. Another reason for moving the family to town and having them come out to the ranch on weekends.

During one of the children's school holidays, children of the school and parents were invited to the ranch; few turned it down. It had rained hard for a few days before the party day and no one turned up, so I grabbed a rope and took the Land Rover to see if the wet hill was a problem. When I got to the hill, I saw a traffic jam down below. Once I had towed them up the hill, I let them carry on because that next section was OK. As I expected, for the return most took the way home via Manzini, which was much further, rather than face sliding sideways down the slope and into the river and being washed away, as happened now and again. The party went well.

I think possibly my work in Swaziland was my most enjoyable assignment. I enjoyed playing cowboys and I left with regret, but the team I left behind were quite capable of managing without me. There was nobody 'over' me who thought he knew more than I thought I did. As I said, my 'boss', the director of veterinary services, only came to the ranch for banana plants.

About ten years later, the number two from Nyonyani Ranch came to the UK for further education and visited us for a few days. One day he admitted that he did not like the village I was in. Why? "Look around. I think I am the only black person here." I said that when I was on Nyonyani, I was the only white man and stayed for two years and I enjoyed it. "Yes, but you were used to it." Unfortunately, the university did not think he had sufficient background education. Maybe so, but he was the best stockman I met.

TEN

Kenya

I looked forward to working in Kenya, as I had had previous contacts there in many ways. I have mentioned attending the Nairobi livestock show whilst I was based in Tanzania. I made a few valuable contacts. Other people I knew also moved to Kenya, and friends from my college days, and as it was very like Tanzania, I did not have to readjust a great deal.

I was employed by a German company on a rural development project in Machakos, with the whole of Ukambani as the area. It was a project of many different fields, roads, handicraft, water, livestock, dam building, and engineering. I was attached to the livestock department in the Ministry of Agriculture and I had a good relationship with the district officer. I had been at my office settling in, meeting staff, etc., when a memo hit my desk. The project was expecting me to build and equip a honey-processing 'factory'. Hey? What's that? I knew less about honey and honey factories than camels (or even what camels know of the subject). I had to learn.

I decided to have a few days in the field to get to understand farmers' problems and the mechanisms and politics of living the village life. For my home there I was given a newly built house in a small group with all the other expats. There were eight expats, four German, three Brits and one American; four or five of us had brought our families. My wife opened a nursery school for project children, with about a dozen children of all hues.

Due to the fact that we had a lot of children in a small area and local drivers had taken to using our private road at high speeds, we decided to curb their antics and we built the first speed humps in Kenya. We did put a sign up on entry to our road, but it was usually ignored or not understood. At night we would hear the roar of a speedster, then a crashing noise, followed by the car without a fitted exhaust. We collected quite a number of exhausts during the project life.

I now feel a need to apologise to all Kenyan motorists, as Kenya has speed humps everywhere, some sensibly spaced and others for seemingly no reason at all. Kenya is not known for driving expertise, except the drivers in the Safari Rally there is/was, a local joke saying that in one rally a *mattatu* overtook a rally car. Mattatu is the name for the ramshackle taxis/minibuses abundant in Kenya. They are well known for unreliability, accidents, speeding and overloading, which is less than ideal, particularly if the driver has just come out of a shebeen (rough boozer). The Safari Rally was cancelled for a few years, I know not as to why; however, I think it has recently started up again. It was a really good spectator sport. Occasionally, when some herdsman could be caught driving his herd of cattle across a road, miles from anywhere, then you'd find out if the drivers are any good.

Living in the town of Machakos did not appeal to me and I decided to look for other accommodation, preferably close to town. I particularly wanted to move due to an unfortunate incident on the new housing site, when locals attempted to rob one of the project houses and the wife of one of the staff was hit in the face with a brick. I asked the top vet if he had any ideas or suggestions. He pointed out to me a house on a veterinary dairy farm on the edge of the town. We fell in love with it on sight. By then we had been adopted by a Jack Russell dog. As soon as we unlocked the door, the dog went crazy with excitement, rushed into the house and killed six rats. After that I think that the news went out in the rat world, because we never saw any more.

I started on the honey factory part of my terms of reference. Equipment from Denmark was ordered and the building renovated to something reasonable. My counterpart knew ten times squared as much about bee keeping and honey marketing than I did. He had been stung so often and was now allergic, such that he had to carry a loaded syringe of antihistamine in his pocket at all times. I had made a two-inch hole through the rear wall of my office and a two-inch pipe attached for access to one of our homemade hives on a shelf over my head, which had a glass side panel in my office. The hives are/were trapezoidal in shape when viewed from the end. I always wanted to use that 'trap' word somewhere. There was continual work going on inside the hive; it amused me to see how soon any visitors lost track of our discussion and then asked about the bees working away over my head.

We taught vet staff about honey collection and splitting hives so more than one new queen was produced. I occasionally helped when harvesting or at other times when a head cover was required. I eventually left it to my staff once they were fully competent, because I had also to be dressed for the job, complete with hat and face mask. The issue with face masks was that they were less than a hundred percent efficient, as my nose is much longer than the average Kenyan and the bees quickly found that out. I was tired of walking around with a bulbous, shiny, painful nose.

Very soon we had a working honey factory, not without some hiccups, but it worked. I learned a lot on that job. Germany was the funding nation on that programme, but most of the equipment for the honey factory was Danish.

I unofficially had a government motorcycle with a 50cc powered engine. There were about a dozen purchased for a project, in which staff found them difficult to handle in the mud, sand and ruts. They were unregistered and unlicensed, and I used them to go to work and back, very useful. One day when I was off to the office around one mile away, I saw a police officer standing at the side of the road with his BMW 500cc motorbike, white helmet and his white leather gloves up in the air, ordering me to stop. He was the epitome of authority. He was a big man and my bike could not outrun his, so I stopped. "Get off your bike." So, I got off. He then said he had often seen me on the bike and had always wanted a ride on the Honda. He then said I could have a go on his BMW. I had a mental picture of me on the police bike doing summersaults, as I had to use full throttle to get my wee 50cc Honda to move, so I rejected his offer. Result? I continued to live. The policeman thanked me and returned the bike unscathed with a very sincere "Thank you."

On one trip to the more rustic areas of Ukambani, I was travelling with four of the veterinary department staff, visiting villages, and come evening we found a hotel and booked in. Dinner was chicken stew, which was rather nice. We all slept well and had breakfast, chicken stew. Thinking back on it later, I doubt very much if they had a fridge, and one at a time all of us had to ask for a stop when a suitable bush to hide behind was seen. I think I was last and it was the worst experience of 'dire rear' ever. We eventually reached Machakos and staggered off to our respective homes. Next day I was the only one to show up at the office. Two took one day off and the other had two days off after hospital visits. Ukambani chicken stew, one day old, is a fantastic cure for constipation; I can personally vouch for that.

On the road we followed when we suffered the dire rear was a well-used road but one also frequented by car thieves, there being few villages along that route. One young couple were stopped on the way to Machakos hospital, as the wife had malaria, when they were held up at gunpoint and their borrowed Land Rover was taken. They managed to get a lift for part of the way back home and reported to the police station, who sent a police Land Rover to chase the stolen Land Rover. The stolen Land Rover was found, having left the road, containing four bodies. It was becoming a practice in much of Kenya to leave a bottle of whisky in the car with a strong essence of cattle dip. The four bodies were all police officers from the station of the ones who found them. I would assume that there was no toxicology test taken; it would have been assumed that it was a common motor accident which happened. Not a nice way to go!

There was a central road in the capital, Nairobi, where a banner was stretched across it and in large letters it said, *Kenya Celebrates Forty Years of Birth Control*. It was not hanging there long once it was made public that the head woman managing the birth control unit had twelve children of her own. Experience?

I liked to fish both fresh water and salt. Lake Naivasha is close to Nairobi and I decided to visit the lake with a small inflatable dinghy, a few friends, and a very slow-speed outboard motor. The speed was perfect for the bass of the lake, and an afternoon on the lake would be quite relaxing. We were all aboard and got about half an hour of fishing, all going well, until I decided to head for another patch of reeds. I was looking backwards at the lines and rods when one of the passengers tapped me on my knee, pointed forwards, and gulped like a fish out of water. I looked forwards and realised he was trying to say "hippo." Sure enough, there were two hippos immediately in front by about ten to fifteen yards, watching us. I did a hasty U-turn at full throttle, which was SLOW, and away at around three miles per hour. Knowing that hippo can get up to twenty miles per hour in water, and even more on land, I was very happy to find that pair were in an amiable mood. That was enough fishing for the day; I believe the day's catch amounted to one ten-inch bass.

There was a lot of the short tree/large bush called lantana in Ukambani, which is poisonous to cattle, but leafed late in the autumn when browsing is the main source of green leaf, so it is desirable to cattle. If they eat too much lantana the white parts of their hide peel off. At Nyonyani Ranch we had had a few animals affected, but only a few, and we were able to keep the cows out of that particular paddock. The animals have to be isolated from the shrub, and kept out of the sunlight, until the healing is finished. In the livestock economy for me and most of Africa, browsing is usually the case. Feeding indoors and attention needed is sub-economic and animals generally go for meat. One farmer asked me to visit his farm for advice on lantana, and he had lantana to show, hundreds of acres of little else but lantana. I admitted I had never seen it so dense and could only make a guess as to what to do, which was to bulldoze the lot into heaps and burn it and try to control any regrowth. I was not in country long enough to hear whether he did it, or whether it worked or not. I hope it did. And there were no computers to ask for advice.

I feel we were very lucky when I was driving just a little way outside Machakos when a cavalcade of the president, Jomo Kenyatta, came straight at us. No problem, you just pull over to the side of the road and stop until he has passed. Fine, except my five-year-old son was standing on a car seat with his head through the sun panel in the roof – so far so good – but he had a toy pistol and was 'shooting' at the cars, president, escort, following lackeys, and half of Machakos.

I was intrigued that there were numerous baobab 'trees' in

Kenya but I never found a small sapling until I asked a local where I could find one and he told me that the young trees, saplings, look nothing like a baobab. The baobab is not truly a tree but it does pretend to be one. One man I asked likened it to a giant cabbage stalk. In Ukambani when I was there the baobab was the source of material to produce the fibre to make traditional baskets or *kikapu*. At the time I was there the Wakamba women started to use sisal, which was a great relief to the older women of the tribe.

The project had a handicraft sector and these kikapu became a big hit internationally. The design made a different style of shopping bag or even handbags; it was the 'must have' accessory for a while. Initially a slab of the baobab 'tree' trunk would be chopped out and allowed to dry. Once dry, strips were then cut from it and the women chewed it until they had chewed out the fleshy part and they had just fibres left over, which was then woven into the traditional kikapu. However, sisal production became popular, which was easier to work with and as it was so very much easier (no chewing) on the old folk's teeth, it was a significant advantage all round, more dentine and easier eating for all from then on.

Incidentally, the Kiswahili name for a 'white' man is *mzungu*. Virtually every working European knows that word. Few know where and how it originated. In the early days, Europeans appeared to have no idea where they were going or how to get there. To walk around aimlessly, getting lost, in Kiswahili is *kuzunguka* and that is what the locals thought of us, and maybe still do so.

One part of my job was purchasing milking goats and handing them out to women of families having no cattle. There was a supplier on the coast who claimed that the then-president had purchased half of his farm four of five years previous, soon after independence, and he was still waiting for his money. A wrong that had yet to be righted, and I am sure you can give a good guess whether it still hasn't been or not.

My assistant and I arrived on one of my semi-usual visits, as my supplier had called and told me he had some goats available. A trip to Mombasa. I parked up and walked to my usual hotel, the Venus, and noticed that were many more than usual 'ladies of the night' in town. I asked the receptionist at the hotel what the reason was and he told me that the US fleet was arriving on the morrow after being at sea for three months or so; he then added that the town goes wild. He was right. I met a guy who was in uniform but not enjoying whatever you fancied. The sailor told me that he had been caught with VD on the two previous stopovers, and if it happened again, he would not be allowed ashore until they returned to the USA, which was a long time ahead. I am surprised that the navy did not supply condoms. I was told that the going rate was tripled when the navy came to town.

Apparently, my assistant viewed the goings-on and told me the next day that when the crowd reached the state of naked dancing at the open-air dance club, he went to bed ashamed of his people.

August the first, 1982, was an entertaining day. It was my wife's birthday and she wanted to have lunch in Nairobi. She was born on the wrong date, as it was the day the air force attempted a coup, and Nairobi was hardly the place for a lunch with the three children. We were in town before we heard what was going on and the army man who stopped us would not let us to return to Machakos. I never did find out just why. We became homeless people and begged a bed or two from the previously named Chris, of buffalo fame. On the way to their home a bullet came in my driver's window and out the other side. No broken glass, as the windows were down, nor was anyone given an unwanted hole in their septum for a nasal decoration. Actually, no one in the family knew about it, and I did not mention for a long time just how lucky we were.

I later heard when I returned to Nairobi after a week or so that the photo shop owner where I had my pics printed had been hit by a bullet straight across his bum as he jumped into his shop on opening that morning, and had a burn mark on both cheeks. I did not ask to see it. It also appears that four mutineers entered a bank to rob it and were found two days later, dead on the floor near the safe. It seemed that they had all probably fired at the safe together in an attempt to get it to open. I assume they faced a return volley of ricochets and lost the gunfight. Another business which was attacked by looters, but the looters decided best to leave it alone, was the Mercedes showroom. The manager had a machine gun on a swivel covering 360 degrees, and used it. He had quite a costly bill from the window installation guys but he lost no cars.

We lost a refrigerator. It was taken from our house, and I checked with a place of recovered loot a few days after the first of August. It was found buried in a garden, but before I could collect it, it was stolen again, this time from the recovered loot depot. No insurance was paid out to anyone, because the president announced that it was an insurrection, which is seldom covered by insurance companies??? In my years of overseas work I have lived through three attempted coups, Tanzania and Kenya, which did not succeed, and Afghanistan, which was successful, and that is enough for now, no more, thanks.

I have been sacked just once in my work, by an American project manager on a US aid project in southern Afghanistan who basically had no interest in the cultural background we had to work in, and bulletproof jackets were not standard issue. He never left his office, never travelled by road if he could get a seat on a plane, I doubt if he ever met an Afghan. Jim Black was the worst so-called program manager I met. Elsewhere I did try one

American piece of body armour, so called, nothing fancy, just a half-inch-thick steel plate on a piece of string around your neck large enough to cover the chest. I thought it to be a little 'Heath Robinson'. On later consideration, I doubted any American troops would even try to run away with a plate on their back, which would be an encumbrance when they 'retreated'. Just a few miles on a backroad/track from Machakos was a scenic spot called Fourteen Falls. It was made famous by appearing in two or three Tarzan films of yesteryear. It was a place where a river flowed as normal then came over a waterfall, but not as one torrent; it divided into fourteen smallish channels which seemed to have been softer than other rocks. These channels were deep and fast flowing. The rocks were slippery and the four people I had with me had never seen this place. In the rainy season it is quite impressive. They all spread out to look at various points of interest. One woman of our group, Jennifer (G), slipped upstream from where I stood and she was washed downstream towards me. I found some sure footing and as she approached, as she had nothing to catch hold of in the way of clothing, I had to grab a handful of hair. I heaved her out of the runnel onto dry land. She thanked me for saving her but cursed me for grabbing her hair.

The project manager had a beehive in his garden from which the bees did not bother him in the slightest, until one day just after work the bees went for him in a big way as soon as he got through the garden gate. No one even postulated as to why it took place with nothing out of the routine to upset them. He just managed to call "help" on his radio before he lost consciousness, luckily picked up by one of the team, who got there, was able to get him away from the bees, and used his syringe of antihistamine. He was off work for a day or two; I am not too sure if it was vanity or not (I saw photos later). Ugly!

My neighbour, a local, too had a beehive, quite far away

from his house. He placed it away from his house but close to mine, with only two-metre-high wall away from our entrance gate. The bees were not impressed by a wall and usually came into our garden. When a person entered our garden, the bees did not like this invasion of their territory and often had a go at my family or visitors. We had a couple of "close encounters" but my neighbour did, after a while, move it away.

In the 1890s, some hero decided that a great chunk of land, thousands of acres, should be used for the production of foods to be sent to the UK, and, a bit like the Kongwa scheme, it failed miserably. A large area of bush was cleared in Ukambani (the land of the Kamba) and Kitui to the north. Sadly, it was another *mipira juu* (less than successful) project. I doubt we will ever learn until we put locals in charge. For me the worst part of the shambles was that over a thousand rhinos were slaughtered. Some sources say five thousand. The Wakamba talk about this with sorrow to this day. We did not help much.

I have mentioned one man who supplied goats for the project farm close to Machakos; on one of his visits he told me of an incident with the Maasai, who are well known for their skill in cattle, sheep and goat stealing. Their often-used tactic would be to steal cattle at night and push them through Maasai land, dropping off part of the stolen herd as they passed other herds and bringing replacements in, until all the cattle they were driving were very obviously Maasai cattle, and by then the stolen cattle could be anywhere in Maasai land. My supplier, a European, had a few years previously been to South Africa and come back with some Boer goats, which are larger and meatier than the local beasts. He crossed his Boer goats with the local animals and the cross was seen to be superior to the local variety. One night after his first crop of half local crossed with Boer goats, he had a number stolen and taken into Maasai land, never to be seen again. After his first cross of good-looking youngsters had reached maturity, he used them for breeding; once again, he was producing superior goats. One evening he had someone knocking on the door and, thinking it was one of his staff, he opened the door and there were a half dozen Maasai dressed in their finest. The poor guy said, "Are you the lot who stole my goats three years ago? I suppose you have come for some more." They agreed, but added, "Yes, it was us and we want some more. The last lot were very good and we want more. We will pay for them, and we will pay for the ones we took last time." I think a suitable term would be gobsmacked.

I was driving out in the wilds one day on a sort of track and saw five lions in the shade of a tree at the side of the track. I slowed down a bit to look at them and then carried on. Before long I met three Maasai and told them of the lions on the path. I was then once again on my way. Through my rear-view mirror I saw them picking up a few stones and then walking on. Not for me, thank you.

At our home we had a few wonderful barbeques with thirty-five to forty people of various hues. I have no idea how many children were there, but I think a good time was had by all. Otherwise, there was little to do on weekends.

The best doctor in town and a far greater area was a Dr Jaffrey. One member of the staff of the project had a strange condition that when he had one of his attacks, he seemed to be dead. He 'died' for a few minutes and then came round again. Understandably worrying to all of his family. Dr Jaffrey diagnosed it as something none of us had ever heard of and Mike was medvacked to Germany. I understand they had him in a hospital bed for nearly a month, and then they came up with the same answer as Dr Jaffrey. Mike returned to the project.

Between Nairobi and Machakos was the only commercial meat factory in Kenya, at Athi River, and as you drove past it, it stank. I guess it went the way of many enterprises in Africa –

corruption, politics and bad management. It seemed to only to produce tinned meat and it was shut down the last time I was in Nairobi. Botswana could teach them a thing or two. Botswana sold their best cuts mainly to Europe, the poorer cuts went to the gold miners in South Africa, and the bones were burned to kill all pathogens and then ground up for a phosphorus and calcium additive in bonemeal for cattle. In the desert areas the animals needed a bit of a sweetener before they would take it, so it was sweetened by molasses. To prevent the cattle from taking too much of the mix, salt was added. The cattle knew when they had taken enough salt and wandered off to find grazing. The grazing is/was quite deficient in phosphate.

Cattle owners were reluctant at first to let cattle eat bonemeal, as prior to our project the owners knew that the eating of burned bones by cattle resulted in dead animals; the burning was not at a high enough temperature to sterilise the bones. Their reluctance to feed bonemeal disappeared after they saw the effect of a few cattle being supplied bonemeal compared to none. Growth rate was magical almost. I do not think many Kenyan stockholders tried this supplementation, as many of the animals did not graze, except for nomadic herders, and they would not appreciate lugging bags of bonemeal around as they moved about.

In Ukambani (the area of the Kamba people) during the project life I was working with cattle owners who only had a very few cows. The cows seldom grazed much of the land used for crops, and antipathy had been settled long before our project started, so I engaged in lessons on fodder production, such as crop residues and household waste. Because so many households only had one or two cows, there were few bulls around for mating, so we jazzed up the artificial insemination program to help improve the production of the cattle through up-breeding. Using project money, I had three veterinary clinics built which provided an insemination service using top-class semen to increase milk supply from the next generation. Inseminators were trained in the technique of insemination to ensure good results.

Out in the wilds once again, I was in Maasai land and so far as I knew I was forty or fifty miles from anywhere to put up for the night. I set up camp and started to get my dinner when three Maasai Morani (warriors) turned up with spears and *simis* (short swords) and told me that it was unsafe to sleep here, as there were lions around. I was about to ask for a safe site but they told me I could sleep in their boma (zeriba). I decided it would not be popular to refuse their offer. I thanked them and they helped me pack up and we drove a few miles to their boma and I left my truck outside. I went inside and there were a few rather undesirable mud huts around the edge of the boma, which competed easily with the worst bedroom I have ever met.

However, one of the men came along and suggested I sleep outside, which was much more appealing. I asked just where as, sleeping under the stars with fifty or so restless cattle, I was rather worried that if any lion stirred the cattle, I could be trampled, to which the baddies in bad Westerns are prone. Then he came up with a lifesaver – he told me that I should sleep next to a white cow because she never moves in the night. I slept quite well and was not crapped on in the night by one of the herd. This had been one of my other less than pleasant options. Next morning, I wished them all farewell and headed for the bush once more.

One of the problems of bush work was incessant punctures. All the tyres had inner tubes which were very prone to thorns. Everyone carried two or three spare wheels and well-equipped puncture repair kits. I was once out in Amboseli game park with another officer from the office. We were checking on the impact of recent easing of the rules about cattle entering the game park and how it affected the wildlife. The job entailed a lot of bush-bashing through thorny scrub. We split the job between us and met up back in camp in the evening. After collecting the random number of thorns during the day, we had a wager for next morning as to who had most thorns. The loser cooks breakfast. The one with most punctures stayed in camp whilst the other went to find some meat by stealing from the vultures. Watch the sky for the birds circling and drive to where they have seen a dead animal. It depends rather on which predator was going to provide a couple of pounds of clean meat for breakfast. This often meant keeping an eye on the lions, with the Land Rover right at hand as you cut out a lump of unchewed meat. I was surprised that the big cats did not seem to care too much, but I always gave a sigh of relief when finishing robbing them, as they usually gave nothing to scavengers. It was said that you could pull the thorns from your tyres by soaking them in water for a while. The thorns swell and are forced out of the tyre and can then be pulled out with pliers. Said to work, but I have never tried it. I preferred to take an extra spare or three.

Another source of punctures is the way that dirt roads are treated. When they get to be rather rough, government send a tractor out with a chain and axe. He finds a nice, bushy tree, cuts it down, and drags it for miles. It creates a lot of dust, makes driving difficult, and overtaking is guesswork, but it does temporarily fill many of the ruts and corrugations. On a dirt road the sand often forms ripples similar to the sand on the beach as the tide recedes. If you drive slowly your teeth rattle. Fifty miles per hour and above gives you a much smoother ride, so long as you are able keep on the road. Another hazard is the frequency of broken-down trucks left on the road at night with no lights on. Some unfortunate car driver with poor headlights tries to drive under it, without much success. Kenyan roads are dangerous; it is not that Kenyan drivers are all poor. Many have paid for genuine driving licences. Others pay on the street for one, and many have no licence at all. The main problem I feel is the density of traffic in and around Nairobi. In the UK around this time a Kenyan was asked on the radio. "Which side of the road do you drive on in Kenya?" Answer, "The best." Unfortunately, I still do it in the UK.

I was once driving with a local along a wide out-of-town road when, after coming to a corner obscured by vegetation, we met a herd of goats straggling across the road. I was driving too fast and unable to stop. I slalomed through the herd of goats without touching even one. As we left them behind my passenger said, "Whoo! You earned your driving licence."

Another time I was driving through a village and to my right I saw a child running towards the road. I expected him to stop but he ran straight across. In avoiding him, I drove off the road into a dry stream bed. Many people saw the incident. The kid got his ears boxed and I got applause and waved on my way, but it was close, too close.

ELEVEN

Ghana
A Short-Term Consultancy

This project was to the east of the Volta Lake in Volta Region, and during my short visit there was an earthquake which introduced me gently into quakes. When I looked at shrub growth around the housing during a mild quake for the project area, individual shrubs on the hillside became a blur caused by the shaking of the quake; it demolished a few village houses but there were no casualties. It also took the corner of my brick-made chalet, such allotted to each and every one on the project. The project was in a valley with only one road in or out, and very soon after I joined the project this was blocked by a large square boulder due to the quake, around fifteen feet in all dimensions, and it had landed flat on the road. It took PWD a few days to blow it up and bulldoze it off the road lower down the slope from the boulder, and great chunks of the boulder went careering down to the stream, just bypassing the house of local farmers, each with trepidation. It had left a six-inch-deep hole in the road which was easily filled in. I learned not to be near a mountain during an earthquake.

My terms of reference were to write up a project supplement to introduce the livestock sector to a rural development project into the ongoing programme. The poultry sector was easy. Introduce improved birds and feed supplies, and decide whether to rehabilitate a poultry slaughter house. Result: not enough poultry in the area for it to be feasible, little local requirement and too far from the market. Whoever built the place, I never did find out. The cattle side was not difficult, as there were few large farm animals, mainly due to the hills. I concentrated on small stock, sheep and goats, of which there was abundance. I was asked to consider feed supplies, which were less than abundant. In fact, I was asked to check on animals going to Togo, which is east of Ghana. It was in a holding yard on the border that I saw sheep and goats together with broken-down trucks. In my report I stated that I had not seen a healthy sheep and never an unhealthy goat and as they grazed together apparently sheep could not digest lorry parts.

It was in Volta region that I was waiting for someone at a farm when a donkey started braying. I took out my phone and recorded it. When the donkey stopped bellyaching I played the noise back to him. I left one worried donkey looking round for his competitor.

It was on this consultancy that I stayed at a small village overnight and next morning I was asked what I would like for breakfast. I asked for poached egg on toast. "Yes, sir." It took a little while, enough for me to think they are slow in this kitchen, before the food arrived. I only earned later that it was the only egg in the village and the hotel staff had to hunt for it. That gave me a slight idea about food shortage.

The project put together a soccer team, who had a kick-about most evenings and were very keen. I wrote to Liverpool for a set of old team shirts for the team; I am still waiting and I have not yet forgiven Liverpool for lack of any response. The club blossomed and won the Ghanaian National Cup under the name Voradep (Volta Region Development Project). No thanks to Liverpool FC.

At the time of my leaving, there was unrest in Ghana and it was not really safe to travel, so I left Voradep at midnight, heading for Accra. I had told no one except the project manager that I would be leaving and had to have the Land Rover fuelled up and ready to go next day. I dug the driver out of bed and we set off, seeing nothing but a duck which *used to* enjoy sleeping in the middle of the road. This was a short-term assignment and I was soon looking for a job. I got a very poor view of Ghana.

TWELVE

Uganda

Idi Amin, self-styled King of Scotland, had been 'asked' to leave Uganda only a short while before I arrived, which he had done, but reluctantly. The Tanzanian army just walked into Uganda and asked Mr Idi Amin and his army to depart. There was a bit of resistance but it was again not much of a problem, as few of the public liked the guy. But the result was that the police force and the army ran away with their weapons, which meant there were thousands of armed men alienated from the general public with weapons and nowhere to go, and they were all roaming the country to try to find food and lodgings. Many of the pushed-out police and military are still in exile in Congo. It was said that few of them had much ammunition, as Idi was worried about being shot and as a result the army and police were issued with few rounds per man. When I was in Uganda anyone could have an adversary shot for £5, but bullets used were added to the price or supplied by the person asking for termination of a problem.

The project had been ongoing for quite a while and was to be funded by Kuwait. It was intended to prop up Idi, who was a

Muslim, so said. Once he was ousted the Kuwaitis were rather recalcitrant in providing the necessary boodle in line with their promises; i.e., we had minimal funds to work with. The place was in chaos even before Idi left. The Kuwaiti government had given him money to build a mosque in Kampala but the intended builder disappeared with the funds. Kuwait gave them another sum to build. It was started, but then the second builder left, leaving a partly built mosque with a twisted minaret.

My terms of reference were to rehabilitate three ranches which had suffered during the 'war' with the remnants of Idi's troops and the previous police force, who were running wild all over the country. It was an interesting situation, one that I was new to. There were many men and a few women who were roaming the country trying to find a place to settle safely down, which was difficult, as they had not been very helpful when they had the power so now they were unwanted almost everywhere. A few were able to melt into their previous village lives, but these were few, as the regime had been hated by the public due to the oppression they had imposed.

Idi started as a good guy. He cycled around Kampala on a bicycle and was greeted by all. He had been living very close to his men and I suppose he expected that Kampala would treat him like his men in the bush. He held a boxing match which he, of course, won. He called himself the King of Scotland; I am not sure why Scotland had to put up with the indignity. He was Muslim and I think it was the Emirates that supported him and accepted him when he was pushed out.

Idi was not accepted as a real Ugandan by many; his history was not from any of the Ugandan tribes and as such he was not really Ugandan. History tells us that his family came to Uganda from South Sudan with Sam Baker the explorer, looking for the source of the Nile. Baker recruited Sudanese as he passed through to Uganda as a police force and army when he took over

South Sudan. Years later I moved into a house in Devon, near to Exeter, with a previous owner – Mr Baker. It was not his home but part of his estate when he retired to the UK. History has it that he was well paid by the khedive of Egypt.

Museveni's troops were ruthless with captives; some ex-servicemen or police did face the judicial court; others were not given the option. I dropped into this mess. I was given a Land Rover Discovery for transport which was sadly in need of a service and a number of vital replacements, such as tyres. I packed a bag and set off for Nairobi but got no farther than the Kenyan border, where I needed Kenyan cash to enter for a visa. The Kenyan border officer wanted only Kenyan shillings; Ugandan currency was no use. When I flew in to Uganda from Kenya, I had to hand over my Kenyan money on leaving the country. So, I parked the truck up and waited until they changed their minds, which happened just before dark.

I got the truck back from being incarcerated and arrived in Nairobi later than I liked. After a few days the truck was fixed, serviced, etc., into running order in Kenya and returned to Kampala. Initially, security was a big problem. I was living in a converted garage. From there I moved to a house out of town, onto a coffee and banana estate. There were about eight houses there, all told, with European residents.

My family came out for a visit. Why? Please don't ask. There had been robberies on the half-mile driveway to the houses; desperate men used desperate methods. A few days after the roadblock robbery on the entrance route, I was returning home when I saw a roadblock ahead and swung off into a pathway and then into the banana plantation. I walked to the houses and told a neighbour of the roadblock and he put me right, in that they were the good police. I walked back to collect the truck. A few nights later there was a lot of shooting not too far away, so we put my youngest child in the cupboard under the sink so he would be out of the way. We then forgot him until about two hours after the shooting stopped. He still remembers that incident and reminds me occasionally, usually when in company.

I understand that the biggest and previously best hotel in Kampala was at last starting to function after a lot of repairs and rebuilding; it was now getting almost habitable. The lift had not been used since the shooting started years ago. At last, the workmen got it started. It creaked earthwards and stopped as expected. With an effort, the doors were opened and they found the remains of a Chinese man and his two suitcases.

I settled down in my home and got to know a number of people, both Ugandan and expats. I seem to have been unsettled. I lived for a while in the garage, then to the banana plantation, then I moved again later to a house on 'the Hill' and finally to a five-sided house on the way to the port on the lake. All the houses had an interesting story.

The house/garage was just a kitchen and bedroom. I was seriously thinking of moving when the family, wife and three children, arrived. Obviously, this was not fun, so the garage owner offered his house for the duration of their holiday. Whilst my family were in Uganda, we had fun and the children were taken camping a couple of times, guarded by the British Military Police. Our kids thought it was a great time. On one of the camping nights the guards got a warning that the burglar alarms had gone off of at the High Commission building. Half of the military at the camp immediately set off for the High Commission and found that some other of the military police were there too. They rounded up some of the thieves but some ran for it and escaped. The building was surrounded by metal posts six feet high and chain link fencing, which was about six feet from the wall of the compound and the gap was filled with razor wire. One of the thieves had attempted to jump the wire but failed and finished up in the wire. He was found next morning looking and feeling very sorry that he had tried to rob the place. He lived, perhaps.

My next house was nice, large and airy. By now I had a servant who moved into the servant's quarters. It was quite good until we had been in it for a week, when we were robbed. The sleeping quarters were locked away from the living part of the house and the thieves got in through the kitchen window, which had been left open. (By who?) They stole a few items and a sack of sugar, which was my ration for a year; sugar was in short supply and expensive in the market. The house owner loaned me his handgun and a few rounds for it. The following night I ensured all windows were locked but we were robbed again; entry was through the same window the servant swore he had locked. This time a few items were taken, the most expensive a being an Omega watch. It was decided that it was an army theft, as they had not been paid and robberies were common. The army were reluctant to take any notice of a local being robbed, never mind a European. So, I asked for a policeman to stay over for the nights, which is how we got Fred.

Fred was a nice guy and he came with an AK-47, which had not been treated very well at all. It had a bullet hole through the plastic stock, which was the possible reason it got to the police armoury rather than remaining as military property. I suppose the army, as the previous owner, had no further use for it. R.I.P. Fred left the gun lying around on the floor in the lounge and I kept kicking it as I walked about in the lounge. So, one day I picked it up and looked it over then asked Fred if he would like me to clean it up. "It's OK by me." I set to and cleaned and oiled everything until, apart from the hole in the stock, it was as good as new??? Anyway, he showed it to his boss, who asked Fred to ask if I would fix, mend and clean the police guns. When I had agreed, the next day Fred arrived in a truck with the back seemingly half full of AK-47s. I fixed many so they worked well.

Some needed replacement parts, so I cannibalised and returned others as not in working order.

I next moved to the house in the banana and coffee plantation. The owner of that was afraid to go fishing on Lake Victoria but allowed his number two to use it. I provided rods, lures and fuel and it got to be a regular thing, weekend fishing. Lake Victoria came to be known for its Nile perch, which had been put into the lake by 'King Freddie' quite some years previously. When I fished, the biggest fish I caught had been around for a while and weighed something like 105 pounds, which was enough fish for me. I understand that 105 pounds is a big catch, over fishing. One weekend the boat owner asked us to take a visitor from his company out on the lake fishing. He was Danish and just come through a Danish winter, meaning he was not used to sunshine. After ten minutes or so he took his shirt off. I suggested that it was not a good idea. In thirty minutes his shirt was back on and his head wrapped in a towel. I felt for him. The combination of sun and the reflection of the sunlight off the lake had cooked him.

I moved house again but kept on fishing regularly each weekend. I fished in short sleeves and shorts. After a while my arms definitely became darker than some of the locals. I had a large freezer where I kept the fish with the understanding that my housemaid could take all she wished but they must remain in my garden; i.e., she could feed as many guests as she wished but not to allow them to take any fish away.

My gardener, male, became quite ill, so I tracked his brother down and gave him the bad news that his brother probably had HIV. He died two weeks later. My fishing friend, a Ugandan also named Derek, died from HIV just after I left Uganda. His problem was that he would go heavy on the beer, and when he was drunk he was less than careful among the ladies. I also fed a Catholic boarding school on fish, as their budget could only afford meat once a month for their pupils so the fish were very welcome. I just dropped the fish off on the way from the lake. So far as HIV is concerned, Uganda was hit hard, due mainly to the fact that it was on the main road from the coast to the Congo, with numerous truck stops en route.

My next and last move was into a five-sided house. It seemed very odd. If you looked through one window you had a view. Go to another window on another side of the same room and it would be showing almost the same scene. As you have probably gathered, times were rather turbulent and the government was hampered by what could be called terrorists. There was a woman named Alice heading a hoard of followers roaming around and creating mayhem wherever they went. Alice travelled with a white hen plus a mini menagerie of animals, including a monkey. She had a hard bunch of terrorists that went wherever she wished. She claimed to be a wizard and could turn rocks into hand grenades among other rather nutty ideas. If her fighters were celibate they could not be harmed by bullets, and so on. A dangerous kind of stupidity.

Alice announced that she would attack Jinja, which is sixty miles or so from the capital, Kampala. She did have a go at the defence force in Jinja but did not make much impression, and then announced that she would attack Kampala and it was believed that she would arrive by crossing the lake by boat. My house was on the route between the road from the lake to Kampala port, which would be the road that Alice would take. The police set up an ambush on the road not far enough from my house, as it was noisy, and unbeknown to the police the army did the same; their ambush site was slightly closer to the lake. Yes, you have got it: the army heard some people approaching (the police) and attacked. The police returned fire and perhaps three hours later they realised who the 'enemy' were. There were casualties, of course, who were taken to Kampala Hospital but numerous guns were missing apparently on both sides.

I left for work before the search began so I can only rely on my maid's account of it. The police knocked on my house door and said they had to search the house. She said they could not come in but they insisted, saying they had orders to search every house. She said that this occupant was a European, but they pushed past her. The group spread throughout the house, searching for guns as ordered. They also went into my bedroom. They found nothing, but one of the police told my maid to lift the mattress on my bed. She said, "No." The policeman asked why. "Because it is too heavy." The policeman pushed her aside and grabbed the mattress, then jumped away in fear. "What is that?" he cried, as the ripples of the water made the mattress behave as though it were a beast of some sort. "It is a water bed," he was told, so he bravely prodded it a couple of times and then called all the other men to the bedroom. Apparently, they stood each side of the bed watching the wave going across and back as they prodded. After a while they called it off and departed laughing. The maid told me the sequence of events and added at the end that the boss man's boots were two inches (five centimetres) from my shotgun.

At this house I had two dogs; one stayed outdoors all night and one inside. I reckoned if anyone came to rob me the outside dog would warn me, so I could get to my gun loaded with buckshot in time. I would not open my door until I could see the outdoor dog and that he had not been killed. The thieves often used poison to get rid of guard dogs. I considered that a load of buckshot indoors would be more damaging than an AK-47. Maybe I was wrong, but glad to say it was never put to the test.

As far as my work went, there was little I could do, of the three ranches I was tasked to rehabilitate, only one was possible. The one in the north at Gulu was ruled out by an overflight of the Ugandan air force reporting that it was being used as a training base by Joseph Cony's rebels. Cony is currently waiting in jail in

Kenya for the charge that he had entered Uganda without a visa. The more serious charge for his past misdemeanours is with the International Court to determine his sentence.

The second ranch was closer to Kampala on the eastern side of the Nile, just after the Nile left Lake Victoria. The Nile could be crossed by a ferry about fifty miles from Kampala. I set off alone (why?) and arrived at the crossing but the ferry operator said that we would have to wait for an escort. This stretch of the river was notorious for croc attacks. The escort arrived, six or seven men armed to the teeth. I was glad that they were on my side. Only the week before a priest had been shot dead as he cycled along my intended course. My truck was loaded onto the ferry. They had two heavy machine guns which they bolted to the ferry, and when they were ready, the ferry set off. I thought it was good of them to supply an escort for me. I think I was the only one stupid enough to be standing, but crossing the Nile expecting an ambush was sort of exciting. We got to the other side without incident and offloaded my truck. Then they just turned around and left me there. My 'escort' disappeared in a cloud of exhaust fumes. What else could I do but carry on? After ten to fifteen miles, I found the ranch. The only directions I had been given was that it was a nice little European-style house on a hill on the right. It seems that Europeans like to build nice houses on hills. I am not quite sure why. There are pros and cons to the matter; I still think about it. I mentioned that these Nile waters were hiding a lot of crocs. In earlier days, when passenger planes starting flying to Africa just after WWII, the plane of choice was an American flying boat. These flying boats had to land on water, and the Nile where I crossed was chosen as the place to unload passengers. I do wonder why the lake was not the chosen place. The plane was stationary and a wooden walkway was used from shore to plane and the people walked along this wooden walkway. One lady was unlucky travelling on one of the early fights; a croc took her off the walkway. After that there is not a lot one can do.

I had a mooch round the area and decided that it was a good site for the ranch – good water and excellent grazing – and set off back home. I did not wait long, as the ferry operator was at my side of the Nile. He said that as I had returned safely, he too could safely cross the river, as he had heard no gunfire. Logic?

The Nile used to leave the lake over a waterfall but the topography is ideal for a site for massive electric generators, which are installed. Firstly, a dam was built just few metres from the rock downstream, close to the original waterfall. Maintenance work on the dam and generators is undertaken with the men in a shark cage.

So that left me with one possibility. This one was in the Luwero Triangle, which had been a base for President Museveni during his years in the bush before taking control of Uganda. This area had been attacked many times by Idi's lot without expelling the president; however, the villagers suffered badly. In one specific place where the road was below the level of the land a hundred-yard stretch had a row of skulls, from tiny ones to adult, and I was informed that that sort of massacre was not uncommon. Driving past it was an unpleasant experience no matter how many times I did it. After that I lost any sympathy with the ousted regime.

The ranch was a surprise, as it was on a small river complete with crocs, and had good grazing and not too dense brush. There were signs of someone growing lemongrass, which made a change from marijuana. I took a long look around and met a few tsetse flies. I later managed to get in touch with a newly qualified student trying to find a way to get rid of tsetse flies using traps, which were highly effective. The tsetse were lured by the specific blue colour of the material and, starting from the low level of the tent-like trap, they flew inside to the peak, where they met poison. I got tired of losing the blue material for the trap 'tent' and seeing too many women wearing a particular shade of blue. Before I started this book, I had not realised that the tsetse might start at a low level inside the dress/tent and move upwards. I produced a work plan to make the ranch viable, but there was rather important problem: Kuwait started to be obstructive. I realised the project would not be funded with the past generosity. They demanded that Uganda purchase what was required and then they, Kuwait, would refund. Next problem: Uganda was short of cash, and when I requested funds, I was told that the total government cash in the country amounted to £340, and the president was taking that money with him on a trip to Europe.

The Ugandan shilling was virtually worthless. I took a trip to southern Uganda with one overnight stop. That took a sports kit bag full of notes. I had a block of a thousand five-shilling notes as a doorstop at my office, and when anyone queried it, I told them it was cheaper than a brick. It was never taken away.

One day I was sitting in my office when a European man was ushered in, wanting to know where John, my co-manager, was. I recognised him as the superior, supercilious guy who had been the project manager when I was in Afghanistan, without a clue of running projects. I left due to the imminent Russian invasion. He was a particularly unpleasant individual, with little experience and no knowledge of Afghanistan and Afghans, or of the lifestyle and customs of the nomadic people. For that job I needed to be an anthropologist as well as a semi-desert livestock specialist. He had not treated me well in Afghanistan. I refused his handshake, no I did not know where John was, or when he would return, however I did suggest he return in two or three weeks and John might be in. Revenge is fun. John was actually just down the road at a wedding.

I was burgled once again; this time it was my houseboy. He

was recruited through his church when I asked the vicar if he knew of an honest young man who would like to be a houseboy for me. He worked well for a while until one day he did not come to work. He was absent and so was my TV, my very expensive world satellite radio, a disc player and a few other items, including my gardener's wheelbarrow. (He was incandescent.) The police said they would try to find him. I asked the vicar if he knew where to look for him. In the church records he stated he came from Arua, right at the far north-west of Uganda, on the Congo border. In other words, a long way away.

The Kampala police sent a message to the Arua police, but they could not find him. Then one of the Kampala police came to see me. He said he was soon to take leave back to his home in Arua, but he could not afford the bus fare. If I funded him, he would look for my ex–house servant. In my thinking, the fare was only a small amount and I agreed with low expectations. A couple of weeks later the police told me that my man had been found on the border trying to sell my TV, which was all he had left to sell. However, he was arrested and I was needed in Arua to identify him. At that time Arua would be the last choice for anyone to spend a holiday. There was unrest with the Congo rebels, gangs, ex-Uganda police and ex-army. It was quite a way to Arua and unsafe by road, so I booked a plane ride, but they were full for quite a few days. So, I waited and eventually I was told I could get a flight, so I booked and waited. At that time of the year Uganda was having its wet season. Just at that week it was heavy rains every day and as the runway in Arua was dirt, it was not good to fly. I went to the airport three times when the flight was a possibility but later cancelled because of more rain. Then came the big day: I went to the airport with little expectation but up we went. The future looked bleak. The pilot announced that it was raining again in Arua but, "We will go and take a look." Expectations plummeted, thick cloud and rain all the way. On arrival we could not see any runway, but the pilot reckoned he would try a landing in what to us passengers was a brown lake. So down we went, and I believe all on board were hoping he knew just where the runway was. The people at the airport thought we had crashed, as they lost sight of the plane; it was all spray. We rolled to a stop and I alighted and wandered into Arua, looking for the prison and wishing I had brought my wellies. I was directed to the prison and met the chief warden and sat in his office, chatting, with a cup of tea in my hand. He said he would organise an identity parade. We then went into the big open space in the centre of the compound. The prisoners were all out of their cells, walking around, chatting, a few playing football and so on. As we walked out of the warden's office my ex-houseboy walked up to me, hand outstretched, and said, "Thank you for coming, Mr Massey," and we shook hands. The warden said, "Well, it seems we can do away with an identity parade" and we went back to the office for another brew.

Next job was to find an hotel, so I decided first to try to book a flight back to Kampala. Due to the rains, the flights had been held back and bookings were full for four days. So, I booked for four days ahead and went to find an hotel. It seemed the White Rhino was the best option. It was spacious, but I noted that it had no windows in the outside walls. I gave a resigned sigh and booked in for four days. They told me they were tired of having windows repaired because of the shooting, so there were no windows. The flight crew were staying there too and we got chatting, or rather, I sat chatting whilst they got drunk. We discussed the old DC3 aircraft which used to be the only passenger planes available in East Africa, and I chatted about the plane's availability and the various landing strips. As we chatted, I realised that the flight crew thought I was an ex-pilot, as they promised to get me a seat the next day on the return flight. Yes, they were fully booked but they promised they would get me on the plane next day.

Then bedtime for me. I slept well, but the crew looked a bit worn next day. A quick breakfast and off to the airfield and up and away. There was no seat for me so I got the jump seat in the cockpit. After a little while, because of the previous night's chat, the pilot asked if I would like to take over, as they were very tired and would like to sleep. It seems I had given the wrong impression; I have never flown anything heavier than a paper dart whilst at school. I got out of it by saying I had not taken a conversion course for the Fokker which we were currently in on that flight. A little time later I heard that the pilot was taken off flying duties for six months after that episode.

Later I came to know that an attempt had been tried to bring my houseboy, among a number of prisoners, to Kampala by bus with an armed escort, for his court trial. On the way three of the prisoners, including my man, had tried to escape during a toilet break but stopped running when three shots went over their heads. The trip was aborted because of the condition of the road and they were all returned to Arua prison. Later still I heard that he was released with all the other prisoners because the prison just had no funds to feed them. Justice?

A few of the expats heard that a number of returning Ugandans wanted to play cricket, so a bunch of locals, resident Asians and also-rans, such as UK wannabees and the States, etc., formed a club, which was named after the local bottle of beer, the White Caps. Other clubs were formed as expatriates trickled back home. Local and in-country sportsmen, such as the university and two clubs in Jinja, after they tired of playing each other would come to Kampala and beat the White Caps. All good fun except for a shortage of umpires. Just before I left Uganda there was knock-out competition which got rid of the White Caps early on, so I was called in to umpire. The two clubs were able to nominate one umpire each. I was asked to be the umpire for the university team.

I claimed I was not good enough to umpire, as I did not know how to play cricket or even know the rules. The university club captain said, "We know you are useless at cricket, but at least you are honest."

We, the White Caps, went to Jinja one weekend to play them on their own ground. One of Uganda's top judges, though living in Kampala, was playing for Jinja. He was the prosecuting judge of the Lord's Resistance Army (mad Alice's mob). He had an armed soldier as personal escort who did not leave his side at all, as ordered, and he insisted that he would accompany John to the wicket. So, we locked him in the pavilion, where he could see the game and got very agitated when we were fielding when a shot was heard whizzing across the field. All the Ugandans hit the dirt; the few Europeans stayed vertical. I was bowling and I heard the judge say, "These eff**g whites are mad." I did not hear the 'thock' of a bullet hitting flesh so, "What's the problem?"

There was a Ugandan friend who was to marry on the next weekend and then I heard he had been arrested for the murder of his father. *No*, I thought, *not Isaac*. He was very religious and not at all likely to kill his dad, especially on the day before his wedding. I saw his fiancée and she said he was charged with killing his dad. People said it was ridiculous to think it of him. The local opinion was that what had happened was that his dad and uncles got into an argument over distribution of land after the wedding and his dad was hit too hard.

There was no evidence at all, not even a body, until one of his uncles had a dream the body would be found in the church grounds in a refuse sack. Sure enough, that was where he was found. Now there was evidence. I began visiting at the prison almost daily whilst he was in there, bringing books and newspapers. One of the locals told me afterwards that my regular visits to the prison were what kept him alive. He was moved around a number of times between the police and the military. Eventually he was released by the police, with no apparent reason, and then locked up by the army, which also very soon released him. A group of Europeans made sure he rapidly got a visa for the UK and was on a plane with his fiancée and some luggage.

NOTE: Dreams were considered evidence at that time in Uganda. Honest. I am not sure if dreams are/can still be considered as proof in a court case.

It is said that the soil is so rich in Uganda that if you stick a walking stick in the ground, it will have bananas in the morning. I understand that Churchill offered Uganda to the Jews but they rejected the offer.

I left Uganda not overly proud of doing nothing to help the country due to lack of funding. I had made numerous friends, fed a lot of people with fish and brought rugby and cricket back to the country.

THIRTEEN

Nigeria

This was an EU-funded rural development project covering the whole of Katsina State in the far north. To the north is Niger, which is definitely Sahelian, as is much of Katsina. The north of Nigeria is semi-desert, whilst the southern section does have better rainfall and does yield crops. This is always a matter of dispute and often bloodshed. This occurs when there has been no rain and little grazing. The Fulani herders bring the herds from Niger to the south into Nigeria, which naturally hurts the crop production of the Hausa people, whose farms are seldom fenced. This problem often results in bloodshed as Fulani herds encroach on the crop.

In West Africa, the other states see Nigeria, as a nation, as more than a little arrogant. On a plane to Ghana, passing through Nigeria, I saw a Nigerian woman arguing when checking in, and she was adamant in wanting to take a sizeable refrigerator as carry-on luggage. I once found my allotted seat on a plane occupied by a rather large Nigerian lady. When I asked her to leave my seat, she told me to go and sit in her seat, which was next to another oversized lady. I got my seat back.

The state is 'ruled' by the emir, who is also the religious and political head and a very pleasant gentleman. Very soon after our arrival we were invited to meet the emir, and there was an interpreter who helped us to understand the emir and some of his advisors. It was just a matter of, "You are very welcome to Katsina and if you have any difficulties, please bring them to my attention." The project manager came back with, "We are very pleased to be here and will do our best to help your people." The project was off to a decent start.

All the non-project individuals then filed out and the emir then addressed us in very fluent English, explaining that the interpreter business was inherited down the line of emirs. The emir is not allowed to deviate from the Fulani tribe in that he is not allowed to marry anyone but a Fulani. There are a lot of very good-looking Fulani ladies and beauty among the men. Even today the men have an annual beauty competition. I never thought to ask whether the judges for the men's competition were men or women. That is an interesting item to mull over.

Then followed a discussion on the work expected and how the project would go ahead. The emir's younger brother was to be co-manager of the project, and he too was well educated and fluent in English. Housing was provided. Most of us lived within a compound of just project staff, whilst two of our lot had houses in town. The plot was on Elephant Head Road. A lovely name. The offices were a short walk from the homes and all seemed OK to get started. Some government staff were seconded whilst other specialists would be recruited.

I needed a veterinarian and preferably female, as once again I would be working in the poultry sector among Islamic ladies, but there seemed to be no female vets around. I informed everyone I could that I wanted to interview a woman vet, and at last I got to hear about a woman vet in Zaria – Zaria is central Nigeria – who currently was making a living selling fat cakes on the street, a graduate from Zaria University, 120 miles south of Katsina town. She was ideal, newly qualified and unmarried, so she would be able to carry out field duties without husband intrusion. Just before our project pulled out of the country, she married a Yoruba, the chief veterinarian of the state. This situation was good until the expats were withdrawn, and hopefully they are still married.

The major problem for livestock owners was grazing and the antagonism between crop farmers and livestock farmers. There was not a lot of friction between residents of Katsina. Most problematic were the nomadic herders from the north. This was more a political matter and I was happy to be kept out of it all. Grazing was almost non-existent, so that was one thing I could attempt to rectify. I knew of vetiver grass which made a very efficient dam to prevent loss of topsoil when planted on contour lines. The grasses bushed out to form a mini dam, which slowed up the water so as to drop sediments to form a better soil. The grass grew higher with the deposit of soil, raising the level of the dam. The vetiver, when it has grown some, is not only useful for retaining soil but makes a good windbreak when the grass has bushed out. Unfortunately, we had to get livestock to identify the vetiver, which was not eaten due to the cutting edge of the grass. A cow would walk along, pull out a tuft of recently planted grass, and then spit it out once the cow felt it to be undesirable; it is very strong and has multiple short, strong, sharp, hair-like bristles in the mouth. It was the duty of one of the labourers to go along the planted lines daily and replant any that the cows had declined, which would be found six cow paces away.

The only problem I had on that project was with the project surveyor, who was supposed to mark out contour lines so we could plant the vetiver to best result in holding back water. He started work marking out the contour lines when I was away from the office for two or three days in Kano. When I got back, not even the surveyor could show me which line of little flags was following a contour line.

The brother of the emir was co-head of the project and was well educated. One day he showed me around his and his brother's stables. They had a number of polo ponies and they were in very good condition. I was then asked what I thought of them. I told him I was a cattle man and not familiar with horses. When I saw a horse, I calculated in my mind how many tins of dog food it would produce. That was when I found the Nigerians did not have the same sense of humour as the Ghanaians. He told his brother.

When one of the secretaries heard I was going to Kano, she asked me to get her a James I copy of the Bible. Ever happy to oblige, I said I would do so, and took the first and only opportunity (just one bookshop in Kano) to go book buying. I asked a shop assistant for the Bible and she apologised. "I am sorry, we have no bibles." As I was walking out, she called out, "Sir, we do have a Koran." 'Don't let a customer leave without buying something' is the mantra of a sales person, male or female, everywhere.

I talked to stock farmers about letting grass recover from the annual heavy grazing by fencing in an acre or so of land, and asked the villagers to leave it until the grasses dropped their seeds to improve the amount of grass. We also ploughed some land to plant grass and shrubs to bring back the natural vegetation, which meant that the local people could care for their grass plots until they were desperately needed. I told them that they could start to open the gate to stock but they should harvest the seeds before animals are allowed into the protected area. The seeds would germinate with next year's rain and would yield palatable, nutritious grass to extend the acreage of better grazing grasses.

An easy way to explain the problems of livestock and

crops in the country is to understand that crops are grown in the south, having more rain, and livestock are best suited to the north. This involved trucking vast amounts of food at harvest time to the north, and a regular transport of animals for slaughter to the south. The roads of Nigeria are relatively straight and occasionally surfaced, and other roads are equally straight and are dirt. A lot of this transporting is done at night, when it is cooler and there is less traffic, so the large trucks go blasting along expecting every other vehicle to give way and move to the side of the road. One night there was an accident in the centre of a village close to Zaria, when an articulated lorry was heading north loaded with maize and another articulated lorry was heading south loaded with cattle, and both with main beams on and horns blasting, neither would give way until they met in the middle in a village. It's Christmas, free food!

By next morning the police found nine bodies, drivers and passengers from the cabs, but not a maize seed nor a scrap of meat was to be found.

I took a look at the local poultry and decided that a bit of crossing with more productive breeds would do the business a favour. The local birds, when mature, would hardly make a meal for two, and the egg production was low, with not overly large eggs at that. I decided that an influx of male chicks would bolster the poultry development. I had been told that good-quality Rhode Island red chicks could be bought in Ethiopia, so off I went.

I checked about importing the chicks in Nigeria and for the export from Ethiopia, so no problem just for me to go and collect them. I contacted a supplier and checked if we could meet and I was invited to visit the farm. The birds looked good and the eggs were good-sized. I asked for a hundred chicks. I contacted Ethiopian Airways and no problem there. I told them I would buy an extra seat so the birds would remain warm on the flight.

When we reached the airport and checked in, there was an immediate problem. We cannot carry live birds in the cabin. No way could they change their mind. So, no deal. But I did enjoy Ethiopia and particularly the UK High Commission compound, said to be the best in the world – who said that I have no idea, but it did look good. Regarding the required chicks, I would have to look elsewhere and Britain with its poultry businesses seemed a possibility.

Many male chicks in the poultry industry were rejected as soon as hatched. In the poultry business in the UK, the Rhode Island red is used by many breeders, but they produced too many males from a batch for their purpose, and the excess were dumped. I made contact with a supplier willing to go to the trouble of selling the ones to be dumped and shipping, by air, a hundred day-old chicks to Nigeria.

All went well and I was on hand when the chicks arrived at Kano airport. They were quickly offloaded and immediately on the road to Katsina, where everything was ready for the chicks, but I was dreading the mortality level of the flight. Warm pens ready for them, we took them from the box, dipped each and every beak in a dish of brandy. It worked this time as it has in the past. People might frown on the action but a welcoming tipple never hurt a holiday maker. After emptying the special boxes we had 198 birds and two deaths, so we had an extra nighty-eight birds at no extra cost. It was a rather excessive allowance for mortality, but thank you supplier and British Airways.

The chicks were checked regularly. They got the best of everything, including almost twenty-four-hour attention. For the first almost three months they had a night nurse in the shape of an ex–high school student, Poppy, who was accepted to go on the Zaria veterinary course. Poppy nursed them as though they were her own children.

The accountant to the project had a small swimming pool and

it also came with a child-sized seaside fishing net. The pool was a favourite drinking spot for the local egrets, which unfortunately often had passengers in the shape of leeches which they probably picked up from a marsh somewhere, though I never found the marshes. They did not make welcome bathing friends but a few were able to latch onto any of us. Before swimming everyone had to go 'fishing' for leeches.

Among people working on aid programmes you seldom meet other livestock specialists, as it was usually a one-man posting, and we seldom met other livestock personnel from other projects. On this project there was an agriculturist whose aunt was the wife of the owner of the Chase Me Inn pub in Mahalapye in Botswana, and that is as close as we usually get.

It was interesting to see that the earwig in Nigeria is not like the European one, in that it is not the dull brown of the UK, but is flamboyant with a brown abdomen and a very orange thorax. Nor does it have the fearsome pinchers at the rear end. It is called a 'skirt and blouse'. I never knew what the earwigs ate until Katsina, then I REALLY found out. Over my garden wall was many acres of sorghum fields, and the skirt and blouse love to eat the pollen. Having said that, there was no pollen in my house but I did have earwigs. I think I can say literally they could be counted in thousands, with one of those thousands and more in my house. All my walls were covered in earwigs and I tolerated their presence until one bit me in bed one night and I decided they had to go. Two spray cans later and a brush and bucket got rid of them.

I had made it very clear to the project manager that I was not going to venture anywhere south of Kano. I broke this self-imposed rule on a visit to Zaria University and partially regretted it. We got to Zaria with no problem, with four staff in the Land Rover Discovery, but on completion of business we found that we could not get back the way we came due to a bit of tribal warfare going on. We had to take a very wide detour, as advised by the police. It seems that a rather superior lady from a supposedly superior tribe (unnamed, that is what she thought) was in a local market and picked a 'fat cake' from a vendor's pile and ate it but refused to pay. That was the start of a fight between the two women. It went from arguing to shouting to name calling, through insults to a physical fight, whereupon the vendor picked up her pan of boiling cooking fat and threw the fat into the face of the protagonist. Up to that time it had been entertaining for the assembling crowd, but they thought cooking fat to be a tad excessive. The local people backing the cook protected her from physical abuse, but the mob wanted to kick her to death. After that it escalated into tribal warfare, mutual shop burning and general complete breakdown of law and order. This type of thing happens south of Kano now and again. Hence my reluctance to risk my life.

In Katsina the main tribe owning cattle are Fulani and they are the ones who are migratory, to some extent. The other tribe are the Hausa, who are mainly agriculturists. Obviously with two tribes living together there has been a degree of intermixing. The emir is a Fulani and custom has it that he may only take Fulani women for a bride. There is often friction when the pastoralists begin to suffer from droughts when there is no grass for their livestock and so they infringe on the farming areas. Occasionally it gets rather violent, understandably, as both are fighting for their livelihood.

They could probably take part in the women's beauty contest in the UK. However, the women were better looking, in my opinion. One day I was out with my staff. We were on the Burkina Faso border. I saw a perhaps an eighteen to twenty year old gorgeous lady carrying a bucket of water on her head. I remarked, "I have fallen in love," and we all cracked up.

I decided to build myself a BBQ in the garden of my house.

Bricks, sand and cement were all available and it was soon finished. BUT I was not proud of it. Bricks were projecting out of the wall, nothing was level or straight. It was an utter mess. I decided I could not let the rest of the crew see it and so I called in a builder to cement render the walls. When he first saw it, he laughed and asked who on earth had built this? "It was here when I moved in." His reply, "Hmmm. It hasn't been used much, has it?"

One weekend I had arranged a BBQ for the staff of the project, all invited, and everyone was ready to tuck in, but the project manager had not arrived. I called him a couple of times but still no arrival. The accountant went to see what the hold-up was, and it really was a hold-up. Apparently five or six men, all armed, entered his house when wife was there. He said they did not just walk in, it was more like they danced into the house in a line. They demanded the keys to the Land Rover Discovery and a car that was there and threatened his wife with a knife if he refused. He handed the keys over and the robbers set off on the road to Niger, but they left the main road and took a desert track and the car had to be towed as it bogged down in the sand, which slowed them rather. The project manager told the local police, who set off after them and warned the guard at the border by radio to try to stop them. As if he could – he was armed with a shotgun and the baddies had quite an armoury. I think the baddies did not see him but the gate guard tried for a tyre shot, which went high and just peppered the bodywork, and by then they were away into Niger. I am sure they were not aware that the Katsina police would contact the Niger police, who then contacted the army, who set up an ambush, so with the police behind them and the army in front they were the meat in the sandwich. Two were shot dead on site, three fled to the bush, two were captured, and one was picked up in Jhansi, the next town. What happened to the living guys I do not know, but

I do know the Land Rover needed some attention! There was blood all over and brain tissue on the interior of the cab. It was riddled with bullet holes, without windows, all tyres including the spare had bullet holes. The seats resembled rags. The Niger government demanded quite a fee for its return to Katsina, which for the sake of good relations was paid.

I had problems with trying to get farmers to level their irrigation plots, not that they did not want to do as I was suggesting, but it was in the translation of English word 'level' to Hausa. Actually, it is not very clear in English. I wanted the soil in vegetable plots to be flat/level so that they could be irrigated. The difference between flat and level did not exist in Hausa, so I had to show them using a piece of cardboard. It is not easily explaining in English either. Think about it.

There was another project ongoing in the 'next door' state. Scott had machinery beyond my dreams for ploughing and such. He also bordered Niger and was very friendly with the local police chief, and on one of his drop-in visits they sat chatting and he did not seem to be doing a great lot of policing. Scott asked him why someone such as he should be in the middle of nowhere and where nothing happens. The policeman gestured for Scott to follow him and drew back a curtain into the next room. There were three children sitting on the floor hugging each other, very afraid. The policeman said, "This is what I am here for. These three children are from northern Niger and they had been sold and were being transported to Lagos for sex work."

I visited many villages, talking livestock to the men and poultry to the women, and the programme was getting going well and seeing results. I got to know the villagers and we would chat on various local topics, such as supplies, schooling, marriage rites and funeral rites, almost anything. One woman asked if I had a wife with me. When I said I did not have my wife with me, she then asked if I needed a servant and I said that I did not, but was offered a girl to look after me and who would do anything I wanted her to do. I asked her age and then said there are many girls available who would look after me, how old did I want? All I had to do would be to pay the mother a ridiculously low sum and she would be mine. I have an idea that her price would go towards feeding the rest of the family. Apparently, slavery still exists in Nigeria.

I met up with a pedlar doing his rounds. He called at my house one day and I offered him tea and a biscuit. Thereafter he became a good friend and saved choice items, like brass statuettes, he thought I would appreciate. I did buy a number of items, such as cloths and handmade blankets, carvings and pictures which I still have. He was a very pleasant guy and I heard all the gossip from miles round as we drank tea. He did not mind sharing it and I learned a lot of local news which does not get into the newspapers or even this book.

The project had been working for a few months when there was an Eid festival, which enabled many of the village chiefs to parade their horses and retinues, and for the Emir to meet the people, and everyone had a fun time. A seemingly never-ending parade of horses, acrobats, sword swallowers, jugglers, etc., etc. It was quite a show. Everything and everyone very colourful and waving colourful flags. The day ended when all the horsemen carrying weapons charged the length of the polo field at full gallop, with the Emir sitting high as a horse rider, and he was not to show any fear. The horses were brought to a stop, often rearing, by brutal hauling on the reins and metal bit. It was a Grand Finale.

Another bit of entertainment was the polo matches. I had never before seen live polo, just on TV. TV does not do it justice; it does not come through showing the relationship between rider and horse. It was obvious that the horses knew the game better than me and revelled in it.

I was helping villagers make the most of what they had and

I worked along the northern border, which is not marked at all. I went to where my staff suggested. After about six months, I found that I was working in Niger in one village and it upset no one, but I did not tell the donors or the project manager.

When I was in Ghana, I had been shown a species of tree, which used to be called Acacia albida but someone had proved it to be a different species. I am not sure that the tree cared what we called it, but it became Faidherbia albida. It is a remarkable tree in that it provides shade in the hottest time of the year and is leafless when the crops need the sunshine. The fruits of the tree are highly nutritious and apparently delicious to domestic and probably wild animals. The only downside to having these trees was an occasional complaint that the trees gave a place for birds to sit when raiding the crops.

Among the people in the know, Nigeria and Pakistan were said to be the most corrupt countries in the world, and I have lived and worked in both. I think that there are other countries competing nowadays. I sensed none during the implementation of the project.

There was precious little in the way of grazing in the area, so I tried to help in ways of increasing the grazing. My neighbour loaned me a tractor again with driver and deep-digger share. A largish piece of Nigeria was ploughed with mechanical help until there was a good cover of grass, which took little time. Shrubs and grass seed were planted and I had to emphasize to the village chief and his people that no cattle or sheep were to be allowed in the fenced-off area under regeneration, until the plants were established. I am not sure it was successful, due to the following:

Government in Nigeria was not very popular; in fact, on the contrary, the public were very dissatisfied. President Sani Abacha was quite unpopular, mainly due to corruption which was draining the public to enrich the wealthy – a common affliction in Africa, and government were worried. A very popular advocate for change was a man called Kenule (Ken) Saro-Wiwa, and pressure was on the president. He had Saro-Wiwa arrested, accused of the death of four Ogoni tribal leaders, and with little, if any, proof, not even a show trial, Ken was hanged. This brought international opprobrium, which was not appreciated by Sani Abacha. The EU told us to get out of Nigeria, to close down the project and leave. Getting rid of the cockerels was not difficult but I do wonder how many went for breeding and how many for the pot.

POSTSCRIPT: The scuttlebutt from Nigeria after Sani Abacha's death was that three houses down from the state house was a brothel, with three young ladies living there. He was not an infrequent visitor and one morning, rising early, he picked up his little jar of blue pills and went three doors away and died from heart trouble. I doubt many people mourned his passing; I feel the girls are worthy of a Yellow Rose of Texas medal.

Another story I have heard is that a woman gave him a poisoned apple which killed him. This one I doubt, but then, who cares?

It is understood that he purloined billions of pounds and dollars during his years as president. After his death, the hidden money could not be found, but his two sons said, "If you give us [a rather large number of millions]" – I am not sure just how many millions – "we will tell you where the rest is." I know no more, but who cares?

My degree is in tropical livestock in the semi-arid areas. However, sometimes one must carry out deviations from one's terms of reference if it helps make your input useful. So—

ON DEVIATIONS

Between contracts one had to live and deviate from the terms of reference. Once employed on a project, it usual to be asked by the employing agency or the people you are helping and, seeing their major needs, one cannot ignore their pleading, or the project manager.

One is expected to be able to carry out other duties within the project terms of reference. I have been asked to get involved in the following:

To help the people in semi-arid areas obviously involves providing water where possible; there are many ways of providing water. I have worked on various attempts to provide water, if only to lengthen the grazing period.

1. Well water is the tapping of aquifer water or underground lake water. These are relatively easy, once found, except for actually drilling in the right place. Where to sink a borehole is an art, a craft, or darned good luck. It works best if there are numerous wells already. Dousers are out there aplenty, but it is becoming an extinct trade. On where to drill, seldom is he as good as his word. I have been told many times by different people that there is an immense lake under the Kalahari Desert. I guess it could well be true, because the vast amount of water in the Okavango swamp has to have gone somewhere annually.
2. I taught people how to make a pool reservoir water and retain it for the dry season.
3. In Afghanistan, water was brought from a source in the higher lands, snowy mountains, for miles in tunnels, which were maintained by men who had no other occupation for how many years? They did not marry unless the wife was from a family with the same occupation. Their job was just to keep the tunnels clean and flowing. It was a rather dangerous job and the family were provided with the articles needed to live. They are easy to see from the air, rows of soil heaps and holes where the spoils from the tunnels was thrown, almost

like a gigantic molehill. I understand that this system has broken down with the Taliban regime and was bombed by the Russians, as they could easily be located from the air.

4. I got to know a European who made a living drilling boreholes in Tanzania. He and his wife lived in a caravan for months on end when drilling and had a very boring life. When he could get to town, Bert used to get extremely drunk, which annoyed his wife rather a lot. It got so bad that when he got back to the caravan completely sozzled, she would not let him into the caravan. Bert's answer was to build a mini-caravan, called the dog box, which was hitched to the back of the caravan when changing jobs, and where he slept when not allowed into the 'home'. This happened every time they got near a town. One night they went to a party and somehow his wife got very, very drunk. Instead of taking revenge, he made a big fuss over her, cleaned up vomit and off the bed, off the floor, off the wife and tended to her all night long. Next morning a very contrite wife decided that he would not have to sleep in the 'dog box' and surprisingly he also moderated his drinking.

FOURTEEN

Somaliland

The Somali is a mixture of Yemeni and the African tribe of Chagga. The Chagga are one of the major tribes of Tanzania and have their own language and culture. They are also thick on the ground around the foothills of Mount Kenya.

There are numerous heaps of stones to be seen in Somaliland, which are claimed to be burial ground. Some have been ransacked, to little or no avail, so I guess the Somalis have now given up. I am told that the looters were looking for grave goods but the bodies on the surface had none.

To get there, I took a flight provided by UN in Nairobi on a regular basis. The plane would often land in Somalia before Somaliland. One place they stopped, Baidoa, scared me, as they only had a very narrow dirt strip for landing and houses were just a plane wing's distance from the incoming planes. Children would be playing the in dirt outside the houses, oblivious to the landing plane.

Somaliland is a breakaway province of Somalia. There was a civil war in Somalia starting in 1981 and ending in 1991 in the north. It seems to be ongoing even into the twenty-first century, as fighting in southern Somalia is ongoing and there was friction on the Somaliland border with Somalia, but this is tribal. The war in the north ended with the north deciding to go it alone under the name of Somaliland. The war was reputedly started because the north was growing rich on the quat (khat) trade. They grew large amounts and sold it to the south of the country, and exported too. The southerners were afraid that the north would soon be rich enough to become the dominant part of the country. There were other reasons too – mainly tribal, but wealth and the power which goes with it were not welcomed by the southerners. It was whispered to me that a Somali living in Europe funded by the quat trade supplied much of the munitions to Somaliland.

The war was long and bitter and became a stalemate, and a truce was agreed. The northern part tells me that they were tired of killing and tired of dying and have put away their guns, mostly in the roofing thatch, and there was to be no shooting. This was taken to the limit. When I was there, the northern people would not shoot even a hyena killing sheep. They would not shoot game because, as I was told, the game animals fed the resistance army whilst they were in the bush and have done their part in the war. One less-than-fun experience occurred when I was out in the field near Adad, when a teenager threw a ball of mud which hit me on my back. This worried me. Had he had a gun with him, would he have used it? Needless to say, I never went back there nor did my team whilst I was in country.

I do not know why the political decision has been taken that no country in the world will recognise them as a separate state. I decided that it was like two families in a semi-detached house. One half is occupied by a sensible family, law-abiding group, and the other side by an irrational bunch, fighting, robbing and killing, axe murderers completely out of control. The international 'decision' seems to be, "If you knock the separating house wall down, and join crazies, we will accept you into the international community." Aid funds are very limited and usually only apply to humanitarian aid implemented by NGOs. Somalia and Somaliland have deep-seated tribal affiliations, and generally, relations are not healthy.

I was part of that, as were volunteers from many other nations working in various sectors. I was sent into an ongoing project of livestock and agriculture by a mainly veterinarian organisation. In many ways, it was a good place to work, as interference was limited, with very few visits from HQ. The 'capital', Hargeisa, was in a sad state. Few houses had roofs; everywhere there were signs of war. There was even a couple of SAM-7 missiles standing on a high part of the ridge overlooking the town, and they were reputedly ready to go if the correct switch were to be flicked, but I doubt it.

Ethiopians had looted Hargeisa when Hargeisa was undefended. Roofing, doors, windows, even the electric cables, switches and wall plugs were stripped from the houses. A few houses had been repaired and one of these had become the office for our project. Somaliland has a strange weather pattern; the east is dry, quite akin to a desert, and the western side can support the growing of food crops. There was a serious problem with crop production, in that all the draught oxen had died in recent years due to drought. I never did see a bovine.

The lack of draught animals puzzled me, as there were plenty of donkeys bouncing around looking well fed. In chats with the local farmers, they thought the donkeys were only good for carrying weaponry and could not pull a plough. After a few chats with other well-travelled workers, they told me that Yemen had single furrow plough and used donkeys to pull them. With a bit of effort, a plough was brought in from Yemen with the help of a Somali student who had a student friend in Yemen University.

The plough was hitched to two donkeys that were trained to drag trees, etc., and we organised a farmer's day to demonstrate donkey ploughing. Success, a good turn out and lots of questions and answers, and I suppose now poor donkeys are dragging ploughs around in Somaliland, which is all my fault, though the trade in ploughs with Yemen could be a problem. When the session broke up, the old man, ninety-four years old I was told, sitting on the ground alongside me, was having trouble getting his sandals on, so I helped him. As I walked away a young man came to me and said, "You have embarrassed us."

Many people attended the ploughing demonstration but for some unknown reason the local agricultural lady taking care of the agricultural side of the project did not attend. She was an anomaly; she wore army boots and was seldom seen in the office.

One export that helps Somaliland exist is frankincense. I was told it comes from a tree, but I never saw a tree in Somaliland so I cannot verify the claim. They also produce rather a lot of ghat. It is fun to watch the early morning car race so that when they reach Hargeisa they can charger higher prices.

Somaliland sold small stock (sheep and goats) by sea to Yemen and Saudi. Animal rights organisations became worried about the loading and shipping conditions, and some outfit sent a vet to check the loading procedure. He and I obtained permission to see them loading the animals the next time they were to ship a load. We both agreed that there was really no cruelty. The procedure was carried out at night when the animals are calmer, no hitting, no yelling and no overcrowding. Shortly after our report, a ship went down, with all the animals and crew drowned.

When we had visitors to the project, we would take them to dinner in the evening at the outdoor restaurant where visitors were always taken, seated on a long wooden bench and a scrubbed wooden tabletop. The food was ordered well ahead and eventually the main course arrived. A platter of dates and a knife stuck into the table and a whole leg of camel. "That's it, folks." You cut a slice of meat, wrap it around a date, and then munch. Tastes good and easy to chew.

My Somaliland stay was unusual in that I lived in Hargeisa. Hargeisa banked in Djibouti, which uses francs, and shopped in Nairobi using Kenyan shillings, and in Addis Ababa in their birr and Dubai dirham. I dealt with currency of those and two types of Somali shilling, US dollars and British pounds. That is eight different currencies for the poor accountant to deal with. When my NGO HQ, sitting in the safety of a Scottish capital, asked why I banked in Djibouti but did most of my shopping in Nairobi, it showed just how little they knew about the Horn of Africa. My reply was something like, "If I walked out of a Nairobi bank with £100, I would possibly be dead before getting out of the bank and definitely would be on the street." In fact, I did not do a lot of shopping personally for that reason. I employed a Kenyan, Diken by name, a schoolteacher, who knew the ropes much better than I did in Nairobi. There were frequent UN flights between Nairobi and Hargeisa, free for aid workers and close relatives if there were enough seats.

The money changing system in Somaliland was almost comical. There would be a line of mostly elderly women sitting on the kerb of the main road in Hargeisa with piles of different currencies and they knew all the latest exchange rates. There were no robberies whilst I was there or, I am told, before I arrived.

Djibouti is far safer than Nairobi because the French Foreign Legion were/are based there since the legion had scared the pants of the French government when it was rumoured that they were to stage a coup in Paris in 1961. Since then and forever, I am told, the legion will not be based in France. The legion in Djibouti were there to prop up the government and to ensure their safety, having an agreement with their neighbours, Somaliland and Ethiopia, that they will not cross the border of either, but if either country tries to cross into Somaliland, then the legion will get very cross! They have taken on the task of keeping Djibouti safe for visitors; I have never seen anything, but hearsay reckons that if any expat is molested, robbed or otherwise badly treated, the guilty will not get treated softly. I was walking in Hargeisa town during Ramadan when many Muslims will not drink or even swallow their own saliva. I walked past a man just as he turned his head and spat, which hit me on the leg. I was in shorts, and to the surprise of the pedestrians, I just made him wipe the phlegm off and we went our different ways. So, the presence of the legion keeping the peace seems to work. Nowadays I believe the Americans have a base there, which may be for the better or worse – my guess is for the worse.

I was in Somaliland when a Saudi prince managed to get a hunting permit from the Somaliland government minister. (Cost?) He came in with four 4x4 trucks plus other luxury vehicles and trucks for carting his camping kit, a palatial set-up. Toilets, water and fuel, the lot, a kitchen equipped with chef and a helicopter to spot game for him. Hardly a low-cost shooting expedition. He hunted for two or three days and, in the evening, an elderly Somali wandered into his camp. He delivered his message: "Go home." The camp was gone by breakfast. They had flown back to Saudi.

One very sad sight, which still affects me, occurred on the road from Hargeisa to the coast. I saw an animal far down the road ahead, but as I drew closer the animal did not move. As I slowed and drove past, I saw it was a female warthog standing with her head bowed, 'crying' over a squashed piglet. Warthog assuredly have feelings, if nothing else but sadness; they do have feelings. I was also surprised to see a farmer drawing water for his stock of sheep and goats. He also had a trough for watering the game, including warthogs. I was surprised that he treated 'pigs' to water, knowing of the hatred of most Muslims. When I asked him why, he replied, "All animals are God's creatures, even pigs." Another type of Muslim.

Somaliland had very few visitors, as there was nothing to show, so it was quite a surprise when I was in town one day and there was a minibus of Japanese tourists at the market. I am sure they were feeling a little apprehensive of Somalis gawping at them, and surrounding them. I guessed they came in from Djibouti, across the desert. This trip was reckoned to be dangerous and people reputedly always left in the early morning. I never did find out what the danger was, perhaps bandits, possibly no one stopping to help in the event of a vehicle breakdown; the heat and lack of water were all threats. I doubt they thought the trip worthwhile, as Hargeisa has little to offer.

From day one, I was never wholly trusting of Somalis, even the office staff. An issue raised its head when one of the staff, the woman who wore army boots, was sent to the UK for training; the company, my employers, helped her to get a studying visit for a year when the course was three months only. She went and then returned after two months. Then her sister went using the 'family passport' but did not return. Another sister went to the UK and only the passport and letter returned to Hargeisa by post, and after that I do know what happened to the passport but the original talked my employers to fund a second visit to the UK. Maybe Mother used it, as she would only have to wrap a shawl around her head to get through passport control. Maybe that is the reason we have so many Somalis in the UK.

I was told that there is a place to the south of Somaliland where there are many caves. The terrain is so bad that it cannot be visited by wheeled vehicles. I do not know why it has that reputation, unless the roads do not exist. Locals told me that tourists used to hire camels and a camel master to take them there, but once you get there after four days you still have a problem. Torches using batteries do not function in the caves – bunkum, but I did not try to test the story. All the Somalis know of the story but they do not quite know exactly where the caves are.

Just outside Hargeisa on the Berbera road, before the war, there was a Coca-Cola factory that provided Coca-Cola all along the Horn of Africa: Somalia, Djibouti, Ethiopia and Yemen. It closed for the war and had not yet started production again, and I did wonder why, as the factory was said to be untouched by the war. Another Somali rumour, perhaps? It is said that someone only has to press the right buttons and you are in business.

On the road to Berbera, they were many 'dead' tanks littered about. I knew of one which has a man living in it! The tanks are said to be Italian. Italy had invaded Ethiopia in 1936 and it was not considered a big deal, even though it took two years to declare success. I suppose they were losing face when all other European neighbouring states were collecting colonies like kids getting pimples, so they joined the colonialists. Churchill is said to have remarked, "Mussolini has his tanks, machine guns and bombers whilst the old Ethiop has his spear. It's going to be an interesting war."

There was a murder carried out in Hargeisa when I was there. Two guys got into a fight. I believe they were related, possibly cousins. When one of them stabbed the other they were both members of the same 'group', the name of which I have forgotten. These groups help members who get into trouble, usually financial. He went to court and was sentenced to death. If the dead man's family would accept money to pardon the killer, he could go free. An offer was made but rejected. The offer was doubled but still the answer was no. And doubled once more, which was rejected. The sentence was duly carried out. The murderer was tied to a tree and a member of the dead man's family used an AK-47, and that was it. One thing that puzzled me and others was why the ambulance taking the corpse to the hospital was travelling very fast with blue lights flashing.

In my earlier African days, when I flew anywhere it was usually in a converted DC-3 bomber. Apparently it was one of a few planes where parachutists did not get a smack at the back of their head on jumping; the wings were highish and the tail was high out of the way. They were used by the SAS when jumping into jungle during the Malayan emergency. The last DC-3 I ever saw in flight was in 1999, being used to map Somaliland. It looked to be a boring job, almost like ploughing, going back and fore, and I guess they had terrible pictures of the sort you would send to your mother-in-law. There were no seagulls following the plane as they do the plough in a country with damp soil, the abode of worms. Boring flying, I am sure.

My older brother was in the SAS and fought in Malaya. He tells a story of jumping at night, as they would be shot at if descending in daylight and easy to find, as their location would be known. So, they jumped at night into the jungle canopy. They would fall through the treetops until the chute caught in the trees. They had a rope to get themselves down, and to gauge the distance they were from the ground if they had not reached it, they dropped a bullet and listened for the noise of it hitting the ground. He tells of one unfortunate companion who could not hear the bullet drop, so he went down the rope, but still heard nothing from dropping a bullet, so he returned to his parachute, strapped himself in and awaited dawn. Needless to say he did not have a good night's sleep. With a bit of daylight, he went back down and to his chagrin he found that his toes were just two inches from the very leafy ground.

When WWII broke out, Italy tried to get their army people and weapons out of Somalia. They set out for Berbera, where they were to be met by a German ship to take them to Italy. There was only one road down to the port through the mountains and the Italians were on schedule to meet the ship until they were stopped in a very narrow valley, and the detour would take days. This is a place well remembered by Somalis, where a British gunner officer and one Somali soldier were in a cave in the rock face looking south where the Italian retreat had to pass. They had one heavy gun plus ammo up in a cave – I am not told how they managed stocking up like that – a cave which commands the road from Hargeisa down to the harbour at Berbera.

The cliff face would be difficult to climb for an infantry attack, the bombers had problems putting a bomb into the cave mouth, and any Italian tank was hit before they could get in range for return fire, which resulted in a massive road block. The place is still littered with dead tanks. I did not hear how many planes, if any, ran into the rock wall with the intent to get a bomb into the cave mouth. Whilst the Italians were sitting on the road and unable to move forwards the British were bringing a relief force into Berbera. Eventually, after the Italian army had been bogged down on the road for quite a long time, the Italians did manage to put a bomb into the cave mouth, but not soon enough, as the Brits had by then got a naval force sitting off Berbera in time to accept the Italian surrender.

Apparently, the son of the Somali who helped the British gunnery officer wandered into the British Foreign Office in London after WWII was over and asked for a job of some type and the man on the desk, on hearing the Somali's name, ensured the Somali was immediately enrolled.

I made shopping trips to Dubai occasionally, mainly for project equipment. I could justify going due to lower prices, but HQ had learned their lesson by then and walking the streets in Dubai was the safest in the world. When I left the airport on arrival the guy at the desk checked my return flight and told me it was from Sharjah. Having never heard of the place, I accepted it as somewhere near Dubai and carried on with my buying blast. I slept well in Dubai; hotels are touristic up to palatial levels, as the world knows. Bloody waste of money when half the Islamic world is starving, so I guess others must be on their side. When it was time to leave, I hired a minivan and piled all my shopping in it to take me to Dubai airport. At the airport, I used two trolleys and went to check in. "Sorry, sir, this ticket is for Sharjah." "Where in Hades is that?" "It is in the next emirate; a taxi can take you there." So as my minivan had departed, I was outside looking for a fat taxi big enough for my load. No luck, but I finally found some guy with a normal taxi who was prepared to go. It was dark by then, so I saw nothing of Sharjah except the edge of the desert by peering around the large TV I had on my lap. I made it, but did not have to wait for my flight to be called. The plane was a rather large semi-converted Russian ex-bomber, still having gun turrets, etc. The bomb bay was not full of bombs, which was a nice way to make it halfway to a civilian conversion, seats were plentiful and halfway up the enormous fuselage was a large carpeted open space. I pondered its use. Soon after take-off I found out. The open space doubled as a mosque, but it obviously had no indicators pointing towards Mecca as appears in hotels and I am sure that Allah would not worry about which way their head was turned.

My secretary in Hargeisa was a lovely woman who had been married to a Dane; she was an excellent employee with only one flaw in that she had previously been married to a Dane. She drank alcohol, never at work but after payday at the month end. She would get quite drunk and, living very close to the state house, she would go into the road and hurl rocks at the president's residence until she was arrested and shown the way to the lock-up. She was never charged. She was tolerated, which I found very decent of them. One of my staff needed to go to the jail to get her the monthly release.

When I first arrived in the country, I moved into the upper floor of a very nice house, with the office down below. To my right were two vacant lots, bombed I assumed, and the third lot was the local mosque. As soon as the mullah knew I was not a Muslim, he decided he would convert me; he did not use an endearing way. The loudspeakers for calling the faithful to prayer were on the wall of the compound and he immediately pointed two of them at my house/office. Five times a day was just a bit over the top but I made no comment. He did mention to my secretary that he would convert me to Islam. She said, "You have no chance. He would be more likely to covert you to Christianity." The speakers were turned away. I have mentioned that she was good.

Somaliland is a harsh place to live; the whole world has turned its face away and leaves them in limbo. Even the weather is against them. One evening/night we had an endless rainstorm and it was very cold in the morning. I decided to take a look at the livestock and how they managed in the night; the answer was that many of them did not manage. The Somalis do not provide shelter for their stock except a boma (kraal) for protection against predators but not against the weather. Some may have been taken into the houses for that night but obviously large numbers were out all night. There were dead sheep and goats all over the place and I reckon the death rate could have been around twenty-five percent. Tragedy. This happened not long after all their oxen had died from malnutrition.

Since writing this paragraph, Somalia has been hit by serious drought, and the world has turned its back on the country. They are not my favourite people but they do deserve some aid.

I was visiting a village far from Hargeisa, driving close to the Ethiopian border, when we saw and stopped for a woman wanting a lift. My counterpart knew her and, as they chatted, he turned to me and told me that she wanted to know what I was doing there in Somaliland. She then said that if I were five miles further south in the Ogaden I would be dead by now. I just hoped the border was well known. Not a pleasant thought.

Prior to the break-up of Somalia there was an enormous amount of military equipment in the north-west of the old Somalia; the military had numerous depots of arms and ammunition. When the southern section left the north, they left a lot of weaponry behind. Much of ammunition was destroyed in the fighting, but much was left behind and 'live'. Local people say there was a huge explosion and live ammunition was scattered for great distances. One of the barracks was near to Burao. According to the stories I was told, the whole barracks blew up, showering the surrounding villages around Burao with shrapnel, mortars, ammunition, grenades, extremely large shells and anything lethal. I was taken to see the place when I was in the area by one of the British de-mining team, who were to help people to avoid being victims in accidents. At the time the Brits were collecting up live shells, some enormous ones, grenades and anything else which could go BANG and would be unpleasant for a foraging child. They had dug a large hole and they had two explosions per day at regular set daily times, so the local populace would not be alarmed. This went on for weeks. The ground shook. I gather the Mogadishu government were not overly happy with the situation and they remain so. At the end of our 'training tour' we were playing a game with a stick of C-4 explosive, throwing it to and fro among the group, to see who would be the first to drop it, and then we all shouted, "Bang!" C-4 needs a fuse before it explodes, so we were not dicing with death – just pretending, I think.

There was one escape from people and the town of Hargeisa, which was to take a three-hour trip out of town to a river which had a waterfall and a swimming pool. It was in a place with zero population, zero croc, clean water from where I know not, and going to where I know not. A group of twenty or so of NGO staff would arrange a picnic, swimming, singing and general relaxation. The trip was usually organised so the first and last vehicles had radio. If there was any problem with any vehicle they would alert the lead vehicle and all stopped until the problem was fixed. It was considered not safe to enter that no man's land alone.

I did once kiss a baby camel; don't understand why, as I was not overly fond of them and still not so after that real experiment. It was a baby camel looking very lost, so we stopped whilst I had a chat with the first camel I touched since my days in Botswana.

HQ in Scotland sent a photographer to get some advertising pics to advertise their work in Africa. The photographer brought a young lady, reputably a model, with him and she actually did appear in some pics. When it was time for them to leave, she did not want to get into the plane – to her it seemed so very small. It was a four-seater. She had not realised how small the plane was on the way to Hargeisa. I gave her a short talk of the awful alternative of driving in bandit country, lack of roads and no help if the vehicle had trouble getting to Djibouti, especially for a young lady. She flew out to Kenya.

Whilst I was there a Scandinavian visitor to Somaliland working in the engineering sector was in Burao. I believe he was in Burao town visiting some field staff and as he was getting equipment out of his car a local calmly walked up and hit him with a piece of metal, which severed his jugular. One of my staff, a veterinarian, was at the scene but was unable to stop the flow of blood. The local just stood there and did not attempt to escape. To ensure that this tragedy should not deter international assistance, a Swiss psychiatrist was brought in to investigate and to see fair play. The investigation found that the man had a serious sanity problem and was not jailed but released to his family. I can understand that the trauma of ten years of warfare on your doorstep is possibly enough to turn anyone unstable.

One day I was at the shore of the Gulf of Aden and I took my light fishing rod and cast a lure to see what happened. My lure brought many beautiful fish almost to the edge of the water. It was like a visit to an aquarium.

The Somalis were 'outdoor' people, but there was an underground prison for certain criminal activities on the road to Berbera. Not at all pleasant for outdoor, semi-nomadic people. I did not visit. No, my experiences in Somaliland made me realise that it was not a nice place, but it was heaven compared with Somalia. It is/was definitely not a nice place. I was glad to get out and go to Afghanistan, believe it or not. Somaliland is the only country I have worked in where I often felt not at ease.

FIFTEEN

Afghanistan Second Tour

After the Hargeisa tour, I went to Afghanistan for my second tour there, so it was a matter of out of the Hargeisa frying pan into the Jalalabad... what?

In the break from overseas I was involved in what you could call a bit of road rage, what could have likely become a road rage incident. I was driving along a road where the left-hand side was blocked for quite a way by parked cars. I was around halfway along the single lane of traffic when a Range Rover pulled out of the parked traffic, blocking my way. I was about thirty yards from the car but a rather beautiful lady was in the driver's seat. I waved her to return to the kerb but she fluttered her hands, which I took to mean she could not reverse. So, being a sort of gentleman, I reversed all the way back until I could stop to allow her to pass. I must admit my hackles were rising, when she passed me and she blew me a kiss. My anger flew away and I laughed. Then—

It was a case of 'Back to Afghanistan' for me.

My second tour in Afghanistan was for an American NGO. The team leader went by the name of Jim Black or something similar, ex-military with no knowledge of aid work and even less of the situation in Afghanistan at that time. Recent history tells us that the Yanks have not improved. There were around eight of us based in Kandahar or 'Qandahar', please yourself, all in a house with plenty of room. The staff was based on what used to be called Taliban Row by the locals. Every house in the road had previously been Taliban occupied and now was just rubble, except for one which was the house of the schoolteacher. The teacher claimed that the only noticeable happening for him during the bombing was that the light bulb swung a little. Elsewhere some precision bombing was not so 'precision'.

The office had a cellar, which had sandbagged windows, and bags ready to be put at the door in case of bombing getting close. Though we never were threatened, so it was never used by us.

There was a good example of precision bomb when the Americans took out the headquarters of the religious police in the town centre. A happy band of jolly fellows who had the power to whip women in the streets – any woman alone out shopping, going to work, hospital or any other excuse they could think up were useless. To drive down the main road in the city traffic was a good feeling, as we passed by the religious police offices which were there no more. The precision bombing had taken the whole of the interior of the building and left the rather grandiose outer wall. Inside was just a heap of rubble and I quietly hoped that there were many of the religious police in there too.

The Taliban banned our daily run around the track in the sports stadium. Happiness was not allowed; even two miles in scorching heat was considered to be too enjoyable. They really are no fun. Hardcore Victorian?

As we travelled all around our area there were examples

of bombing. There would be a crater in the road and then a burned-out petrol tanker off the road fifty to a hundred metres ahead. Burned-out tanks and weaponry were on display and other military flotsam. The Taliban were still being bombed, but air strikes were diminished somewhat and it was safer for us to move about the country. In a bid to preserve their transport vehicles, the Taliban housed their vehicles in a large go-down (storage building) and painted red crosses on the roof. It was successfully bombed. The ruse failed, but initially the raid was censured by the not-knowing Western media, or perhaps they thought it was unsportsmanlike to destroy the Taliban toys.

This was the time of the Tora Bora caves bombing, which made everyone happy; few Taliban were killed but the Americans took the opportunity use up a lot of ageing bombs and let the world know how effective they were(n't). The Taliban, in the main, escaped. It was rumoured Osama bin Laden became a goat herder at the time, riding a donkey out of mountains into Pakistan.

I took a trip to Lashkar Gah, which was always an iffy place to visit. I had been there a number of times during the 'golden era' on my previous tour out of Herat, so I went to look up old friends and see what they needed that the project could provide. Only a few days after my visit, the place was raided by the Taliban and the populace were told to accept no aid from outsiders. Shortly afterwards the project had a truck there with an overnight stay. Our driver opted to sleep in the house used by the police, where he felt safer. He wasn't. The police were attacked and everyone in that house was killed. Odd, but not a surprise, as the police did not at that time use a sentry for the nights away from 'safety'. Mistake.

I had visited an old castle on my previous tour in the golden era that I had enjoyed, particularly on hot days. We headed south for twenty-five miles or so as there was to be found an old mud castle/walled city covering perhaps ten acres; most of it was fallen down. The old gateway was beautiful and was the motif on the currency notes for Afghanistan at that time. There had been defensive towers every hundred yards and there was an immense heap of soil with a small 'hut' about a toilet size at the top. The 'almost closet' had a door which opened and gave way to a spiral staircase going down, and down, and down. The lower we got, the colder it became. There was absolutely no light. The staircase had rooms coming off all the way down, which we did not investigate. When our teeth started to chatter, we thought discretion and so on was needed, so we returned to the top and out.

It was definitely not a holiday visit. I was travelling with staff and they wanted to stop for water, as one of them knew of a spring nearby. When we were off the road for just a little way we found the spring and also four Taliban soldiers, who were not at all threatening, and we stopped and the staff chatted a while. I saw a man crawling around the camp doing chores and he puzzled me. I decided not to question the situation until we had left the camp and I was told that the man was a captive and he was a spy. When he admits he is a spy they will shoot him and they had broken his legs so he could not run away.

During my stay in Afghanistan, I got used to hearing about 'night letters'. These were notices nailed to a post or anything wooden during the night. They were informing the public that the Taliban would pay many dollars (prices differed), dependant on how good the writer's imagination concerning the value of an infidel was. We had a weekly game of volleyball and one day I reckoned I could be a very rich man if I could find a bus and load the whole lot up and head for… where? It was never specified, nor was place for payment, so I decided not to bother.

There was always the possibility of an attack, so I planned an escape route out of the area without going near the city and on the way to Pakistan, all cross-country, using river beds and orchards. It would probably not work, as the Taliban would attack from that direction, but it gave me a bit of pleasure to think that there was a way out other than the city.

The gate out of Afghanistan on the border with Pakistan was where we changed over from driving on the right side of the road to the left. I never found out how it was accomplished, but it worked; you suddenly found you had changed sides, but when, and how? Very odd.

I was the only one of the staff of the charity who went into the field, and as such, the only one to see all the devastation. Visiting markets on market days showed that not only had the people suffered, but so had their livestock. Livestock were kept close to home or they disappeared, and anything grown close to home was needed at the home. No edible crops were grown away from the 'kitchen garden', so they grew poppy, being a very high value crop and readily marketable.

I met a farmer not too far from Lashkar Gah who was trying to get me to give him a tractor or something useful for ploughing his farm, "as he could not afford one." He invited me to visit his farm; he had about seventy-five black and white cows, poor-looking Friesians, obviously under nourished. I asked him where he sold his milk and he told me he did not sell it but he gave it away to the villagers. I later learned that most of the villagers were his relatives; philanthropy begins at home, I guess. Then he took me away from the homestead to show me his lands. He had a thousand acres on which he grew poppies and he needed a tractor to bring another thousand acres into production, also to grow poppy. I suggested I would have to ask the office whether this was possible and never saw him again. Off one year's money from the opium crop he could plough with Rolls Royce cars. I seem to remember that the next profitable crop was onions, as they were able to be transported on the road to Pakistan. The farmers could get $250 per acre from onions but they could get $2,500 per acre from poppies. Soooooo? Can the Afghan be blamed?

I was to take a trip up into central Afghanistan to Oruzgan Province, I have forgotten just why, as I would normally avoid places like that because they were extremely unsafe. It was very wild country! Medicines Sans Frontières got to know I was going and they asked if I could do them a favour and check on some disease outbreak they had got news of. It was in Oruzgan town, and they suspected meningitis. I, having never had meningitis, asked the symptoms, which would help. A couple of days before I left Kandahar, I was told that I need not go, as they had managed to get a helicopter to take them. I suggested they would hardly get beyond Kandahar city before being shot down in a helicopter. So, they decided it might be better if I went instead. It was quite some trip; I went north for about one hundred miles to Oruzgan town, where the mayor was surprised to see me. After a long chat he eventually told me that the local hospital had diagnosed the problem and it was not too serious.

Oruzgan seemed to be quiet, and I then moved on to my destination, Dasht-e Nawar, after letting the mayor know where I would be. However, communication in the mountains was poor and I was warned that until the previous week he would not have allowed me to leave Oruzgan, but now it appeared to be safe to travel. I travelled; it was some of the worst territory I have ever seen for potential ambushing; in fact, I had rather bad dreams for a while. Even the satellite phone did not work, because the mountains on each side of the road would only give access to one and at most two satellites. Great lumps of rock had been turned on edge, so providing a very good place for ambush almost around every corner. However, I did see something which amazed me: a hemispherical hill such as half of an enormous ball, perhaps forty metres high. It was rather beautiful. I reckoned it to be a sample of the striped underground strata which had been turned over ninety degrees. The colours were black, red, white, brown and yellow. We did not stop to explore, as it was off the track, and in those mountains, you cannot walk. It would be a climb.

We arrived safely at our destination, met the district officer there, and discussed matters pertinent to the project. A school and market were his top requirements. Plus water and a decent road. I questioned how a road could be built in the middle of such a rocky area. I even questioned myself how or why anyone would like to live there. Whoever decided that place would be a good place for project assistance I cannot imagine; I would bet a month's salary that they had never been there. Maybe a pin, a blindfold and a map had something to do with it. I returned to Kandahar after accomplishing nothing. I was supposed to be looking into the problems of livestock and saw about ten animals only. Grazing there was definitely not.

To be honest, the whole project was a shambles. I have a feeling that the project document was written for somewhere else, such as Minnesota or Oklahoma, whilst sitting in Florida.

There were a few veterinarians looking after what pets there were in Kandahar, which I assumed to be few. There were also dairy cattle, but only one farmer with more cows than were needed for home milk supply, and few who had got the past the level of bucket and stool. The vets were poorly trained, as I assumed, in Kabul, but probably better in Kandahar. Most were sitting on their backsides or working on their own farm and drawing a government wage. The notion of growing fodder for livestock never entered the equation; milk hygiene was a pipe dream. Calf production was not up to scratch, mainly due to the lack of milk from the mother, as their diet was very poor too. First milk, colostrum, went to the dogs, not humans or calves. Colostrum is the early milk after the cow had calved;

the perfect, essential first milk carries all the antibodies against local conditions. It is thrown away. As a child, whenever we had a calving cow, the calf got its fill and the rest came into the home and was consumed, called 'beastings pudding'. None of us children ever suffered from cow's diseases. Pasteurisation became the fad, and the cattle jabbed for tuberculosis did not enjoy the pantomime.

I often stepped out of my line of work. The child death rate in Afghanistan at that time was something like twenty-five percent. I may have this wrong; it could be higher. And some NGOs had women in the field trying improve the birth rate for both mother and child. I believe, but I could be wrong, in Afghanistan, having given birth, a woman was not allowed to wash for three weeks, not allowed out of her room for four weeks, and only fed the child with (usually) unclean water until the child's faeces lost its black colour. Only then was the father allowed to see wife and child. I did what I could to get them to understand the concept of feeding a calf and a child from day one. To the Afghan, the first faeces being black was not a good sign, and only when that was long past could a child be given breast milk. It is very difficult to get such a seismic change, of thousands of mothers for thousands of years telling daughters how to do anything in the Afghan society, and so few women working on projects. I spent twenty-five years in Islamic countries and was able to meet and talk with the Islamic womenfolk, except in Afghanistan.

I was working on getting a short course for Afghan vets in Pakistan, to get them on their feet and away from home and office, and get them back to fieldwork, without much success. I had a feeling that this project was not going to get very far. I think it was at the wrong place at the wrong time, with the wrong manager. I eventually realised that it was the American military trying to make amends for all the chaos they had perpetrated upon the Afghan. It was said at the time that it was all about

Osama bin Laden and the bombing on 9/11 in the USA. What few Americans seem to know was it not the Afghans to blame. Osama bin Laden was Afghan born but raised in Saudi, and fifteen out of nineteen terrorists taking part in the atrocity were Saudi Arabian. They left the Afghans to suffer under the Taliban.

I quit this project and after a short while in the UK I joined anther NGO, who had a better grasp of Afghan affairs. I hoped.

SIXTEEN

Afghanistan Third Visit

The bombing of Tora Bora was a short while before I arrived, but it was close enough to worry about errors. I was based in Jalalabad, at the top end of the Khyber Pass and about thirty-nine miles from Tora Bora. At the time, the country was reasonably stable. I would not say, "Not a cloud on the horizon," but it seemed settled. We were advised not to go to Nuristan, where there was a war going on, which was just next door over a mountain range, and I dropped the idea of a weekend's walk in Tora Bora too due to the obligatory minefields as yet de-mined.

Accommodation was a large house just a short walk from the office. There were six of us on the Jalalabad team. It did have HQ in Kabul, and another field office in Taloqan in the north, carrying on a similar project as in the south. I was the only livestock guy on the project, so I travelled between the two, visiting HQ as I meandered through Kabul, usually spending a night there.

The house in Jalalabad was a rental and had been in use by

the programme for some time, but there was a new building going up next to 'our' residence, which I thought too close for security's sake. In addition, we were having problems with our neighbour, who thought the men in our team spent most of the day, other than when at work, spying on his women. Barry went and had a word with him and told him we were not watching his wives and we would put up a tarpaulin to block any view. Neighbour said:, "I don't care about you looking at my women, but other people will be saying that I do not care about my wives." It led me to wonder just how much of the protective attitude is genuine.

Soon after I joined the team, I explained my worries about an empty house adjacent, which could be used as a gunman's roost. We all agreed that a move would be a good idea and after a while a pleasant residency was found. The move was quite a sight; we hired ten donkey carts, as there was little room to manoeuvre in the 'new' house drive and parking spot, so lorries would not be efficient. The donkey owners were very appreciative of the funding. Considering the number of donkey owners and their helpers, we did well in that we only lost a crate of beer and one blanket. The distance was around a mile and the 'trek' of ten carts in line astern would have amused the Afrikaners. On thinking about it, I never met an Afrikaner in Afghanistan – not surprising, I suppose.

The new place had plenty of rooms, one each for everyone, four toilets, a lounge and dining room. There was a balcony on two sides and a flat roof. There was little to do in Jalalabad after working hours, so I painted a squash court on the roof. It was a good way of relaxing and, as none of us were any good at squash, we did not deter people who were not very good or learning. That's logic. We often had spectators, mainly the American Apache helicopter crews that used Jalalabad airfield for refuelling and possibly, definitely, rearming. They would come and, holding their height, would sit and watch the game for ten minutes or so before going over the mountains into Nuristan, where there was a war going on, and unloading. The Apache helicopters are nasty little things. The Apache 'copter looks like an aggressive dragonfly, with guns and missiles visible. Having one of those hovering fully armed just a few yards away did not seem to worry the squash players.

I was at the Jalalabad airport one day, waiting for a passenger; firstly, an Apache helicopter flew overhead, then went away, after, I supposed, reporting all was well. Next, the passenger plane came into view, followed by the helicopter, which checked the airstrip, and then the big one landed. The helicopter was between the plane and the arrivals building, and arriving passengers got off to be ushered around the chopper to the building. What impressed me was that the helicopter remained in the same place, at exactly the same height of around eighteen inches. Quite a feat, I thought. Passengers were offloaded and first the 'chopper' departed and then the passenger plane went away.

I was at the airport on another day collecting someone coming to visit the project whilst there was a grass fire along each side of the runway and their parking space. Lost ammunition was going "pop, pop, pop," rifle fire all the time, with the occasional bang of a grenade. Even in Kabul people were told not to walk on the grass at the airport. It reminded me as being similar to the DO NOT WALK ON THE GRASS signs of UK parks, except it was landmines to beware of, not the park keeper.

Between the Jalalabad office and Taloqan is one of my least favourite bits of road in the world, leading to Parwan; the old Salang path through the pass was awful. The Salang Tunnel, which made the Salang Pass obsolete on foot, was to be a more attractive way to ease the problems of uniting north and south Afghans, and now this tunnel was awful too. I understand that it is considered one of the worst tunnels (Jeremy C says so) in the world, at 11,154 feet in altitude and 1.66 miles in length. Both ends of the tunnel have been shelled and bombed, so it looks very iffy. Going through the tunnel is no fun and can be quite dangerous. It was constructed, dug, by the soviets in 1966. I was told it was a good and safe way to travel, but believe me, this was not the case when I last went through it. It is through the mountains of the Hindu Kush. It is awful. In theory, it should have been a two-lane road. It may have been so years ago, but it generally was only one-way daily, by local agreement that worked OK. Occasionally some idiot who thinks his journey is of paramount importance can be the cause of hours of hold-up. Also, breakdowns were relatively frequent. Hours of hold-up in a tunnel without ventilation and blocked solid with old trucks and cars, vans and pickups belching out fumes, creates an atmosphere foul enough to kill, and kill it does. The walls are perpetually iced and the road is usually ice, except where a puddle remains liquid due to engine oil or such in the puddles. 'Puddles' can be and often are as much as two feet deep. There were some rockfalls where some noble people had braved the atmosphere and moved the rock to the side of the road. It must be understood, to appreciate the hazards, that the Afghan lorries should have been taken off the road twenty years ago. In Europe or almost anywhere else these absolute wrecks, most of them, would be considered scrap metal.

To break down can be and is often fatal. There is no lighting, no ventilation, and no assistance offered. Overnight breakdowns are bad, as people keep the engines running if they have in-car heating. The temperature plummets. Even if you are not yet in the tunnel, the roads to and from are narrow and mountainous, and turning around is usually impossible. Both ends of the tunnel were bombed to stop the northern faction going south, and southern factions going north. I did wonder what would be the outcome if two tanks had met nose to nose. They would be very close before they realised it was a tank, as the smoke and lack of lighting limits visibility. If they decided to be belligerent, it could be nasty within a collapsed tunnel. I thought that a tee shirt should be produced for the occasional traveller: "I SURVIVED THE SALANG TUNNEL. I'm a nut." I thought three "I'm a nut" tee shirts would suffice, even for the Salang. The only good thing about that tunnel was the exits.

In a village meeting not far from the northern end of the Khyber Pass, I was sitting in a circle of a dozen of male villagers discussing all sorts of topics, some selected by me and other topics by the villagers. I brought up the topic of schooling for girls, as we were building schools on the project. They all said they were in favour of education for girls. It could be true, or an attempt to keep me satisfied. Then I tried the topic of bride price and asked what was the current bride price of unschooled girls, and got a figure between $200 and astronomic. I then asked about educated girls and I was surprised; the answer was nothing for the schooled girls. Uneducated girls were more subservient, perhaps? Could it be that girls with education were liable to find their husbands ignorant and were not able to hide their contempt?

I was often told that girls from both Afghanistan and Pakistan have to learn to lie from the very beginning. They live in a precarious situation. There are a number of 'kitchen' deaths from boiling water or very hot fat. And they could die, killed by a close relative, if caught misbehaving. Misbehaving can be as simple as the woman or girl even taking a look at a man on the street. I saw one incident when a woman was returning home and heard a man running behind her. She turned to see what was going on. When she got to her home, which was close to where she looked at the runner, she was beaten with a stick, presumably by her husband.

Whilst I was in Jalalabad during the winter months, there was often a problem at the Salang Tunnel, and one memorable extra-cold night resulted in 143 people frozen to death, both in the tunnel and in both entry roads. That tunnel was evil. A little before I left Afghanistan, a new tunnel at about three thousand feet lower altitude was completed, and a few works trucks were using it. I suppose it is open to the public now. But the nomads still have to walk their livestock over the ancient pass to take animals to their summer grazing.

Northern Afghanistan is a beautiful area and could become a world-renowned holiday resort if it were peaceful. Mountains, rivers, snow, fishing, vast views, good local cuisine. It would be wonderful for hiking or pony trekking, etc. And vast acres of poppy fields, bright red and *papaver somniferum*! I was in the north, farm visiting, and managed to catch a fish with a circular casting net the owner of the net demonstrated, and I was super lucky. We were walking along the stream with many *somniferous* poppy fields on both sides when a farmer came out to see what we were up to among his poppies. He was not belligerent, perhaps because there was an American B-29 bomber overhead doing figure of eights, and him thinking it was my top cover. I assumed that the bombers were just waiting to be told exactly where they were to drop their cargo. Incidentally, the Afghans refer to smoking opium as 'eating flowers'.

In Taloqan, our northern outpost was very close to Tajikistan and Uzbekistan. The project house was in the town itself, and as usual the garden was watered by a *jui*, a small stream diverted through the gardens of many of the houses in the village. It is often used as a toilet in extremis, but this one was quite clean. It was Olympic Games year, so we held our boat race, choose your own boat, for Pooh sticks. It was fun for people who live on their nerves; it is useful to have a bit of distraction.

One unusual feature of that house was a Nebelwerfer parked

at the corner of the garden, roadside, obviously defunct. It made a good landmark if you got lost in town, though what Nebelwefer is in Farsi I do not know, and am glad I never got lost.

I worked from Taloquan in a village about forty miles south of the town, not far from a village called Burka. There was an earthquake whilst I was there and the programme was involved in aid to villagers. I learned one lesson from this one: if you see any amount of aid gifts on the village markets, then they have received enough aid. I was building a veterinary clinic, as I did in many places, around thirty miles from town. My brother informed me that the number of house sparrows was declining in the UK, so I told him where they all were. The road to the village where we were building a clinic had about eight miles of driving up a dry riverbed. On each side of the river was a vertical soil riverbank with small rocks in the wall, around forty feet high, which had literally thousands of holes drilled in it by the house sparrows as nesting sites. I suppose this was their fortress away from people and away from snakes. It was a fantastic sight to see thousands of sparrows returning to the nesting site in the evening. They flew in a continuous stream fifteen feet wide and five feet deep, with little if any breaks in the stream.

The birds were about fifteen miles from the village I was heading for, and on one of my visits, I drove past a kuchi encampment a hundred or so yards off-road, and a small boy came running across to us, waving his arms. I said we should stop but the driver said not to do so. We stopped. The child told us that his sister was very ill and would I come to treat her. I told him that I was not a doctor, but he was insistent. I walked across to the tent, which held eight or ten people, all men but one female, the mother, and the girl of about thirteen. The child was lying on the floor on a carpet with a blanket over her, and there was a saline drip attached to the tent post but not to the girl. Now, in Afghanistan you do not mess with the kuchies, even looking at one of their women can invite a bullet, so I asked permission to touch her, which was agreed. I could not raise a vein to put the needle in; it had collapsed, and I told them so. She was very dehydrated. I asked if I took her along with one of the people, a relative, I could take her to the next village, where the doctor was a friend of mine. I told them that I was returning the next day and would check at the hospital to see if she could come home.

That was agreed. After I said I would not take her without a relative, brother-in-law was nominated. No problems on the way, but she was very ill and I drove straight to the doctor's house. He answered the doorbell and told me it was lunchtime and he was eating. I suggested I wait outside but he would not have it. He said, "If you will have lunch with me, I will treat the young lady for free." How could I refuse that?

After lunch I dropped the girl and her chaperone off at the hospital and went to see how the vet clinic was coming along. There was one minor problem, in that the water table was about thirty centimetres down and we could not move the site, though I never found out why, which puzzled me and still does. Otherwise, all was well.

Next morning, I collected the young lady, who was remarkably sprightly and far from death's door. I dropped her off on my return trip. She ran from the car across the field to the tent with the four bottles of water that I had with me. Her problem was cholera, and she had been very dehydrated. The doctor said the river water was to blame and she would very soon get cholera again. What a life!

The usual line of project transport was a Russian type of Jeep similar to the old Autodacia of my first visit to Afghanistan. Very cheap, and showed it. The Taliban would stage a hold-up on the road, take the satellite phone off the Russian-style Jeep, and send the 'Jeep' on its way. I considered that to be an insult. They obviously had better vehicles than we had.

Jalalabad had an Indian Embassy; we never did work out why it was there, as there was only one Indian in Jalalabad and he worked for us. One day someone threw a hand grenade over the wall. I guess India was not seen as friend by someone.

The soviets had left behind a beautiful sauna, which I never tried out. I have never had a sauna. No water. Jalalabad previously had a fruit and tomato sauce bottling plant for export. The roads are not overly conducive to getting soft fruit out of country, and Afghanistan desperately needs a market. Most of the machinery was still there but would need a checking over before it could work again. The tomato sauce machine apparently was unscathed; it looked as though it had someone taking care of it.

The project was asked to see what could be done about supplies for the university, which was waking up from fifteen years of 'slumber'. (That would suit some students.) I was most involved with the livestock parts of the requirements. There was literally absolutely nothing in the building except rooms. My list was rather long and all I did was write it out and hand it to the powers that be. One of the first items from my list to turn up in Jalalabad was almost a truckload of computers. There were other donors busy in Jalalabad, headed by an Iraqi lady working for a Lions Club out of California. I was surprised, but the Iranian was paying way over and above the going rate for supplies – perhaps an over-Americanised Iraqi.

Afghanistan and Pakistan have a very different attitude as to what the mosque is for. In Afghanistan they use the mosque almost as a village hall; both sexes are welcome. I had a talk in one mosque about trying to get people to stop growing poppies and get a plastic tunnel and grow soft fruits all the year round. There was an Iranian woman in the mosque talking about the new school the village would have and encouraging parents to send their daughters to attend school when it opened. A short while after this meeting, I was in Pakistan at some sort of meeting and the Iranian lady was there too. I introduced the lady to a top surgeon I knew and mentioned that I met her in a mosque. He nearly blew his top! "In a where? And for what it's worth, what the heavens were you doing in a mosque?" These two reactions were only the length of the Khyber Pass apart.

I was responsible for a few veterinary clinics being constructed and the equipping them with drugs, etc. Much of the bulky stuff, like cement, had to come from Pakistan via the Khyber Pass, which lives up to its geological reputation but is not as worrisome as other passes I have used. But I could imagine it with an armed Khyber Pashtun behind each and every boulder. That was another *Mpira juu Kabisa* (Kiswahili for 'less than successful') British transfer of sovereignty to the rightful owners. My apologies to any Kiswahili speakers.

Opium was the most profitable crop by far. We did consider getting the bottling/canning plant up and running again, but it would have no chance of competing with opium as a primary export; unfortunately, farmers were reluctant even to discuss it. They were much less reluctant to talk about plastic tunnels for the production of out-of-season soft fruits and vegetables. Poly tunnels were competitive so long as the project produces the tunnel fabric, which had a finite life in the Afghan summer sun – and so did I. It could really get hot.

I was out on a trip in western Afghanistan with three project employees and a driver at the hottest part of the year that, unfortunately for the Muslims, was also Ramadan. I was surreptitiously sipping water from my bottle, but none of the lads accepted an offer of water, and then we met a *jui* (streamlet) between villages and the staff asked to stop. They all dived into the shallow water and I thought they had their faces in the water for a rather long time but did not comment on it, as it was a matter between just them and Allah.

On my first tour in 1978, I met a guy in Kabul who had a team in the Bushkasi league in Kabul. Bushkasi (rugby on horseback with a goat carcase as a ball) being a rather physical game, I was interested. He told me that the game in Kabul is for softies. The real games are in the north around Mazar-e Sharif. The game in Kabul is for the tourists, according to him. They had a league table, twelve horsemen per side and limits to the area of the field. One thing he assured me of was the horses loved the game, and he showed me a photograph of one of his horses galloping ahead of the field with the goat in his teeth. The goat is dead before they start, so do not worry. After a Bushkazi game the meat would be well tenderised. I also hear from other sources that one of the more serious games in the north has up to a thousand participants. It is not uncommon for there to be one or two deaths – not horses, but riders.

In Mazar-e Sharif there no limits to numbers and the playing field is/was the whole of the north. To be a spectator you needed a driver and a Land Rover, as you may need to get the hell out of the way of a horse stampede, as the game could go in any direction. The horsemen, riders, participants, call them what you will, carried a wicked short whip for use on the horse, and also other riders. A slap across the eyes was enough to deter some people, or at least make their eyes water. It turns into a melee around the body of the goat until someone makes a breakaway, then it is a mad gallop to the goal. The Afghans I spoke to were as enthusiastic as the wildest soccer fan, and retired players were disgusted with their children who did not wish to follow father's footsteps. I said nothing but I reckoned it showed common sense within the next generation.

The project had a forestry interest, so I took the forestry specialist to see some forestry. We parked and had to walk when we reached there, and as we walked across a meadow, we were walking through a sea of knee-high, reddish-purple flowers. My friend picked one and, very excited, he said, "These are orchids. Ask him [our driver] what he calls them." The answer? Weeds.

On the north end of the Salang, plus a few miles, is a small village, not big enough to be on the map but an essential stop for people who have survived the tunnel. The food is Afghan and very good, but it is the restaurant that leaves memories; I do not think I have had such fun elsewhere. The restaurant is circular but in itself nothing special. The perimeter is a platform about one metre above floor level, where the Afghans sit cross-legged and spend hours chatting and eating. The centre circle has chairs and tables. The tables have metal plates and cutlery laid out for any customers, such as me, who cannot sit cross-legged. For me the big attraction was the waiter. He was enormous for an Afghan, almost two metres tall, well built, bald headed with a shiny dome, bare chested and wearing a grubby wrap-around cloth and bare feet. He carries a tea towel–sized cloth with which he cleans the plates and the tabletops, table by table, wipes the sweat from the top of his head, wipes a few more plates and tabletops, then wipes the sweat off his large chest, then back to the tables, all with the same cloth. I always stopped there, not just to see him – the food was excellent, unbelievably so. In Afghanistan I always ate Afghan food at home or out and about and, so far as I remember, dire rear was never a problem. Why?

One of my out-of-town trips took me to Bamiyan. This was after the destruction of the two giant Buddha statues carved from the solid rock. When we got off the plane, we were standing amid a locust plague, not exactly crunch-crunch as we walked, but they were rather thick on the ground and usually they moved away. The landing was an experience; they were still using one of the WWII steel landing strips that were laid down where an earth/sand strip was not viable. I was expecting a nice smooth landing, but as soon as we touched down the plane rattled like a tin of shaken gravel. However, for a 'temporary' wartime strip it was in remarkably good condition. Even the locusts enjoyed it as a holiday resort or something.

One day we were driving along faint wheel tracks across the Farah desert when we noticed something up ahead. It turned out to be a camel trotting along, blissfully unladen and unaccompanied, towards us. We discussed it for a while and then later we passed a man running in the same direction as the camel, but not particularly fast; we asked if we could help. He rejected the offer, as we were going in the opposite direction. His camel had escaped and he was hoping it was close, not knowing what 'close' meant. We reckoned they were about five miles apart. He was without water, and there was nothing obvious in the way of a horse trough. I still wonder if he caught it or someone else did.

One close escape and completely due to the lack of thought happened one evening when my neighbour and I were refilling the fuel tank of the generator providing our houses with electricity. It was dark. The garage was darker, and we were pouring petrol into a small hole with minimum idea of how full it was getting. We never agreed who did it, but a match was lit so we could check the level of fuel. I was left holding the fuel can, which was belching flames; my neighbour was a long way away in a very short time. I put the cap on the jerrycan and put it down and walked out of the garage. The only time, as far as I know, I was grateful for the lack of quality in any Russian product, including the octane level of petrol, in those days being little better than kerosene. Thank you, Russia.

I was sitting chatting in a village in south-east Afghanistan, talking about all their woes and difficulties and also their better matters. We heard a helicopter come and, as it approached, it got lower and landed in the village. It had American forces identification signs. No excitement noticeable. I asked the villagers what they wanted. Nonchalantly one said, "They have come for the opium."

It was here that I saw a donkey with a cart attached which was obviously heavier than the donkey was. The donkey was hanging in the air. It did not seem to take umbrage, as it was not complaining, so I reckoned that it was not the first time he had been airborne. In both Afghanistan and Pakistan, the life of a donkey seems to be almost universally miserable, even compared to African methods. The worst I saw in Africa was a donkey being ridden by his owner heading for his village, fully loaded with stuff from a shopping spree. It was quite a distance and the owner accepted a lift by a lorry, leaving the donkey behind. This area was pretty thick with lions. The donkey was probably twenty-five miles from home, but I doubt if it saw the next morn.

Back to Afghanistan. I was wandering about with some staff and decided on a visit to the Panjshir Valley, which had held out against the Russians and the Taliban. There was a road out which crossed a riverbed, dry at my time, and it had been heavily mined in the past. We crossed using the wheel tracks as a guide and then met up with a five-hundred-pound bomb, which was still live. I sat on it for a photograph. I reported it and it was defused. We were shown around schools and hospitals, hotel and offices all carved into the mountain rock and seriously never hurt in the bombing raids. Apparently there were numerous live bombs deliberately lying about, ready to be used in case of invasion; this being the case, they would detonate at a pertinent time.

The hold out against the Russians was achieved by their leader, known as the Lion of Panjshir. Unfortunately, he was assassinated by a couple of so-called journalists from Libya who had a bomb inside a camera which killed all three. He was extremely popular in the valley and would probably have become the next leader of Afghanistan, as he had thwarted the Russians. I do often wonder how that area of South Asia would be if the Libyans had not got involved.

I met the head of a village I was visiting who only had one hand, so I asked him how he got that. He told me that he was driving along a road and saw a 'rope/fuse' across the road. He got out of his truck and started to wind the fuse up, using hand and elbow, when some nasty-minded individual lit the fuse. The 'blue sump fuse' was basically a tube filled with explosive and goes off like a bomb; it is instantaneous, and took his lower arm off. He had four AK-47s in his office, three on the wall and a loaded one propped up by his chair. I understood why.

The project did quite a lot of construction work – schools, markets, rural roads and in Jalalabad a refuge for women. As it was a US donor funding, on completion of the refuge a colonel was invited to officially open the refuge, showing the American flag. I was asked to attend as the local representative. What I was not aware of was that I was given the rank of colonel in the US military whilst I accompanied him, which I feel my wife's relatives, Americans, would disagree with, as her brother was a real colonel. After the opening the colonel and I chatted for a few minutes and he asked what else we were doing. I offered to show him around our office, a short walk away, and he would get a better idea than me just telling him. It took a few minutes to get bodyguard personnel on the rooftops along our walk.

The stroll was uneventful and I gave him a chat, showing maps and photos of finished projects and projects as yet incomplete. He asked if he could meet the staff, so I offered to show him around the block which was one floor up. From my flat office roof, I usually entered the offices through a large window and I suggested we use that route. He agreed.

The colonel appeared to be very interested and the Afghan staff explained their duties. All went well until we exited the office block via the main door. His bodyguards were running around all over the place; they had lost their colonel and by the excitement raised it seemed that would be important. As the colonel got into his armoured vehicle, the senior rank of the bodyguard came to me and said, "Do that again and I personally will shoot you." It seems to happen quite often to me; I think I had three such threats, but this one was likely to be genuine, though the other two could have been so – but I very much doubt it.

I was with a car full of staff on the way to visit a government farm, and in doing so passed through a village where there lived an elderly man unable to walk. He scooted around on his bum. I would give him a bit of cash each time I went past. On one time, on the way I took some cash and put it on the dashboard so I did not forget him, but being distracted by some other matter as we passed him, I did not give him the cash. On realising I had forgotten and saying so, I was told, "Don't worry, if you really did forget you will still be credited in heaven." Now that really made me think about the rich Muslim giving alms to the poor – perhaps not a matter so much of generosity as self-interest. Camels and the eye of a needle.

This project did not seem to be of much value to the Afghans, nor of much interest to me. I was offered a better job in Pakistan and decided to leave Jalalabad and check the opportunity in Pakistan, so I hired a lorry and loaded my junk and took a tourist route through the Khyber Pass. I was glad to be doing the journey without any enemy waiting for me, as was the method used a few years earlier when the British left after overstaying their welcome. There were a couple of villages on the way down where I was advised by the driver to duck below the window so as not to be seen. It was an educational journey.

On arriving at the border, I had no problem and was very surprised that the Pakistani customs were still using typewriters when I passed through in 2004.

After I resigned, my replacement arrived in Jalalabad and resigned the next day. His replacement on the project was man described to me as being mad, and the Afghan does not use that term lightly. I hear he lasted three months. I do admit that I was not sorry to leave, but it was not that bad. I don't think.

Pests and Other Problems

During my time out of the UK, I met a number of pests for which my UK MSc did not prepare me (e.g. the Taliban).

1. The armyworm is a major problem in East Africa. It is actually a caterpillar of a type that does not enjoy being lonesome. They come by the acre, not numbers, and are hungry at that and just munch along until it is time to become a rather nice white butterfly. There is nothing to dislike about the armyworm; it is the number of friends he has which are the problem, millions of them. The caterpillars are a hungry bunch. When they hatch to butterfly state, they do it in unison, so many flying as a mob it is like a snow blizzard, so much so that if you are driving it is better to stop and wait for them to pass, perhaps for up to an hour. I guess the same goes for elephants, but Jumbo does not squish on your windscreen; he might squish your vehicle. Incidentally, Jumbo does not appreciate car horns, nor do rhino. It gets them upset and you should not upset either. There was a photograph in the newspaper in Tanzania of a car perched in the top of a tree, put there by a jumbo which objected to being told to get a move on. Also, a rhino got very upset by a Land Rover on the road between Mbeya and Dar which hooted at him. He kept charging, modifying the model for over an hour, and walked away with a door of the truck stuck on his/her horn.

2. Locusts are regularly a major problem. When I first went to Tanganyika (Tanzania), the government had recently

disbanded the locust control squad. They had been constant aerial locust surveillance over the known breeding sites, and if the number of hoppers went beyond bearable, they would spray them from the air. This ensured minimal numbers the following year. Now it is out of control. True or not, I do not know, but there was said to be an ageing pilot who could see the hoppers from the air and decide whether to spray or not to spray. When he retired, the aerial survey was not to the previous quality. I met this swarm of creatures for the first time when I landed at Bamiyan in Afghanistan, the place which used to be a hotspot for tourists to see the giant statues cut from the rock face. The locusts were there, but not the statues (thank you, Taliban, I don't think). Often a swarm is a matter of walking crunch-crunch-crunch. I was little apprehensive about taking off in such a cloud of insects at the Bamiyan incident. I think if they were a bit more palatable it would be a good source of food in a dry area. I have heard of them being eaten, but without custard I would not try it.

3. The corn cricket is very like the locust, but slightly larger and more corpulent. They have a hopper stage when they have a limited area to damage, but the flying swarm can cover a much greater number of football fields (or whatever is the current yardstick with which to give an idea of a size larger than a front lawn). A swarm arrived in Botswana close to the swamp. They were everywhere and eating the newly to be harvested maize and other plants. The roads were covered and every green plant around was unrecognisable or just a bare stalk. Schoolchildren were let off school to kill as many as possible. Some people ate them, but it would not be the choice of *haute cuisine* – too much gristle and not enough meat. Then one day an Abdim's stork appeared. He/she gorged for a fortnight and then flew away, returning five

days or so later with an army of pals. This was their holiday. When they had filled out somewhat, they returned, from whence I know not. It was postulated that they came from three hundred miles away, as that was the nearest haunt of these amazing birds. I am not sure if they like to eat locusts, because if so, they must wait for the clouds of these insects. It seems the swarm sends out scouts to find their whereabouts. Buffalo, elephants and other species definitely send out scouts, to return to lead the way to a desirable location.

4. Spiders around the eastern side of Lake Victoria are a pest. Periodically the lake would produce clouds of lake fly, black flies which were so numerous as to appear to be a black rain cloud and could be seen miles away. The fly breeds in the lake and the hatch get out of the water and fly. They are blown by the prevailing winds to the various shores; multiple swarms can be seen on some good days. Spiderwebs are so thick in the bush, shrubs and trees, etc., which calmly stand around the lake, awaiting the lake flies. Their webs are so numerous that they can cover agricultural fields to such an extent that the hedge, the bush or whatever shuts out all the light out, to the extreme extent that crops die or are reduced in quantity, with lack of photosensitisation ensuring a low crop or death of 'perennial' shrubs which are obvious in the hedgerows.

5. Earwigs, as I have dealt with in my earlier text. Unbelievable. I met them in Nigeria. Skirt and blouse is the local term, and they bite.

6. Today tsetse fly no longer exists in the Okavango due to spraying, but are still found in Africa. In my time there the tsetse fly was very much there. It has a painful bite with an everlasting effect, if you are unfortunate. Actually, it is not a bite. They saw away until they draw blood – it is not a puncture but a mini crater. They were a major protector of the game in the swamps; game animals were not overly

troubled, but for cattle, horses, sheep and goats it meant death. I tried numerous types of insect repellent but none seemed to work except one. This kept away the tsetse but, in the heat, it gave off a vapour sufficient to stop your shooting or driving (and I do not mean golf). You could not see due to painful running eyes.

7. Ticks are not actually insects but masquerade as one. Insecticide does not 'doofor' the precious little arachnid. They vary in size from pepper to larger fingernail size, and even bigger when bloated with blood. My least favourite one is the pepper tick. Very tiny and red, hence its name. It is one of the least appreciated in that it heads straight for the crotch. Pepper-sized ones on your testicles are no fun, I can promise you (unless you are female, which I have never personally been). Pepper ticks never come in singles; they come in hoards. Ticks are found over most of the world in various colours, shapes and ferocity. De-ticking yourself after a day of walking through cattle land is no fun. A vaccine was produced in Kenya years ago (1997) and it has probably been improved upon, but I left Africa soon afterwards and am not aware of what has happened since. A friend of mine almost lost his life during the process of getting the jab for farm animals against tsetse.

8. Then there is the ubiquitous mosquito, carrying several diseases, such as yellow fever and dengue fever as well as malaria, nasty little females. Said to be the biggest killer in Africa and possibly the whole world. My personal experience with the 'mossie' was enduring it as a pest and an itchy bite or seventy, or thereabouts. In some countries with cold or very dry areas the ubiquitous nasty is self-isolating. In fact, in the high Himalayas there are zero to add to the count. In the evening, I often changed from shorts to long trousers, thick socks and boots, plus a half gallon of mossie

repellent, in the bush. I used nets at night in towns and just occasionally in the bush if I was camped close to pools and non-running water. However, there was a usually a choice between a mosquito or a lion. Where there was a possibility of a lion or two visiting my camping spot, the net would hinder me getting set to fire a gun. This wee fly is Africa's biggest killer, ahead of the hippo and the croc together, is my belief.

9. Other diseases lurk in the stagnant pools of water. Bilharzia is one, and the treatment for that makes it feels like your blood is boiling, as experienced by a friend of mine. Hopefully the treatment is less painful now.
10. Another is the guinea worm, which is ingested in poor quality water and lays eggs which hatch to become a worm, which grows to as much as thirty centimetres. The worm travels within the human and can turn an active man into a cripple. It is a horrible beast and once noticed and found can be extracted by getting a hold of the end and, over days, slowly twisting it around an instrument (a twig perhaps) until it is fully out. Filtering drinking water through sand can help to stop the egg getting into water taken for drinking. Boiling also kills them in the egg stage. I have never met one, thankfully.
11. There is another bug which hibernates in drought situations for as much as eight years. A bite from one of these bugs (name forgotten I'm afraid) can and does slowly kill. I believe this is most prevalent along the Botswana/South African border and perhaps by now there is a cure; I do hope so.
12. Bedbugs seem to have become less frequent of late. Maybe my poisonous 'Gamatox' was more useful than recognised. However, the occasional biting spider and other wee beasties are there to remind us that we may not be at the top of the food chain.

13. In Tanzania I met the red-billed finch, a small bird about the size of a house sparrow or smaller, also called quelea, which eats seeds such as grass seed, and they love sorghum seed. They are present in enormous flocks, especially in harvest time, and farmers engage children to drive them away from the fields. At night the flocks roost in trees and occasionally the numbers are so great that the tree branches cannot support them. Farmers would take a forty-four-gallon drum of kerosene or kerosene/diesel and wait at night until all the birds were settled. Dynamite or a stick of C-4 produces an entertaining and spectacular blast. Another ploy during the nesting season is to burn the nests and fledglings before the young can fly using a 'flame thrower'. A tank of kerosene as a backpack and a burning 'lance' is used at night to burn the nests. This method was popular until one of the people using the flame method had a leaking lance, which soaked the man, who then caught fire. I once went to meet a guide from his village in Tanzania. When we arrived, I saw quelea going down in his field. I asked if he would like me to shoot a few. He agreed. I threw a rock into his crop and a great big cloud of birds rose, and I used a single barrel and on that one shot many birds fell. I was about to drive away when the villager said, "Nini acha nyama?" "What leave meat?" We collected seventy-three and I am sure we left a few. I did have sympathy for his wife, plucking those seventy-three small birds. More recently research has shown that destroying vast numbers of quelea is not a very effective method, because if the numbers in the flocks are depleted the following breeding season produces extra fledglings to compensate.

14. One beast really impressed me during my time out of the UK. I went fishing off uMhlanga Rocks near Durban, South Africa. I was fishing, or rather just going a distance further

out to sea to fish. We were running at a reasonable speed and distance out to sea somewhere to start fishing when a hammerhead shark came to take a look at us in the boat. The shark seemed to be about fifteen or so feet long and just slid alongside, not aggressive, just curious and was watching me with his/her right eye. I stared at the fish with both eyes and was impressed – VERY! It was staying close to the boat, about three or four feet from me. It then glided away and came back again from astern, showing no effort whatsoever. I saw this immense fish just gliding along with the occasional swish of its tail, compared to my thrashing around like an idiot when swimming. I am sure the shark was laughing, not eyeing me up for supper, but I was very impressed. Since then, I feel like an idiot even putting a toe into the briny when I get to the seaside. I have never even walked in the sea since that day. The sea belongs to fishes, not people; and sharks seldom encroach on our bit of the planet. I have stopped fishing now; I consider it inhumane. I am rather disparaging when I hear of people trying to hunt a shark if it takes a piece of someone. We do not belong there. There are many sports where there is a possibility of injury and the risk is accepted, but for some reason the shark is exempt from this very same reasoning. Since this experience I have turned away from fishing and have seen other nasties like sea snakes in the briny. I do not even paddle in it. I reckon there are only two beasties you cannot reason with: one is a crocodile and the other a fish.

15. The other nasty would be the scorpion – horrible beast. I first had the pleasure of meeting one when me and my passenger came upon a 'gutter' too deep to attempt with the car and we had to fill in the enormous rut across the road. There was a nearby pile of stones which we carried to fill in the ditch, but unfortunately the pile of stones was the

home of a black, enormous, scorpion. He/she objected, and I objected to being stung. We had a fight and I won. I was lucky in that it was a big black one rather than a small green one, which is said in certain situations to be a killer. I used to stay reasonably often at the Outspan Hotel on Lake Rukwa. There was a child, three or four years old, who carried a pair of scissors on a string around his neck as a necklace. He successfully hunted the scorpions and just snipped off the spike at the end of the tail.

16. Depending on where you are, and if wading through less than clean water, leeches can be a bit of a bind. The little brutes catch hold as you walk along worrying about larger creatures such as croc. When you start to undress later you can find any amount of the little blood suckers. They do not hurt when they catch you, unlike a lion. I would assume that the bite could be infected if the water was stagnant and stinks. Infection could be a thing to remember and you can lose a lot of blood if the matter is not quickly dealt with. The remedy? Send the cook for the salt cellar and give each a decent share. This is a slow method, slow torture for them, but the use of a lighted cigarette speeds up the process. Stamping on them is an effective way to go. It is not always fetid water.

17. I think crocodiles could be called pests, because they are. Many people aware of the brutes believe that the croc is the biggest cause of death throughout Africa. A few make the news but many in the more rural areas are not reported; such events are considered nothing much out of the usual by the locals, something to be put up with and uneventful. Another factor to label them as a king/pest is that, though they mainly inhabit water, they can and do move between water sources. Crocs are often believed to be the cause of unexplained deaths and disappearances in rural Africa.

There are examples proving the distances croc will move between water sources. There are examples of people being taken by croc miles from water. Croc are unbelievably fast on land and to my feeling a croc death is about the worst possible. I decided quite early on that if I saw a croc take anyone I would not hesitate. If I shot at the croc the person might get away; if I were to hit the person it would be a better death than that provided by the croc. And the time in which the decision has to be made is very short. I feel that it would be an instant reaction were I carrying a gun, large or small, preferably 0.375 mm or more. I am told it is the only remaining creature from the dinosaur era, and their demise would not worry me.

18. A pest is something that interferes with your duties, and in this definition comes people 'in charge'. I have worked under a man employed as a livestock specialist provided by the UK government. This was in Botswana. He was completely lost in what was required by the government. Just one example was when he dithered and fussed giving me instructions as to where, east or west, we would visit and told me to book rooms in hotels. From memory he was not sure which way to go, where to stop, and on what dates. I spent a morning calling various towns in South Africa and on average three hotels per town, if in fact there were any hotels. This guy had a secretary but considered her to be incompetent, so I got lumbered. He was eventually medevacked out with appendicitis that he had self-treated and disbelieved all advice. He crunched antibiotics over a few weeks and at last it got so bad that he died in the UK stubborn. He lived much longer than we expected compared to my bout earlier. He was not replaced, which gave me a much-improved position to sort out the problems he created.

SEVENTEEN

Pakistan Khyber Pakhtunkhwa, Now Known As Kp Or Kpk. Aka North-West Frontier Province

I have always been interested in the time during the colonial period when NWFP residents were not overly excited to be ruled by the British. One of the tribes beyond the Khyber Pass was particularly upset with the Brits and causing problems. An expedition duly set off towards Afghanistan up the Khyber Pass, but staying on the heights rather than in the pass – that shows that we can sometimes learn a lesson. The Brits had to fight their way daily, and to construct some fortification each day to be 'safe' at night and then to push on the next day. This went on for a couple of weeks, I believe, and then one of the tribesmen walked up to the Brits and asked why they were fighting. The

Brits said that they wanted to punish a tribe beyond the pass. A meeting was arranged with the Khyber headman and the matter was explained that a tribe beyond the Khyber tribe territory was giving problems. During the meeting, it came out that the Khyber tribe were enemies of the ones the British wished to give a hiding. The agreement was struck that the Brits could pass without any more fighting. The Brits were able to continue and punished the more northern tribe. After the Brits had moved on, some Khyber tribesman had suggested, "We only gave safe passage going that way but not back again." This is a joke of theirs even today when you get to know them. Is it a joke or true?

This was an ongoing EU project, which initially had a problem keeping staff. I had worked with the project manager previously in Botswana and we were on good terms, but unfortunately he fell out with the EU rep, which was a carry-over from previous employments. I was not too fond of the EU representative, not that he did anything to me; he just did nothing.

There were two posts for expats available and I was given a choice. Punjab was one and the other NWFP. I visited Lahore in the Punjab and was not unduly impressed by the attitude of the director of veterinary services towards the project. Next, I went to Peshawar in NWFP and felt that I was back at home in Afghanistan. Here their interest and friendliness were not needed to win me over; I was sold as soon as I entered the compound. Pashtun hospitality is legendary. My staff in Peshawar was among the best I met in my working life. I always had my office door open, which was a sign that anyone could drop in, and in particular the female staff felt safe. If someone was having problems at home or with their health, I would tell them to go and get better and come back when they were ready. They were honest with me and trusted me, and I got to know things which other people, local or expats, do not appreciate.

My first job was to return to Lahore and explain to the only

British female expat vet on the project there that it would be best for everyone if she were to resign. She did not want to leave, but she was having problems with the male head of the veterinary services there and it could only get worse. I did feel for her, as she was a good vet, but females in Pakistan often do have problems regardless of their competence.

The head of the veterinary department in KP was an Afghan Pashtun, as are the majority of the population of the province, and we made a good team for the duration of the project, which by the end was recognised as the best livestock project ever in NWFP or even Pakistan. I am indebted to my co-manager for his help to run the project, as well his regular position as veterinary director of NWFP. Thank you, Muqarrab Ali Khan.

I understand that NWFP was part of Afghanistan until it was ceded to Pakistan on a hundred-year lease, similar to Hong Kong, which expired around the end of the twentieth century. At the time there was no Afghan government to request its return, and so it has remained as part of Pakistan. Pakistanis a number of times told me this. Am I shit-stirring?

The project was national, covering all four provinces of Pakistan, with a staffing of project director and four provincial directors. It was embedded in the government structure, with project managers like myself on equal footing. In this form, success, or lack of, all boils down to individual relationships. There has often been friction between animal health staff and animal production; fortunately, my counterpart was a production specialist for six years or so. We maintained a very comfortable relationship, if not with the other veterinarians we met up with.

OK that has settled my introduction and now for a bit of fun.

My daughter had gotten married soon after I started work in Pakistan. I missed the wedding in England but the two decided to have a confirmation ceremony in India, where they had recently had a wonderful holiday. I took a short leave and a short flight to Goa. They had one of these fancy dressed-up elephants in attendance, and daughter decided she wanted a photo with her and myself together, one each side of the elephant. So... I put my arm around her shoulder and under the elephant's chin/jaw, and Jumbo thought, "Oh, goodies" and bit me on the shoulder. Suffice to say that elephant jaws can rip up trees daily and shred the bark and eat it; obviously they have strong jaws. I can vouch for that. As soon as Jumbo realised that I was not a titbit, he spat my shoulder out so I could groan unhindered. I can personally confirm that elephants have no incisors or I would be short of one shoulder now.

Checking on the 'net I found that elephants have been known to batter people on numerous occasions, but I have only heard of one case where an elephant ate a human, a woman, according to Peter Capstick (RIP), a professional hunter, in his book *Death in the Long Grass* (p. 64). He tells of a certain Bertha, a typist in Zurich Zoo in 1944, who had such a good rapport with an elephant named Chang that she was allowed to sleep in a room next to him – a rather strange relationship. But one morning Bertha did not report for work. The fact that the stall area was doused in blood, fingers and toes scattered on the floor, did not convince the Swiss authorities of the happening until later, when among Chang's droppings were parts of Bertha's half-digested dress.

It is a good book, well worth reading.

There was an incident in Tanzania when I was there where a hunter lost his life. The jumbo caught him and trampled him to such an extent that when he was found, 'he' was just a mess of dried blood and soil – mud. It was probable that scavengers disposed of much of his remains, and some passing local went away with the gun. But it is well known that to tangle with Jumbo without a backup gun is not a good idea.

My counterpart was not a veterinarian; his qualification was the same as mine, in tropical livestock production, and it is fair to say that the many veterinarians were not happy that a non-veterinarian was in charge of the veterinary services in NWFP. I backed him one hundred percent and we made a good pair for the implementation of the project. Regularly the veterinarians were trying to oust him from his position because he was not a vet, but by suggesting other breaches of service behaviour, such as paying too much for inputs. It was all nonsense but it wasted a lot of time proving that it was nonsense. I had no problem with the field staff in NWFP once they realised that I knew what needed doing and the project would help them with farming requirements. The annual audits were always a problem. The auditors were from a reputable international company but used local staff. I once asked one of my staff how much bribe other parts of the programme had paid to get a 'clean audit'. He replied, "Thousands." NWFP never had a faulty audit. All sorts of queries were raised but honestly solved.

I occurred to me that there were *no farm-raised vets* in NWFP and likely few elsewhere. Almost all started university courses for human doctors but could not make the grade, so they changed course and went for veterinary medicine. I found that they were afraid of animals; I had a number of examples of their fear. One was when I was talking to a group of veterinary staff in a cow shed, standing by a cow. I was partly leaning on her, scratching her back whilst facing the audience, chatting to vets and farmers. One of the vets suggested I should get away from the cow, as "you never know what she will do." I knew what she would do and said so; she enjoyed having her back-end scratched and raised her tail as a 'thank you'. A second incident was as I walked among a grazing group of about twenty young buffalo that I had reared. Not one of the fifteen or so vets would come with me. In reality, with few exceptions, they were a feeble lot.

The final nail in my feelings about the national veterinary branch of government concerned the use of diclofenac sodium, a pain-relieving treatment. The use of this painkiller is widely banned in many countries, as is its manufacture, but Pakistan continued to produce it. I am not sure whether it is currently still being marketed for use with livestock, but is known as Voltarol in medical practice. Due to lack of knowledge in the profession, veterinarians, when called out to treat farm animals and had no ideas as to the problem, would give the animal a shot of diclofenac sodium to remove any pain. The patient will temporarily get over the problem, all pain disappeared but not cured, and will be OK for a couple of days, then drop down dead from the initial unrecognised problem. Pakistan being almost ninety percent or so Islamic, they will not eat meat unless the animal is slaughtered whilst living. So usually, the carcase is left out in the open, which attracts scavengers and specifically vultures. Unfortunately for the Indian vulture, the diclofenac wrecks their kidneys and the vultures die. They have died in vast numbers, almost to extinction. Diclofenac sodium has destroyed the vulture population of Pakistan and when I asked the national head of veterinary services why he allowed the use of such an awful medication that is banned throughout the world, his reply was, and I quote, "I do not know what you are worrying about. They are only vultures." I do wonder sometimes just how many of nature's cleaning up squad died; it would probably be measured in millions. It also hardened my feelings about the low knowledge level of the vets of Pakistan.

The project ran a few forage trials, with seed provided by my Kenyan supplier, Diken, mainly grass seeds. Rye grass was an obvious one but it only grew in the shade and I decided the heat of the soil cooked the germinating seed. In cooler parts of the country the rye grass did well, and a big positive of this grass is it is able to be grown in saline soils, which were prevalent, caused by years of irrigation. It returned wasteland to productivity to the extent that Pakistan started exporting hay to the Emirates. Other grasses were successful due to their deep roots, some as much as three metres, allowing them to get deeper water sources. I was thinking back to my old friend in Ghana with his acres of Faidherbia albida tree, with goats competing for the fruits as they fell off the tree, very helpful at a time of the year when the goats of the village have little available grazing or browsing. I planted out a few of these trees, imported from Kenya, on a government farm but I left Pakistan before they matured sufficiently to produce fruits. The foliage is also notorious, but if cut for fodder they lose out in the amount of fodder in the fruits, and as such they were advised that cutting should be used only under dire conditions. It is an excellent tree and should be used more often by tropical and semi-tropical livestock owners.

The project held a livestock show in Sindh Province. I believe the farming community enjoyed it, but my lasting memory was that the project's marquee was blown away by a strong gust of wind, which was barely noticeable elsewhere on the showground. I was also deputed to judge a milking competition to find the most productive dairy cow on show. The owners were to milk the animal under supervision of a vet. The milk weighed was to be in public view. I am not sure if I gained credence or not when I went along next morning and upturned every milk bucket to drain the cleaning water out before they started milking. Noone was prepared to upturn the bucket over his head. It gave many of the competitors and spectators a laugh.

One of the biggest inputs of the programme was to enable people to get their evening milking to market in good condition next day. Heat was a major problem, so cooling tanks for overnight storage were essential, with a generator to provide for the cooling of the tanks. Next day morning milk was added and then taken to town for sale. Some sold to individual households, to distributers and standing orders, such as hotels and shops. The delivery of milk to town was completely in the hands of the villagers after two of the villagers who were trained by project staff learned how to check that nothing was added to the raw milk. For farmers, distribution of the income was a matter for them and I never heard of any trouble.

I was living for a while in a rather nice house in the wealthier part of town. It was situated on a quiet road and across the road was the home of a leading politician. One evening, towards an election in just a while, one of his usual meetings was in progress when the shooting started. It was an attempted assassination, which failed. The politician's house was often noisy and could have involved me unintentionally, which was not a comforting thought. I therefore moved house, but not too far away, taking the second story of a Pakistani's house opposite a CIA residence. The CIA were not overly friendly – in fact I considered them to be miserable ***** and amusingly my balcony overlooked their abode. It also amused me that the CIA (or the FBI) always used identical make and model vehicles for travel; incognito they were not. Though they changed their number plates, as if that mattered.

I understand that the USA has around seventeen secret service organisations, so it could have been any one of those.

My balcony was a great place to be in the evenings before the local house sparrows went to roost in a small grove of rubber trees behind my house. I literally had a fly-past of the first degree, a sparrow 'murmuration'. The sparrows would collect up and head straight at me, very fast, then when they were close the flock would spit and pass closely each side and over my head from where I was sitting. I would have this display, six to ten fly-pasts, each evening. There were more than just 'many' birds and I would hesitate to claim to be accurate as to the number in the flock but I would suggest many thousands. I am aware that starlings are noted for this sort of display, but I had sparrows to keep me content.

Peshawar was considered relatively safe for foreigners, but it became less so over time, as with much of PKP. An American neighbour living just around the corner from my residence was shot dead, along with his driver, as he left his home for work. I was often told on employment that my first responsibility was for my own safety. His mistake was to go to work at a set time. Another thing was that he had a driver, and drivers could be forced to give information for the kidnappings or shootings on the driver's morning pick-ups by capturing their family and holding them hostage. The Taliban obviously knew of his routine, waited for him one morning, and shot him dead along with his driver as he passed through his garden gate.

There is a tale that a captured Taliban, when asked why a certain American was never targeted, replied that the American was a hard target and explained the he could not be bombed, as he inspected his car each morning, even underneath. The American could not understand what he was hearing until he realised it was when he was looking for the cat which liked to sleep in or under his car, and he was just checking the cat was not going to be run over. I tried to make it more difficult for an ambush. I had no driver, so there was no one knowing what time I would leave for work. I took as varied a route as possible and had no set time to leave for the office or go home. My timing varied from 5 a.m. to not going to the office at all or returning home at all hours.

After a short while, the regional project manager for Baluchistan decided to depart. We assumed he had no intention of staying for long. His excuse was that there was no English school for his child. He could have found that out before applying. He was not overly industrious. I was asked to take on Baluchistan until someone else was recruited. Baluchistan is the land of the tribe Baloch. The British had promised them a degree of autonomy at the time of partition, a promise that never materialised once Pakistan was self-governing. Baluchistan was the largest and richest province in minerals, which Pakistan mined. The Baloch received nothing in return and it had periods of attempting to become independent. It was not a happy place to work in and I was glad when the EU decided it was too dangerous for us to work there.

As I had no superior in PK, when I tired of the traffic, the atmosphere and security problems I would take to the hills and work in the mountains. It was akin to taking an illicit holiday. When I was young, I saw a few hills that impressed me. Then I went to Wales and saw their mountains. Even going up Snowdon was wonderful, except I had to carry one of the scout troop down much of the way with a sprained ankle. Later I was impressed once more with the Munros of Scotland; the mountains were something special to a farm boy. After college, I went to Switzerland for a couple of months working on a poultry farm and saw the Alps. Wow, they were magical mountains, particularly the north face of the Eiger, and I thought things could not get better. But then I saw the real mountains! Unbelievable, majestic and scary – it was a quality geographical, ecological education. The Himalayas.

Driving into the mountains was not good for the nerves, as the Karakoram Highway was enough to stop you thinking of any future. I therefore went by plane, and it was not long before you wondered if you were going to miss Nanga Parbat or not. One or two planes had run into mountains for various reasons, and one has not yet been found when I was there. Landing in Chitral was so different from other stops in Pakistan, slow, easy-going, do-it-yourself style, very laid back. Just outside the town, beyond the end of the runway, there is a restaurant in the shape of a Fokker 50. It seemed to have lost its brakes on landing, but it is a very popular eating venue.

The restaurant plane went down before my time, but one did go down not long before I left the country. The gossip is that the loaders at the Karachi airfield loaded too large an illicit cargo of mangos, flown in privately for the unloading porters – not unusual for a bit of private enterprise. It was seemingly more weight than they told the driver.

Hotel accommodation in Chitral was a series of huts on a riverbank of clear snowmelt. The rooms were about three yards from the river edge (no croc there) and in those three yards were fruit trees and it was a matter of help yourself when the fruits were ripe. They had a good restaurant, which was not normal once out of Peshawar, and one evening there were many senior school youths who were taking care of an aged expat. He turned out to be a relic from the early years of Pakistan, just after the break-up of India, the partition. He was about to retire and the students had organised a slap-up 'goodbye' party. He was enjoying it immensely.

It is in this area that the supposedly highest game of polo in the world takes place. It is an annual match between the team of Chitral and the military team of Northern Area. The field is halfway between the two places. One rule of this match is that there is no changing of horses during the game, so the horses spend early summer grazing at altitude to acclimatise them. I saw games in Chitral but not the big match.

My paymaster, the EU, requested that I try to help the Kalash in any way I could. Never having met a Kalash, I was happy to do so. Occupying just three valleys in the mountains of Chitral District, there is a 'tribal' group of people that are different from Pakistanis, in that they have their own religion, some have fairish hair and lighter colour eyes, and have their own and a different lifestyle. They are the Kalash. If you Google the name, you will enjoy it, as it is difficult to get a full picture in print. It is said that when Alexander came from Afghanistan heading for India, he passed through Chitral. There was a big battle and he had many killed and many too badly wounded to go further. He wanted to get to India as soon as he was able, lured on by all the wealth he knew was there, so he left men to guard the wounded and women to care for them, and they are still there. The women dress in long, very colourful embroidered dresses, but not particularly for tourist – they are worn all the year round. It was until recently that they were not burying their dead, who were placed in coffins and left above ground. When I asked about their religion, my Kalash interpreter said, "We worship the same God that you do." I can assure you it is in a different way, as I was permitted to enter the temple. They have been pressured to turn to Islam for many years, but just a few have done so, and they tell me it is mainly for business purposes or employment.

The Himalayas have a fascination for me. The people there are very different from the ones down on the plains; they tend to be less rich, but happier.

One thing intrigued me, that in such a mountainous region there are no major waterfalls; once the snowmelt reaches the river valley it never goes over any falls, and it is a long way to the sea. There are few, if any, lakes. There is one place where the river water slows down and widens, which is said to be a lake, but not in our accepted form.

There is a village called Garam Chashma (Hot Water) where the water is used for laundry in the village, and also channelled to some houses for heating in winter and supplies the only hotel for many miles around with a swimming pool, a dip for all seasons.

Sheep and goats play a large part in the mountain economy, though there are a few domestic buffalo and, in the higher areas, there are yaks. Any remotely 'level' patches of land are cultivated, usually for home fruits, nuts or vegetables. The livestock exist on natural rather than cultivated grasses and anything green. I even found some cocksfoot grass there. I did find some possibly 'wild tulips'. I say this because they were nowhere near any villages or other habitations. There was a patch of tulips, maybe fifteen centimetres tall, red with white stripes on the petals. I did not have the heart to dig up a couple to take home.

The project built a large shed for the machinery and storage. It was winter by the time we got the machinery into the shed, and the mechanical parts were spread around the walls. It was time to call it a night. Accommodation was scarce and I slept in an unheated schoolroom with a mound of quilts and a hat, as it was less than cosy. In fact, it snowed and snowed and snowed. It was so heavy, it was not only our shed that collapsed, but many houses all having flat roofs went down. Owners spent hours during the night sweeping snow off as it settled. It was difficult opening the door in the morning so I exited my 'bedroom' through a window. I believe someone up there was on our side for once because the collapsing roof of the shed did not fall to the floor. It was propped against the wall and all the kit was in the safe triangle. It was a large example of the triangle of life, which has saved many, fortunate to get through.

Due to the number of sheep in the mountains and wanting to help the mountain folk, the project provided a wool processing machine which took in raw wool and turned out yarn. The local women knitted a lot of the 'harvest'. Once through teething problems they did well.

The sheep in the area were a very small 'breed' which were ideal for the mountains. They look to be around thirty-five to forty centimetres high. The fleece was soft but the animals were shorn five or six times each year. They were sheared whenever the family needed cash for shoes, clothing, an event, school fees, etc. The sheep are their bank account. I tried to tell them that the longer the fleece is, if the animals are shorn less frequently, the more valuable it is. They even sheared during winter. I tried to explain that the fleece was grown to keep them warm but... When I discussed this in a Kalash village meeting, outdoors, in weather close to winter, I decided to give a small demo. I primed one of the villagers, who was happy to help, and I got into my spiel and when I said that the lack of fleece would be like "one of your people being like THIS for all the winter" I tore off his waistcoat and shirt. Laughter all around. I try to leave any meeting all laughing, as I think that by leaving them laughing the people may remember what I have said.

The people there asked if I could get some larger sheep for them, thinking that a larger sheep should provide more wool, but I did not think this would help as these sheep are acclimatised to the mountains and the mountain climate is as rough as can be imagined.

The goats in the mountains seemed to be better adapted to the mountains than any introduced sheep; they provided milk too. Their hair is rather rough and of little use commercially, and some carry quite a lot of it if not sheared. I scoured Pakistan for angora goats, which, if close to pure angora the 'wool' is akin to a poor cashmere. By the continued use of an angora male, after a few generations of these cross-breeds the wool would become close to pure angora and of high value. I distributed them to farmers I knew who would help their neighbours and give their first-born males to a neighbour, so this goat could eventually become an acknowledged part of Pakistan livestock.

I visited Hunza, which is the ex-capital of a small kingdom set high in the mountains. There is a fort there of vintage years and still the home of the would-have-been king of Hunza; he gave his small kingdom to Pakistan at the time of the partition with India. Myself and my travelling friend, the head of veterinary services in the area, were shown around the fort and even went to meet his herd of yaks. I had seen only one yak previously, in

Kabul Zoo, and that one suffered due to the 'low' altitude. In the heights of Hunza they were at home. I managed to get a bit of hand milking of one of, I suspect, the quieter animals.

If a yak male is crossed with a European cow, the offspring is called a zo (sic), which could be very useful for a Scrabble player to know. I wonder what they would/do call a calf from a yak dam and bovine bull. "Eh?"

Later that same day after meeting with an ex-king, we stopped on the way and were approached by a village elder known to my companion and sat on rocks at the roadside, chatting. We were there for a little while before the local influential villager decided to take off his shoes, which were hurting him. I wished he had not done so. The stench was awful. In my time, I have known a lot of awful smells, but this one came close to being a winner. Sitting in the clear, clean mountain air then, for politeness's sake, having to stay rather than depart almost came in the realms of torture. I still shudder to think of it. It is rumoured that certain Afghan and Pakistan living in the highlands bathe once each year. I can believe at least one does not wash his feet.

On one trip returning from the foothills, we came upon a number of standing vehicles with people in the vehicles looking at a wild goat chasing other people around the vehicles. I got out of our Land Rover and went to see the goat. He was enjoying chasing people and came at me. There was no malice in him as he tried to butt me. I grabbed his horns and we had a push and retreat bit of exercise. I allowed him to push me about and then I pushed him to the side of the road, which had a five-metre fall to a river. Then I finally let go and he went to chase other folk and butt cars, etc.

Very sadly, I heard about one month later that some very *brave* Pakistani (I refuse to call him/her a hunter) *idiot* had shot it.

I never travelled the whole of the Karakoram Highway, but

met it when it was at quite an altitude when I would get off the plane in Gilgit. Along with the local district veterinary officer, we headed for the Chinese border where there is a dry port, visiting the odd small village and farmers on the way. Close to the border, perhaps by thirty miles or so, we saw a very pleasant grove of pines which turned out to be a cemetery for Chinese workers who died making the track into a road – now 'Highway' – capable of taking transport trucks to the border. It was a nice enough place for a burial but too far from home for relatives to ever be able to visit, even if they could get a visa.

On the way up to the border we passed a young couple sheltering from the cold and brisk, 'no very brisk', breeze. To be honest it was damned cold. I believe it is around sixteen thousand feet. At the border is the dry port where Chinese loads are dropped off and collected by Pakistani trucks. On the way back the couple were still there, so we stopped and asked where they were going. Silly really, because there was only one way to go and that was down. They clambered aboard, and when I asked what country they came from, their answer was that they were Japanese and come to see the cherry trees. We set off but stopped at a few villages on the way and eventually stopped to meet a farmer who had said he wished to see us on the way back from the border. He invited us into his house and found a few of his neighbours too. I realised that this was going to go on for a longish time and mentioned that we had two passengers and, if he agreed, I could ask them to come in and out of the cold. Invitation gratefully accepted and we all went into the house; the fire was welcome, and the hot tea. Then we started chatting. The hitchhikers were included but their English was not too good, so I jokingly asked if anyone spoke Japanese. One man sitting high upon some sacks said he could. He was a bit of a shock considering where we were and how far they had travelled to see the cherry trees.

Travelling in the mountains is never safe, as almost all the roads follow the rivers, and roads are carved out of the hillside and prone to rock slides and snow avalanches. In my time I realised why the drivers always seem to be looking at the hillside, in case of rolling rocks. I was in the mountains visiting farmers when we met with a recent snow avalanche completely blocking the road. The snow was about six metres deep. We turned around very carefully due to the height above the river and the narrow width of the road. We did manage to turn around and set off back to our hotel, and after four miles or so, we met another avalanche which had come down since we passed that way. Problem. No mobiles in those mountains and no radio connection. The driver had the answer and set off to get help from our base, bless him. We spent a rather chilly (sarcasm) night. He returned the next day with a bulldozer and a driver who set to immediately. The dozer carved a way through the fall enough to get our truck through and back home we went. The dozer driver stayed to move both avalanches, even if he had to spend days at it, when that part of the valley was defunct of households.

At the partition of the country of India in 1947, Kashmir was a country of Muslims and Sikh and Hindu, Buddhists and a few other beliefs, including Christians, who lived together apparently happily. Since partition this cohesion seems to have been assigned to history, with Kashmir being split in two parts – one assigned to India and the other to Pakistan. It has been a fraught period. Pakistan and India have fought over the two parts to little avail. The Pakistan portion was within my geographical area of operation. I went with an idea of improving the poultry sector in the villages and, after my first visit, the housing had improved. Later, with better quality Rhode Island red males, they got busy and progeny, when hatched, would provide larger eggs and more meaty males for the 'table'. We provided chicken feed for the first few months. Under the tender care of a lady veterinary field officer, the project went very well. One idea the people had was that until their hens began producing eggs, they would not get fed poultry food. This was a hard one to get across but eventually we got the people to understand with a lot of laughter.

As a farm-raised lad, I can understand the ignorance, as in Tanzania, when the UK-trained surveyors went into the bush for months on end, I was asked numerous times how many cockerels were needed for twelve hens before they could get eggs. I used the metaphor of their girlfriends' menstruation in my answer, which caused giggles among my audience.

I enjoyed the people of Kashmir and when I asked whether they would prefer to be Pakistani or Indian the reply was uniformly, "We wish they would both leave us alone."

Swat Valley is not very far from Peshawar and it is north through Mingora, a thriving town. When there were tourists visiting Pakistan, it was a popular tourist attraction, and has Buddhist relics such as a stone carving which suffers abuse when passing Muslims take offence. The population of Swat Valley are almost ninety-eight percent Islamic of the Pashtun tribe and most of the inhabitants consider themselves as Afghan. People of this tribe are proud of their hospitality. If a Pashtun says he will look after you, he means *he will* look after you to the *death*; then you are safe to travel and stay in homesteads overnight. As one enters the valley there is a river alongside the road, as is common in Pakistan, and as there are no bridges crossing the river, people go by a ropeway, precarious and even dangerous. I once asked how often the ropes or cables were replaced. I was told, "When one breaks."

Swat Valley is where Malala Yousafzai, the fourteen-year-old schoolgirl, was on her way to Mingora School, but the bus she was in was stopped by Taliban and Malala was shot in the head, and two other girls wounded. The reason was simple and ridiculous: it was because she was a known advocate for education for girls, which for some presumably sexist reason the Taliban are/were against. She has become known worldwide, and the strength of the misogynistic attitude within the Taliban is no secret. My personal opinion is that the men are afraid that the wife, if educated, could be more knowledgeable than the 'head of the household'.

It was interesting to see that there very few houses at riverside, at the level where all the farming was carried out. The houses were built up on the side of the valley of, at my guess, forty to fifty metres from the valley floor. I did wonder why, then in my imagination I saw cold air come rolling down the valley from the heights of ice and snow and decided, rightly or wrongly, that the houses were built away from the valley bottom to avoid this river of freezing air. Winter cropping was not an option, whereas in other parts of Pakistan two crops per annum are common if there is water.

The project's interest was centred on the dairy problem in the valley. In the tourist season milk is in great demand. In winter, when there are very few tourists, if any, the livestock are down in the valley. In summer, the cattle have been taken to the high ground and to verdant pastures on each side of the valley. It is a two-day walk to get to the valley bottom, so no milk is carried down but made into cheese. It means that tourists and villagers do not get fresh milk in summer and are dependent on milk powder, whilst the available milk is made into cheese on the high ground along the valley sides.

Our solution was to erect rope transport from the top to a central place in the village. A suitable site was located and all the equipment, cables, pylons, etc., were purchased. The ropeway was definitely not a form of transport for people. The company supplying the materials were to install it, but due to Taliban activities, the erection was put on hold until the area was safe for the company's staff to work there. It was seldom considered 'safe' whilst I was there and since then the situation has worsened.

With the veterinary department having recently been taken over by a veterinarian who was notably not interested, all the equipment will still be there or has been taken away by some local magnate who feels he can make use of it. Whilst the ropeway was still definitely a plausible answer, visitors from the EU visited the project and wanted to see Swat. The visitors wished to see how efficient the services of the department were in winter. We had visited a few veterinary offices on the way and, where a veterinary assistant could be found, the visitors chatted about local problems. When we got to Swat village, the snow was deep and untrodden at the door of the veterinary office. When we eventually made contact with him, he was sick and had been for some time, or that was his claim. We met with villagers and discussed all their winter problems, especially the milk issue, and they were enthusiastic with the idea of a ropeway.

In the evening, we booked into the only hotel in Swat. It was closed, but opened up for us. As they'd had no customers for weeks, the heating was off, but to our surprise there was a cook. Dinner was a stew, which I believe was probably intended for his family. Rooms were freezing cold and I, at least, slept in my clothes, though I took my boots off.

Morning was even colder and a breakfast was prepared for us with the choice of cheese omelettes or nothing other than coffee, made with powdered milk, of course. We all wore our full outdoor clothing, including gloves and woolly hats, as we sat down to eat. I even have a photo of that taken by the cook; surprisingly we all looked quite happy. Shortly after this visit, it was decided that visits to Swat should cease due to the presence of the Taliban.

The atmosphere in Peshawar was disgusting, which was

put down mainly to the presence of forty thousand tuk-tuks, the three-wheeled 'taxis' based on a motorcycle engine, poorly maintained, and each belching its share of pollution at the rear. The government were making all these vehicles convert to gas instead of petrol/oil mix as used in motorbikes. It was always a pleasure to get into the hills and away from that atmosphere.

I was told that corruption was so bad that a man wishing to be a customs officer at the Pakistani end of the Khyber Pass had to buy the job and, knowing that others would be wanting and paying for his job, he would only be in post for a limited time, so he knew he would have to gouge as much cash out of truck drivers as possible. When I came through, I was amused to see that the border post, with all the traffic going through there, did not have a computer. Records were handwritten, but I did get a rubber stamp of clearance.

The border between Afghanistan and Pakistan is a bit of an anomaly; it is almost no man's land. I believe it is supposed to be Pakistani territory, but they have very little influence there. Along the border are a series of tribal lands which are virtually uncontrolled, where the Pakistani government fears to tread. The tribes are Afghani but any Afghan government tolerates them or uses them when required. Smuggling is rife and so far as guns are concerned, they are sold quite openly; neither Afghan nor Pakistani law prevails. If Pakistan sent in the military, the locals would just disappear into the hills and the troops would get battered from on high. The project employed an elderly man who was from the Khyber tribe, and the project hoped he could help with getting into contact with the local people. The idea was shelved when he demanded a toilet to himself. The one used by the senior staff was offered but no, he wanted his own. I asked him to go into the area and talk to farmers but he delayed leaving the office and eventually he admitted that he was afraid of meeting even his own tribe. He did not last long on the project.

My staff gave me guidance as to where and when I could visit any village that I would like to, but if internal conflict was in the air, I was advised not to go, so we went somewhere else. The border was not marked in any way, and after a year or so I found I had been meeting people in the tribal areas with no bother at all. OK, some of the guys at the meeting were cuddling AK-47s, but I decided it was such a commonplace matter that it was like a woman taking her handbag to a meeting. The area itself is little or no threat to Pakistan; they trade and Pakistani law has little, or no, influence. In the tribal areas people live under Sharia law. I always felt safe, partly because the villagers had been briefed before I arrived, and also because I was promised safety in the tribal areas. They knew my job and I never got into political or religious matters, or even tribal matters. I was completely neutral and the locals wanted to see me. I regularly had visitors from the tribal areas to my office, and the market in Peshawar has many customers from there. It is apparently a part of Pakistan culture and the residents wish to live as they did a hundred-plus years ago. I was informed that when men from the tribal areas left their area, they generally travelled with a small boy. Do not ask me why.

It seems that, internationally, the Afghan nation is not fully understood. For the Afghan his first loyalty is to Allah, second his family, third to his village, and then his tribal area, and then the country. I could accept this and kept it in mind when I was visiting the tribal area. I found them welcoming and interested in the fact that I was trying to help them and not wanting anything from them. My accompanying staff were accepted and there was no animosity at all. In the past, the Pakistan government have sent the army in to punish some tribe for some misdemeanour or other, so the tribesmen take to the hills, where they are safe from tanks and armoured vehicles. The invaders find the terrain to be the biggest threat, and then have a little show of strength, just to show their muscle. They shoot or blow up a few acres of hillside then go back to base, chastened.

The Afghan tribes will join to eject anyone invading the tribal area and will fight together, but once the threat has been shown the way out, it will be a matter of back to the old days. The mullah is very important in the village and national life. Anyone who has sufficient funds to build a mosque can call himself a mullah, and he will have the people in the palm of his hand despite his lack of formal education. He would usually know the Koran by heart and that would be it. I feel that it is the religious training given to children by parents who have no or little education, particularly of Islam religion, and once that religious worm gets into someone's head it is hard to shake it away. I was lucky that my parents did not indoctrinate me in my early years, as I have met so many religions in my work and can look on religion objectively.

Pakistan is not noted for serious earthquakes. I experienced a few when I was there, particularly once in Islamabad. Sitting reading on the balcony of my one-floor-up hotel room, it started to shiver. I decided the stairwell would not be a sensible option when I had a nice green lawn to land on if I had to jump off the balcony. However, it stopped shivering after perhaps one minute, but seemed longer. I went back to my newspaper. This was before the quake of 2005, which was a serious surprise.

Then the October 5th, 2005, earthquake, measuring 7.8 magnitude, hit my area of operations.

Seismologists reckon it was the biggest ever to hit South Asia, and it was registered as 'severe'. The centre of the quake was under Muzaffarabad, about thirty miles of mountains north of Balakot, and was two hundred twelve kilometres deep, affecting Kashmir, Pakistan, Nepal, Afghanistan and India. The official Pakistan death toll was said to be 75,000 dead and 86,000 injured. Local estimates said 220,000 in Balakot dead and a similar number injured. I would suggest that the truth is in the middle.

I was in England on this fateful day of the 7.8 earthquake, which ripped through the heart of my area of work. I caught the first flight available back to Islamabad to see what our project could do to help. There were a few after-shakes, recorded as five or six on the Richter scale, for a few days after I got back to Peshawar, but nothing compared to the big one. It was very unpleasant and frightening, so much so that many residents slept outside for the next few nights. It was cold, not seriously however, but very worrying depending at what altitude you are.

Firstly, we had to decide what we wanted from our livestock budget and secondly whether the EU would allow this expenditure, as they were the project donors. Initially the news in international press or broadcasting was only interested in one building in Islamabad. The news from the north was 'not a lot'. The builder and owner were nowhere to be found, which usually means that the building was not built to specification and usually it was a matter of pilfered cement. I then drove to the worst affected area in Pakistan for a quick look around, to find the needs and what we would be allowed to buy for the early days of the relief. Winter had set in and it was very cold there, particularly at nighttime.

In Balakot, which was a sizeable town, every building was damaged except for the mosque, which seemed to be untouched. I put this down to the builder being honest during the building of the mosque and not thinning out the cementing and concrete. That builder had not fled the country, so I was told, but most of the others had. Talking to local people who wished to talk about it, they said it was terrifying and I can believe it. The quake was just after morning school time, at 8:39 a.m., and children were in the classroom when the school collapsed. When I got to Balakot I was walking across a large slab of concrete with one of my staff whose home had previously been there when he told me that there were 243 children under that concrete slab, plus teachers, that we were walking on.

One of the saddest things I have ever seen was a message eighteen inches high, written on a low wall to show drivers where the edge of the road to Balakot was. FORGIVE US LORD FOR WHAT WE HAVE DONE. That still hurts, that these people thought it was their fault.

As far as the livestock were concerned, many had just been turned out to graze on the hillsides and many lost their footing and rolled down the mountains – not so many sheep and goats but a lot of cattle and buffalo. All in all, the estimated number of livestock deaths was 250,000 cattle and buffalo. The main requirements were metal sheeting for houses and, for livestock, winter sheds. For the cold nights, the larger surviving livestock needed blankets. Our project purchased every blanket in Peshawar and distributed them among farmers. This disaster was seen as a great chance to make money, and the price of blankets was tripled or so the day after the earthquake. I toured the few shops that sold rough blankets and told them they had better reduce those prices or they would not benefit from future government purchases. Personally, I was not overly worried if the blankets were shared among the household and the livestock, as both needed warmth. The project also supplied roofing sheets and timber, in fact anything to provide shelter through the winter for people and their animals. It was a terrible time.

One happier story coming out after this quake was that, in a hill village miles away in the mountains, a family of two sons and an elderly mother living miles from Balakot lost their house, flattened. After getting out from under the wreckage, the two sons could not find Mother, so they left the farm and went down to where they could safely stay with family, thinking that Mother had gone to stay with her family. Two or three weeks later the sons returned to the house to salvage anything of use and, when moving the wreckage, they found Mother under the kitchen timbers. They placed Mother under some sheeting and covered her with a blanket, I understand. After spending the night there, next morning they realised she was a little warm; they made a litter and carried her for three days to a place at which a helicopter could land. She was airlifted to Islamabad and hospital, where she revived. After a while, she was discharged, and was never quite right in the head, understandably, but able to look after herself as before. The whole nation was cheered by this episode. The old woman suffered mentally but not over severely.

I drove around the area where the project was active to check how the local people were getting on and what assistance we could provide. We were driving along a road cut into the mountainside overlooking a lake, rather pretty and a beautiful shade of blue. When we could see the end of the lake, my guide pointed out a mudslide down the opposite side to us, the mountainous side of the lake, and said that the mudslide was where a village used to be; now the mud made the dam wall. The dam 'wall' is believed to have 263 people in it; my companion could appreciate the beauty of the lake, but hated it too.

Pakistan has the rather dubious honour of being one of the most corrupt countries in the world and external funds to assist the people who suffered from the quake are the ones that suffered. It is rumoured that $4.5 billion was given to Pakistan to help the people afflicted by the quake, and six weeks after the quake, $4.5 billion went out to Dubai banks. I would suppose that one reason people of the affected area were still living in tents two or three years later was due to lack of funds for building materials.

In Kashmir it is reported that thirty thousand houses collapsed during the quake, and when I visited Kashmir there was devastation all around. However, the only hotel available was the one our group stayed in overnight. Even the lift was still functioning, or was it? After dinner, as we went to our rooms, we took the lift. It had no doors, which was not much of a surprise. I was allotted a room on the second floor whilst my friend and co-manager on the project was one floor above. The lift behaved when I pushed the button for my floor and it stopped obediently. I turned my head to say, "See you at breakfast." I stepped out of the lift, still looking over my shoulder, and I became airborne. I realised the floor had either dropped or the floor of the lift had risen. It was the latter; it had raised itself three feet or so. I hit the floor leaning forwards, did a 'rugby tackle' roll, and escaped unhurt. Luckily, I stopped rolling before I got to the flight of stairs, or someone else might be writing this book.

I think I was one of the last Europeans to see Osama bin Laden before he was killed. One day I was returning from Abbottabad on the 'motorway' to Islamabad and stopped off at a string of roadside stalls selling fruit and vegetables. There were only two or three other cars and I stopped across from a car going north as I was heading south. I walked across the road and as I passed a rather less-than-new blue car, I saw a man in the rear seat and nodded to him as I walked past; he nodded back. I had seen numerous photos of bin Laden and I am sure it was he. I was unable to raise the alarm even if I had wanted to. I had no way of contacting the Americans, as I had no phone and no number. In retrospect, I think I am glad I was ill-prepared; I prefer living to $23m and looking over my shoulder every few minutes.

I have heard that going to war for the Americans is to teach them geography. I do not know why the Americans attacked Iran in revenge for the 9/11 episode. Seventeen of the nineteen hijackers were Saudi Arabian, so America attacked Iran. Admittedly, bin Laden was born in Iran but living in Afghanistan, so how come it was Iran's fault?

In my work, I regularly visited Abbottabad, as we were working with many farmers there on cattle and poultry. We also held a project meeting with staff nationwide. The hotel many of us stayed at was a mere half mile from bin Laden's residence. We found out later when the Yanks made it known. The house was also not too far from a major military barracks.

The Peshawaris are not particularly good drivers, as few take a driving test but driving licences are cheap to buy; consequently, the driving standards are not high. The observances of traffic lights are not common. There was a Pakistani recently back from the UK who stopped at a red light. The car behind had a driver who was incandescent with rage and hooted continuously. Eventually he got out of his car, smacked the driver holding him up on the head with a tyre lever, and then drove away. A pedestrian took the tyre lever wielder's number plate and the case was taken to court. The verdict was 'case dismissed'. The judge said that the hospital discharge form did not say the man had been hit by a tyre lever, even though a witness claimed he had seen it. Pakistani justice at work. (Cost?)

I was in a village in the hills when, after a really good lunch, my host asked if I would like to go shooting. I asked to shoot what and he said pigs. As, being Muslims, they will not have anything to do with pigs, I therefore thought I would stock up my freezer. I was handed an elderly rifle and a handful of bullets and up the hill we went, and found nothing. We discussed walking further and decided not to, but just for the experience of shooting in Pakistan I aimed at a particular tree and 'click'. So I checked the load and all seemed well. I tried again, twice. Click... click. On further investigation I found there was no firing pin. I am glad it was not a tiger hunt.

On one of the higher altitude government farms I was visiting, pigs were a nuisance, as they spent much of their life rooting up pastures for food. The manager asked if I would take the farm 12-bore shotgun and get rid of one or two, hoping they would move on. He gave instructions as to where the herd of pigs might be found at that time of day, and off I went. I found a nice, secluded patch of scrub and made myself comfortable. The manager knew his farm, as the pigs came down the hill towards me as I waited. The herd was one older male, about four or five almost mature boars, presumably last year piglets, and three or four mature females. A dozen or more youngsters were chasing about, chasing each other, squealing as they played. I sat and watched the youngsters having fun. I decided pig shooting was not in the terms of reference of my employment and left the pigs alone. I waited until they wandered away to dig up pastures elsewhere, then walked back to the office feeling very pleased to have been able to enjoy the piglets at play. Back at the office, "How did it go?" "Never saw them."

Meanwhile, five or six thousand miles away, secluded in their wee burrow in *Brussels*, an out of touch bunch of *experts* concerning Pakistan were having a meeting, and they agreed that no EU employees were to visit NWFP. (An *expert* is a drip under pressure away from home.) Then one person, probably a security guard, realised that they had an employee living there. That is when the *SH one T* hit the fan and a frantic phone call was made to Pakistan, to the EU office, then, as the phone was working, through to our HQ in Islamabad. I was told to get out of Peshawar NOW! Being a good and faithful servant, I left five days later. My co-manager and all the office staff had to have final dinner, plus other essential delaying events. On my last day at work in Peshawar, I was driving to Islamabad via the Peshawar office when I was stopped at traffic lights. I saw a motorcycle coming up rather too fast and knew he was going to hit my pickup. That is a common suicide bomber tactic. I felt the thump but no bang. As I waited for the lights to change, in my mirror there was a motorcycle and a man rolling on the road. The lights changed and away I went. Were it not for the EU warning, I would have got out to help him.

I went to live in Islamabad and tried to run the NWFP from there, which became impossible. The project was nearing its end of life, so I was preparing to leave when a USAID project was looking for a livestock consultant to operate in the tribal areas and I went to the office in Islamabad, had a chat, and was employed.

The objective was to help farmers in the tribal areas to replenish their cattle which had been killed or stolen in recent fighting in the area. I was employed to buy/procure cattle in the NWFP or Punjab and check that they were healthy and producing milk before sending them to farmers who had lost cattle in the recent fighting. For this, I needed places to hold them for assessment before transport to the tribal lands, and some way to ensure that the animals went to the more needy farmers, as I was forbidden to go into the tribal areas. Actually, officially, I was not to go outside of the Islamabad city limits, which did also enclose some countryside. A very poorly thought out programme.

There had recently been a downturn in the poultry industry, leaving numerous large, vacant poultry houses, which were visible from the roads. The owners of these empty poultry houses were then contacted to see if they could be used as holding sheds for cattle. The owners were sometimes in the local village, but sometimes they were in the city, which could be a problem. I also bumped into USA environmental regulations. I wanted to dig postholes to put in a cattle crush for vaccinations or treating less than passive cows, but I had to complete forms covering this, and then what was I to do with the manure? What would be the effect of having animals so close to villages? And so on and on… daft.

I been granted permission to proceed when, on orders from

on high, the programme was cancelled, so pack up and go home. I never found out why it was closed, but a rumour was it was a mishandling of financial matters in the USA.

All my staff from Peshawar came to Islamabad and we had a goodbye feast. It was at that 'goodbye' I was presented with an engraved plate, the only one I ever received, and the only one collected by anyone else in my business. I was extremely appreciative.

SO, I RETIRED.

But...

I received an email asking if I were interested in a short-term consultancy in Karachi – Pakistan again. Once again funded by USAID. The problem was a 'cattle colony' in Karachi. Government were worried about it being in the city and wanted to know what to do about it. I told them perhaps I was the wrong person to look into the matter, as I was known to be very much against cattle colony projects. I was not in favour of cattle colonies and whilst head of the recent livestock development programme I had grave problems with the whole concept. The reply was, "We think you are the right person." Which set in motion the process of packing and away to Islamabad.

My brother Bob had stopped for while at Karachi when he was on his way to Malaya with the SAS in the fifties to sort out their troubles. (Incidentally, as kids we had four comics weekly at home and after reading them, we sent them to Bob, who says that all his SAS cronies read them too, namely the *Adventure*, *Wizard*, *Hotspur* and *Rover*, and occasionally the *Beano*!) He assures me that Karachi was just a small fishing village of half a million population then. Now it has grown somewhat and has a population estimated by government to be sixteen million today, but there are so many refugees from Afghanistan that no one has any accurate figures. Suffice to say there are a lot of people there. The local estimate is thirty million. The problem in the early nineteen hundreds was that the village existed on a fishing industry, and as fish do not produce milk, the locals wished to keep cattle and buffalo for a milk supply for consumption. The then-headman granted permission, allowing a few animals to be kept in the village centre. Unfortunately, as the population grew so did the demand for milk, and so did the livestock numbers, so much so that when I arrived the owners of these city-dwelling animals had become a major problem – a forty thousand buffalo/cattle problem in the city. Not only do cattle/buffalo produce milk but also manure. Lots of it, for which there is not much demand in the city. There was a plan mooted to use the manure in biodigesters and produce gas which, converted into electricity, would supply much of the city. However, whoever put this forwards did not take in the fact that Karachi had not enough non-saline water for the city already, never mind water for biodigesters. To do this if they used seawater, the slurry left behind would be saline and no use for growing anything. There would be a short time before the mountain of manure became an embarrassment. I do agree that the waste manure could be dried out and used for fuel, but by who?

During a short briefing by the NGO, which was the organisation deputed to do 'something' about this problem, it boiled down to the fact that the animals in the city were a damned nuisance, and what can we do about it? Another probable nuisance would be due to the rather unsettled situation in the city determining that I would be limited to two trips to see the colony, and no longer than two nights per trip. Hardly enough time to be certain that your guesses are correct.

After a few meetings with heads of government and other organisations, I was booked on a flight to Karachi and booked into a 'safe' hotel. Karachi is always as hot as Hades, so I was glad to see, and to make use of, an outdoor swimming pool. Next day I had the sqitters/dire rear, which was a bit premature to my thinking. Then I watched the pool for a while, and found that when there were no swimmers the overhead hoard of red kites dropped in for a drink, which was not the only thing they dropped in. A few years before, it would have been the Egyptian vulture, except for the 'genocide' campaign carried out by the veterinary department of government by refusing to ban the use of diclofenac sodium, as mentioned previously. They will have killed off millions of scavenger birds who got rid of rotting carcases throughout Pakistan, showing no guilt whatsoever – ignorance. This yells poor training once again.

I took a look around the colony – animals mainly in good condition, owners living nearby and the stock fed well compared to many livestock in Pakistan. The green food was brought in from surrounding farms, usually early morning or night when there is less of a congestion problem. Many farmers were feeding compound feedstuffs. Obviously, there was no grazing, but farmers had arrived at a decent system of producing milk. Sale of milk was through agents who supplied the population and businesses. There was to be a vet or two on call twenty-four-seven.

That is the end of what was good. Now read on.

1. The best milking buffalo and cattle are kept for one lactation, then sold off for meat.
2. Keeping them through a gestation period is not profitable, so they are disposing of the best animals in Pakistan within one year, so the quality of the national herd is being destroyed year on year.
3. Keeping animals in close proximity can result in cross infections (zoonosis) detrimental to humans and vice versa.
4. So many animals are kept in such close conditions that

any disease spreads immediately within the buffalo and is difficult to control.
5. The price per litre is the same right through the marketing chain. The profit to the handler is how much extra volume of milk compared to what he bought he could get away with. I heard stories of anything between water and white paint. Adulteration is rife and the first thing the consumer does is to boil the milk on receipt.

Domestic water is very limited, adequate for drinking water only. Salt water, seawater, is used to wash out the manure. I calculated that around six hundred tons of manure per day is washed from the yard to the monsoon drain into a streambed, which flows twenty-four hours each day, and then into the Indian Ocean. On the way to the ocean there is a small water *SH one T* fall about three metres high, and I have a beautiful photograph of it on my office wall.

I later met the city governor of Karachi and asked him if he thought this pumping of untreated manure directly into the ocean to be healthy. He told me not to worry, as they also pump fifty cubic metres of untreated human excrement per day into the ocean too. I rather facetiously asked if you could buy fresh fish from the market, which he assured me that I am able.

If the USAID had decided to go ahead with my suggestion, the project would be an enormous enterprise and, having experience of the level of corruption in Pakistan, I doubt if it would get anywhere near the objective.

Inputs required for a successful project, assuming one-third of the current farmers decided that the Karachi life is better than outside the city? First, a very large acreage close to water for animals and domestic use. Are there such places within reasonable range of Karachi? The list is just to give the reader the near impossibility of the scheme. There would possibly be only three thousand farmers agreeing to leave the city. And forty thousand head of cattle/buffalo moving from the city.

There would be two options. One is to move them, lock, stock and barrel, and establish smaller colonies, but water would be a problem. The other option would be providing three thousand farmers each with a normal farm needing water, fodder, feed, fencing and all the services required by a commercial enterprise.

Either of the options would require the following inputs mainly on site before any moves by the farmers.

1. A dwelling akin to the one they left in the city, with all amenities for a working farm. Full twenty-four-hour electricity supply for house and out buildings.
2. Fencing of the area of land allocated, sufficient in size to be accepted by the farmers. This would be determined by his head of cattle.
3. All the amenities of a small town: mosque, schools, veterinary clinics, roads, at least from the 'town' to Karachi, suitable for milk tankers taking milk to the city. A medical help for people, so a house and surgery for an onsite doctor.
4. Each farm would need an appropriately sized milk dairy with a cooler tank, as milk would be held overnight and collected by a tanker next day. This would cut down on the pollution of milk, as it could be tested before being pumped into the tanker.
5. It is assumed that such as various shops, garages and markets would arrive without being provided by the project. Twenty years down the line, there could be three settlements of relatively happy dairy farms. Just before I left Pakistan I was asked what the cost would be. I made a quick off the top of my head costing between $2 and $3 billion. Today as I write, it will be nearer to $10 to $15 billion, after factoring in the reputation for corruption.

USAID decision: too expensive.

I believe that I am very lucky to have such a diverse and fulfilling life.

The old system of selecting a 'jury of his peers' – finding one could be a problem had I been sent to court. Here is a list of experiences I have met with, and I doubt that anyone has met with many of these:

1. I have been bitten by an elephant.
2. Played and refereed a rugby match at the same time.
3. Never smoked.
4. Got a vulture through my windscreen.
5. Suffered a broken neck when I headbutted a ship, broken ribs three times, a broken finger, a dislocated collarbone and broken spinous process.
6. To have driven for 240 miles on a road and met one only vehicle.
7. Shot a charging lion dead with a single shot from a 0.243 calibre rifle.
8. Lived in forty-one houses since leaving school.
9. Survived two attempted strikes by a mamba.
10. I think I can claim to be the last European or American to have seen Osama bin Laden alive, other than that American army patrol guy who shot him.
11. I have milked a zo.
12. I have been through an operating cattle dip.
13. Indulged in a play fight with a cheetah.
14. Landed a 105-pound Nile perch. I have forgotten the exact weight, but it was quite a tiddler on rod and line.

I would love to meet him for a good old natter.

THANK YOU FOR PERSERVERING.